The Fruits of Grace

The Fruits of Grace

The Ecumenical Experience of the Community of Grandchamp

Sister Minke de Vries

Translation, Preface, and Introduction by
Nancy S. Gower

Foreword by
Thomas F. Best

The Lutterworth Press

The Lutterworth Press
P.O. Box 60
Cambridge
CB1 2NT
United Kingdom

www.lutterworth.com
publishing@lutterworth.com

ISBN: 978 0 7188 9533 4

British Library Cataloguing in Publication Data
A record is available from the British Library

First published by The Lutterworth Press, 2018

Copyright © Minke de Vries, 2007

Published by arrangement
with Pickwick Publications

All rights reserved. No part of this edition may be reproduced, stored electronically or in any retrieval system, or transmitted in any form or by any means, electronic, mechanical, photocopying, recording, or otherwise, without prior written permission from the Publisher (permissions@lutterworth.com).

Contents

Foreword by Thomas F. Best | vii
Preface by Nancy S. Gower | xi

Introduction: The Roots and Early History of the Community of Grandchamp | 1
The Author: Minke de Vries (1929–2013) | 35

Introduction | 39

Chapter 1: In the Beginning | 42

    When the World is Troubled and in Distress . . . God Acts | 42
    Signs in the Church | 45
    The Great Field (*Grand Champ*) of the World | 48
    From "Yes" . . . to "Yes". . . | 52
    Monastic Inspiration within the Churches of the Reformation | 54
    Call to Life in Community | 57
    Presence to the World: First Steps | 61
    Taizé, Pomeyrol . . . | 63
    Through the Prayers of an Apostle of Unity: Abbé Paul Couturier | 69
    The Call of God . . . the Commitments | 76
    Here Am I, Holy Spirit, Creator of Life | 81

Chapter 2: The Adventure of Open Communion | 84

    Putting Down Ecclesial Roots Far and Near | 84

Rooted In the Same Ecumenical Dynamic | 87
Easter, Feast of Feasts . . . of Unity | 92
Easter Sunrise at Grandchamp | 95
Community Worship and Personal Prayer | 98
Personal Prayer As a Source of Communion | 102
The Eucharist | 104
The Eucharist, Foundational Act of Nonviolence | 110
From the Desert to Communion | 113
Becoming a Parable of Community | 122
Reconciliation and Gospel Nonviolence | 130
Steps on the Road of Gospel Nonviolence | 134

Chapter 3: Together in Solidarity with a World in Travail | 138
On the Road to Eastern Europe | 138
Three Pilgrims in the Spirit of the Beatitudes | 142
"Memory for Peace" at Auschwitz | 147
Pilgrimage for Peace in the Holy Land | 149
The Mystery of Israel | 155
Our Ties with the Community of Imshausen | 159
The Winds of Renewal | 162
From Visitations to Visitations | 165

Chapter 4: Testimonies of "Otherness" within the One Love | 171
In Places of Brokenness | 171
The Daughters of Abraham | 176
The Spiritual Family of Grandchamp | 179

Conclusion | 187
Toward the Fruits of Grace | 187
The Creation | 189
Watch Over the World | 190

Appendix: Several Communities Introduce Themselves—2007 | 193
Bibliography | 197
Index | 205

Foreword

Thomas F. Best

THIS BOOK IS A precious gift offered by the Community of Grandchamp to other monastic communities, to churches of all traditions, and not least to the ecumenical movement. Sr. Minke and the Community have given us a work combining recollection, reflection, meditation, church and ecumenical history and more, all offered in a highly personal and engaging style. It brings us in a unique way *into* the Community of Grandchamp, exploring the faith from which the Community lives and how it puts that faith into practice: in life together, in worship, and in service to the world.

For those familiar with monastic communities, *The Fruits of Grace* will deepen their understanding of the unique rewards, challenges and opportunities for service in this distinctive form of the Christian life. For those unfamiliar with monastic communities, I cannot think of a better introduction to their life and to their importance for the whole Church. And for many in both groups, this book will open a new world: that of monastic communities within Protestant churches—within the Reformed churches (as is Grandchamp), but also within Anglican and Lutheran churches, and perhaps more. Such communities have recovered, for the Protestant world, a form of Christian life and service which has been integral to the Church from its earliest days. For this the whole Church owes them a debt of gratitude.

Reflecting on my own experience with the Community of Grandchamp, I am moved to mention two aspects of its life in particular: its worship and its ecumenical commitment.

First, at the heart of the Community's life is *its life of worship*. This takes place in the chapel ("the Ark"). This is a large, open room with warm wooden walls and a high ceiling braced by soaring wooden beams. On entering one sees the altar, lectern with Holy Scripture, and a large cross standing against a wall; then a modest number of profound icons, most familiarly that of the Trinity; and candles. The overall impression is one of simplicity, of focus on the essential, and of welcome to a place of encounter with God. In daylight the space is bright, sparked by splashes of color from strips of colored glass set into the walls; at nighttime it is a space of holy mystery, a darkness illumined by God's light. Even during non-Eucharistic services, Bread and Wine seem to be present on the Lord's Table. God is present; Christ is present; and the Holy Spirit is moving within. For me it is a precious and beautiful space, one which transcends the divisions of our churches. One could say: the chapel itself is an "icon" of our unity, filled with Sisters and visitors from various churches and countries, all coming together in the presence of Christ.

Notably, worship has been a center for renewal at Grandchamp. Drawing on the Community's experience, the liturgy has been modified over the years to include additional elements, particularly from the Orthodox tradition, while (as Sr. Minke says) "keeping its evangelical simplicity." The latest fruit of this continuing liturgical renewal is the book *Louange des Jours à Grandchamp: Temps de l'Église* (Communauté de Grandchamp and Éditions Ouverture, 2015).

Second, the Community's understanding of the Christian faith, and of its own experience, means that *its life is inherently ecumenical*. Over the years the Community has included Sisters from many Christian traditions and from many different countries. Small communities of Sisters have extended Grandchamp's presence, notably in Jerusalem and Algeria, but in several other places as well—and, crucially, always in contact with local churches. There are extensive contacts with other monastic communities, Roman Catholic, Orthodox and Protestant, with Sisters sometimes sharing in their lives for periods of time. In addition to extensive ecumenical contacts, there are links also to inter-religious dialogue and to movements for reconciliation in the human family and with the natural world. And the fact that Grandchamp, in French-speaking Switzerland, has its spiritual retreat house, the *Sonnenhof*, in German-speaking Switzerland is itself an ecumenical statement—as those with some familiarity with the country will understand!

All this diversity is no accident. In forming its own distinctive pattern of life, Grandchamp has drawn from the experience of other monastic communities whether Protestant, Roman Catholic or Orthodox. Remember too that the Community's earlier years coincided with a time of great ecumenical ferment and hope—the First and Second World Conferences on Faith and Order in 1927 and 1937, the emergence of the Life and Work movement in the 1930s, the formation of the World Council of Churches (WCC) in 1948, the Second Vatican Council in the 1960s . . .

Formed in this ecumenical climate, the Community has made a significant impact ecumenically. I mention only a few examples which I know from personal experience: a Sister of Grandchamp produced the beautiful Vesper services for the 5th World Conference on Faith and Order in 1993 (a highpoint of the entire Conference); Sisters have accompanied the Graduate School at the WCC's Ecumenical Institute, Bossey; and Sisters have contributed to several WCC Assemblies. Nor can one forget *The Way of the Cross*, prepared by Sr. Minke at the request of Pope John Paul II for this celebration in Rome in 1995, and republished in 2015. (Typically, she included material adapted from Mère Geneviève, so important in the earliest years of the Community, a Passion hymn beloved by Protestants, and a text from Dietrich Bonhoeffer's *Life Together*.) Examples of the Community's ecumenical witness could be multiplied in local, regional, national and international contexts.

The ecumenical engagement practiced by the Community of Grandchamp is not a "programme." It is simply the sharing of the Community's *faith and interior life, put into practice*. It is simply the sharing of the unity-in-diversity which the Community *already* experiences within itself, within the one Body of Christ. That is why its ecumenical witness is so authentic and effective. There are lessons here for the rest of us.

Worship and ecumenical commitment are, of course, but two central aspects of the Community of Grandchamp. This book carries us into the history and life of the Community in all its dimensions, revealing the truly astonishing range of contacts, relationships, and commitments which have marked its life over the years.

One thing is abundantly clear: this is a Community which looks toward the future. Recent events abundantly confirm this. It is great communities which produce great leaders. Sr. Minke was succeeded by Sr. Pierrette in 1999, and she in her turn by Sr. Anne-Emmanuelle in 2016: the Holy Spirit is at work. Since the original language versions of *The Fruits of Grace* were published, signs of continuing renewal abound, some of which are mentioned above. And, perhaps most heartening of all, women continue to explore the possibility of entering the Community in order to follow its vocation of unity and reconciliation. Surely the ministry of Grandchamp to the Church and to the world will continue to flourish.

It has been an honor to be asked to contribute this Foreword. The Community of Grandchamp has inspired and nurtured me—and in equal or even greater measure my wife Isabel—for more than 30 years. It gave her special pleasure to say "thank you" to the Community by translating its texts and annual Newsletter. And here, in my own way, I join my heartfelt "thanks" to hers.

Rev. Dr. Thomas F. Best

Former Director, Faith and Order Commission,
World Council of Churches and Pastor of the
Christian Church (Disciples of Christ)

Preface

I VISITED GRANDCHAMP FOR the first time in 2005, just after Brother Roger's memorial service. I wanted to interview Sister Minke on the history of Taizé, the subject of my doctoral thesis. I was struck at once by her sparkling, honest blue gaze, her attentive listening, her caring, her concern for the unity of the church and at the same time her love for her own part of that church, her strength of character, the quality of her leadership as a woman. I admire her greatly for leading the community of Grandchamp during those difficult years of the sixties and seventies. With strength and love she built on the foundation laid by her predecessors, especially Mother Genevieve. Sister Minke's leadership was formative for the Grandchamp pilgrims find there today: open, welcoming, inspiring, engaging, stimulating, healing, loving—beautiful and comfortable and yet simple. What a place!

She must have sensed my admiration; a few days later she asked if I would be willing to translate her first book into English. I agreed to do it thinking American readers would surely benefit from knowing of Grandchamp. There was a significant complication: the initial version is in Italian, translated from an early French version, there was a published French version, and a manuscript in French with significant additions to and deletions from the earlier versions! Generally, the later manuscript has been followed, unless that reading posed problems for understanding the text.

I am grateful to Sister Minke for the assignment and the many hours of conversation about the history of Grandchamp, to the Archivist, Sister Anneke, and to the Prioress, Sister Pierrette. I am also grateful to the multifaceted support of Dr. Catherine Clifford and Anne Louise Mahoney, but especially their editorial suggestions. I am also grateful to my friend and research collaborator David Bundy for assisting in the final preparation of the manuscript and for hours of discussion of Grandchamp and its context.

Nancy S. Gower

Pasadena, August 1, 2016

INTRODUCTION

The Roots and Early History of the Community of Grandchamp

Nancy S. Gower

THIS INTRODUCTION PRESENTS THE pre-history of Sister Minke's book, *Vers une gratuité féconde* translated here as *The Fruits of Grace*.[1] It is a chapter in the history of women striving for freedom during the nineteenth and twentieth centuries. Protestant women in Europe were seeking to shape a distinctive spirituality where they could develop their own culture and forms of devotion to God.[2] It is a story of women networking and cooperating to achieve those goals, often with the support of individual men. The concrete result of that struggle is the Community of Grandchamp, literally the "community of the large field," near Neuchâtel, Switzerland. It is also the story of the Protestant Christian women of Grandchamp extending the network of their relationships beyond the Swiss Reformed Church to include all Christians and eventually, during Sister Minke's time, fellow seekers of God among Muslims and Jews.

The Context of Grandchamp: The Bovet Family

Without the Bovet family, the Community would not have been at Grandchamp. The Neuchâtel branch of the Swiss Bovet family began as merchants

---

1. Minke de Vries, *Vers une gratuité féconde*. This was originally published in Italian as Vries, *Verso una gratuità Feconda* and in Dutch as Vries, *Christen zijn vandaag* and reprinted in Dutch as Vries, *Mijn leven in Grandchamp*.

2. This concept has been discussed, by Freedman, "Separation as Strategy," 513–29; Keller, "Creating a Sphere for Women," 246–60; and Kerber, "Separate Spheres," 9–39.

of painted muslin (called *Indiennes*), a business that expanded quickly during the eighteenth century.[3] But for their religious and intellectual interests, the family would have been just one of many recorded in the annals of Swiss international businesses whose enterprises closed due to changing technologies and tastes. The story of the family, its businesses and religious perspectives has been told in detail by Pierre Bovet and Sister Gilberte de Rougemont.[4]

The family sent daughters to the Moravian school at nearby Montmirail[5] and promoted and protected the *Réveil* in its local expressions.[6] For example, when the *Indiennes* business that had filled Grandchamp saw closure in the 1840s, they rented some of its lodgings to *Réveil* advocates such as industrialist Émile Peugeot (1815–1874) and Neuchâtel professor Abram-François Pétavel (1791–1870).[7] Other buildings of the closed business—drying barns, hangars, workshops of various kinds, the washhouse, a dovecote—were later filled with charitable and educational enterprises, the same buildings that are today the Community of Grandchamp. As Gilberte de Rougemont, an early sister of the community observed, "The dynamic that animates this family can be summarized in two words, the motto of the Bovets: *Pour autruy* (For others)."[8] The Bovet family felt compelled to use its resources to encourage mission and spirituality, and to care for the less fortunate in society.[9]

Bertha Mumm (1813–1874) married Philippe Bovet and soon became the driving force and inspiration behind many of the family's charitable and educational initiatives, including a hospital for the poor and an orphanage, the first two ministries to move into the disused buildings of Grandchamp. The models were Kaiserswerth, a deaconess house founded in Germany by

---

3. Berthoud, *Les Indiennes*.
4. Bovet, *Un Siècle*; Rougemont, *La Geste des Bovet*.
5. Senft and Reichel, *Souvenir du jubilé*; Senft, *Ceux de Montmirail*.
6. The *Réveil* (revival) in Francophone Europe dated from about 1815 to 1870. Bundy argued that it is a re-appropriation of Moravian spirituality and practices, initially within the churches, developed with an awareness of Methodism, while knowing little about Methodism. Networks of evangelists and laity worked to renew the church and encourage personal devotion. See Bovet, *Un Siècle*, 24–43; Bundy, "Should the Methodists"; Encrevé, "Le Réveil en France"; " Robert, *Les Églises Réformées en France*; Leonard, *Déclin et renouveau*.
7. Bovet, *Un Siècle*, 196. On Pétavel, see Bundy, "Should the Methodists," 189–90.
8. Rougemont, *La Geste des Bovet*, 3.
9. Bovet, *Un siècle*.

Theodore Fliedner,[10] and the Moravian center, Herrnhut.[11] They maintained close relationships with other pietistic centers such as Mannedorf where their son Arnold was sent, and healed, when suffering from tuberculosis of the knee.[12]

Félix Bovet (1824-1903), nephew of Philippe, made a lasting imprint on Grandchamp and Neuchâtel.[13] A scholar of theology and history, he was brought to Grandchamp as tutor of the Bovet children. He had long considered Bertha to be his spiritual mentor and with her encouragement, married her daughter Hélène. Félix dreamed of applying Herrnhut's methods in Grandchamp. "We aren't Zinzendorf, but the Lord is still the Lord: let us pray, work and have faith!"[14] He put into practice Moravian educational insights on family care, instruction, education, business apprenticeships, and Christian formation.[15] Félix invited Jules Paroz to Grandchamp to found and direct the school whose motto was *Ora et Labora* (Pray and Work).[16] A refuge for former governesses was founded in 1867 and a nursery school teacher training academy in 1874.[17] The last ministry to be added to the village was called *l'Andalousie*, a refuge for Spanish Protestants fleeing persecution.[18]

> In 1880 activity at Grandchamp was at its peak. The number of inhabitants had grown from nine in 1850 to . . . 200 in 1880 . . . Alongside this educational and charitable hospitality had grown up a network of cultural and spiritual friendships. An elite group of thinkers, poets, pastors, Christians of all types, were attracted to this place . . .[19]

---

10. Fliedner's deaconess house at Kaiserswerth became the model for most Protestant deaconess houses in Western Europe and the USA. See Meyer, *Deaconesses*.

11. Rougemont, *La Geste des Bovet*, 25; Bovet, *Un Siècle*, 207-69.

12. Bovet, *Un siècle*, 271-75. On Mannedorf, see Cullis, *Dorothea Trudel* and Kober-Gobat, *Samuel Zeller*.

13. On Félix Bovet, see Berchtold, *La Suisse romande*, 74-83; Schlup, "Félix Bovet," 50-56; Bovet, *Lettres de Grandchamp*. Félix Bovet served as librarian at the University Library in Neuchâtel where the main reading room was named in his honor.

14. Rougemont, *La Geste des Bovet*, 25; Bovet, *Un Siècle*, 207-69. For Bovet's analysis of Zinzendorf, see Bovet, *Zinzendorf*.

15. Rougemont, *La Geste des Bovet*, 25-39; Bovet, *Un Siècle*, 93-173.

16. Bourquin, *Des portes qui s'ouvrent*; Bovet, *Un Siècle*, 299-305; Rougemont, *La Geste des Bovet*, 65-66.

17. Rougemont, *La Geste des Bovet*, 70-71.

18. Ibid., 68; Bovet, *Un Siècle*, 319-24.

19. Rougemont, *La Geste des Bovet*, 4.

Genevan writer H. F. Amiel admired "the patriarchal life" and "the biblical clan" of the Bovets of Grandchamp. Félix Bovet was the great patriarch of this family at the height of its pietistic enterprise. Each refurbished building of the former fabric painting business was fitted with a chapel where daily prayers were held by the directors of each ministry. New residents received Bibles and Sunday worship was led by Félix Bovet who also created Bible games for the children and played with them himself. Residents, friends and neighbors joined in the Sunday worship of the village whose spirituality sprang from and was expressed in these communal prayer and teaching times.[20]

> Strong ties connected Grandchamp with various Christian communities in Germany, German-speaking Switzerland, and French Catholics. Ecumenical before his time, respectful of all beliefs, Félix and the Bovet family developed friendships with everyone. The erudition of Félix and the richness of the family's traditions made of the village of Grandchamp in the nineteenth century a spiritual center of French-speaking Switzerland.[21]

Félix and Hélène had two sons who became professors.[22] Jean married Mathilde, who had been raised at the orphanage in Grandchamp, and in 1910 they moved back to take charge of it. Pierre married Amy Babut, a pastor's daughter and lived in Geneva where Pierre was director of the Rousseau Institute.[23] They retired to Grandchamp where Pierre published its history.[24] Accustomed to life in a community of prayer and service they rejoiced to see their beloved buildings filled once again with a "new thing" God was doing.[25] A great-great grandson of Philippe and Bertha, Jacques Bovet, spoke of Grandchamp, paraphrasing Samuel Gagnebin, friend of Pierre Bovet: "Grandchamp should be seen as a formational training ground, a place that invites us to healing and even more, to self-transcendence; a place that allows us to discover within, one who is greater than ourselves." [26]

---

20. Ibid.
21. Ibid., 5.
22. Ibid., 47–48; Bovet, *Un Siècle*, 333–73.
23. Bovet, *Vingt ans de vie*.
24. Rougemont, *La Geste des Bovet*, 46.
25. Ibid., 6.
26. Jacques Bovet, "Quelques mots en introduction au vernissage de l'exposition de photographies anciennes du hameau de Grandchamp," September 10, 2011 in Grandchamp. Courtesy of Anne Bovet Nussbaum, who currently lives in the Grande Maison at Grandchamp and knits sweaters for the sisters.

The Community of Grandchamp, which views itself "to some extent as the heir to what preceded them in the old houses they renovated,"[27] was viewed by the family, and the region, as the best way to continue the vision of the Bovet family for prayer, service and intellectual inquiry. It was to this place that Swiss Reformed women came, first for retreats, and then to form a women's monastic community.

A Tale of Three Women: *Réveil*, Retreats, and Community in Protestant Switzerland

In the turbulent years of the last decade of the nineteenth century and the early decades of the twentieth, Protestant women in Switzerland began to create space for women to develop their lives, intellects, and spirituality. The women able to do this were of the privileged classes, financially secure, and influenced by the *Réveil* and its institutions, such as the École Vinet at Lausanne. Three of these women, Hélène Laufer Gautier (1882–1959), Geneviève de Lacroix Micheli (1883–1961), and Marguerite de Beaumont (1895–1986) developed life-long friendships which intertwined in such a way as to create something entirely new: a women's monastic community within the Reformed Church in Switzerland. Together they pushed the boundaries of what was possible for women and women's spirituality.

After years of fruitful collaboration, they eventually focused on the idea of silent retreats for Protestant women, organizing the first such in Switzerland in 1931 at Grandchamp. The idea of the silent retreat was new in Protestant circles. Just a few years earlier, in 1929, Antoinette Butte, founder of the women's community, Pomeyrol (France), had opened a very small retreat house near Paris for offering silent retreats.[28] She was a member of the lay spirituality group the *Veilleurs* (Watchers) founded in 1923 by Wilfrid Monod and his son Théodore. This group encouraged silent retreats for the purpose of drawing near to God as part of the normal spiritual discipline to be practiced by all Christians. In 1933 Wilfred Monod wrote, with amazing foresight, "Before long, we will see houses consecrated to spiritual retreat open in diverse areas. And when this happens . . . the next generation will bless the obscure efforts of the *Veilleurs*."[29] The validation by the *Veilleurs* of the idea that a community of Christians living together the teachings of Jesus Christ through a life of prayer and service to one another and to others can be a powerful witness to the truth and matchless value of Christ's

27. Bovet, *Un Siècle*, 5.
28. Butte, *Semences*, 24.
29. Monod, "Les Veilleurs," 16.

message, played an important part in the development of both Grandchamp and the Community of Taizé.[30]

Hélène Laufer Gautier (1882–1959)

Hélène's father, Lucien Gautier, was a faculty member of the evangelical free-church seminary[31] founded in 1847 by Alexandre Vinet in Lausanne, the school attended by Roger Schutz (Brother Roger, founder of Taizé). Vinet is a name as familiar to the French-speaking Swiss as that of Calvin. Sometimes called the French Schleiermacher because of his emphasis on the primacy of experiential knowledge for theology and Christian life,[32] it was Vinet's conviction that once ushered into the presence of Christ, the human soul recognizes that for which it has always been longing, the truth of its deepest intuitions. The Word, the Bible, was for Vinet, not a written code, but rather the story of a person of irresistible attraction to the soul. "In a word, Christianity is Christ."[33] Hélène's family belonged to the denomination founded by Vinet.[34]

As a result of her education at the *École Vinet*, the girls' school founded by Vinet, Hélène had a precocious confidence in the abilities of her own gender. She went on to study at Neuchâtel, and the University of Geneva. As a college student she experienced the power of Christian community at *Fédé* conferences organized at Sainte-Croix,[35] the students hosted by its Moravian influenced congregation of the Église Évangélique Libre.[36] Hélène first attended in 1906, one of only five women among ninety-three men.[37] When no longer a student, she participated in the Montricher conferences founded by Sophie Vernet in 1910,[38] with the help of several teachers from the *École Vinet*. The summer camps were for unmarried women only, aged 18 to 35. After many positive communal experiences from school days

---

30. For more on Taizé see Gower, "Reformed and Ecumenical"; Laplane, *Frère Roger*; Gonzalez-Balado, *The Story of Taizé*; Paupert, *Taizé et l'Église de demain*.

31. Faculté de Théologie de L'Église Évangélique Libre du Canton de Vaud.

32. Rambert, *Alexandre Vinet*; Latourette, *The Nineteenth Century*, 213.

33. Alexandre Vinet, quoted in Colomb, "Un siècle de prédication," 120.

34. The *Église Évangélique Libre* of Vaud was founded in 1847 by Alexandre Vinet because the civil power in the Canton of Vaud interfered with the church's autonomy.

35. World Student Christian Federation (WSCF), founded by Methodist layman John R. Mott. In francophone Europe, it was called the Fédération Universel d'Associations Chrétiennes d'Étudiants, known as the Fédé.

36. Wernle, "Les Frères Moraves," 140–42.

37. C., "18–21 septembre," 6.

38. Laufer "Témoignage," 60.

through 1912, the year of her marriage, Hélène Laufer Gautier could not be satisfied with less. She invited a few married friends during the winter of 1913–1914 to discuss their need for sharing and support of one another. Forty women answered her invitation.[39]

United by strong friendships and a shared spiritual vision, they formed a committee in view of organizing at Morges, Switzerland, an annual retreat of thirty-six hours on the model of the conferences of Montricher.[40] The result was the *Dames de Morges*, the women responsible for founding the Community of Grandchamp. Hélène's close friend Geneviève Micheli was invited to that first organizing meeting, but declined to attend because she was so recently widowed and did not want to affect the others with her sadness. She did accept a speaking assignment for the first conference and took leadership in years to come.

Geneviève Micheli de Lacroix (1883–1961)

Geneviève de Lacroix was born into a mixed Catholic-Protestant family of privilege in Paris. She married (1902) Léopold Micheli, a member of the upper middle class (*haute bourgeoisie*) of Geneva, head librarian of Geneva. Léopold's family had been influenced by the *Réveil*; in 1900 he attended the Bible conference at Sainte-Croix.[41] He worked with the *Jeunesse-club* (Youth Club) in Geneva, a ministry to students, which Geneviève continued after his death.[42]

Léopold struggled with depression. In November 1909 the couple were invited to hear Georges Boissonnas, French pastor and evangelist. His message was "a revelation to Léopold and Geneviève."[43] Genevieve wrote, "We were deeply moved by his heartfelt words and for the first time I felt Christian joy, the happiness of believing . . . For Leopold there was complete, absolute deliverance from his dark thoughts and discouragements."[44] Summer 1910, they vacationed in Bretagne where Léopold died in a swimming accident. Boissonnas came to counsel and pray with Geneviève. It was her mystical experience of the love of God overcoming the terrible pain of this tragic death that she eventually brought to the *Dames de Morges*.[45] She

39. Westphal, *Nos fondatrices*, 3.
40. Laufer, "Témoignage," 61.
41. Gardy, *Léopold Micheli*, 22.
42. Aubert, "Léopold Micheli au Jeunesse-Club."
43. Minke, "Historique," in Boissonnas, *Expériences d'un évangéliste*, 14.
44. Laufer, "Témoignage," 48.
45. Genevieve Micheli's account of her experience is found in *The Fruits of Grace*,

never ceased seeking that love and trying to connect it with all the tragedies of human life, for herself, her community, and all the lives she touched. The young widow and her three children returned to the Geneva area where she developed a close friendship with her neighbor, Hélène Gautier. "These two single women got together and began to share . . . their need to deepen their spiritual lives and share it with others. The two, rich in youth, culture, tradition and faith would seek to support one another and to share their spiritual search and then lead other women into it."[46]

She developed a deep and fruitful relationship with Dr. Marguerite Champendal (1880–1928), a pastor's daughter, one of the earliest women to receive a doctorate in medicine from the University of Geneva. Her organization, *Goutte de Lait* (Drop of Milk), which worked with mothers and babies, grew to include a nursing school, the *Bon Secours* (Good Help) where Geneviève Micheli helped by giving classes in religious and cultural human development.[47] There she met Marguerite de Beaumont, a nursing student. Both women adored Dr. Marguerite Champendal whom they called "La Doctoresse." Their friendship intensified after her death as they shared memories of her and her teachings.[48]

In 1930 Geneviève took up residence in Paris where her children were in school. There she formed other friendships which would be important for the development of Grandchamp. She attended the *Oratoire*, the Protestant church where Wilfred Monod preached and joined the *Veilleurs*, the spirituality group he had created in 1923. She met Antoinette Butte, a *Veilleuse* who had opened a retreat house at St.-Germain-en-Laye in 1929. Wilfred Monod introduced her to his ecumenical circles including Russian Orthodox and Catholic scholars.[49] She met Mother Elisabeth de Wavrechin, also a widow, and founder of the Benedictine monastery of the Sisters of Sainte-Françoise-Romaine, nun oblates of the Abbey of Bec Helouin. Geneviève was struck by all they had in common:

> We love the same God, we want to serve him as we are. We love the same Lord, Christ who came to tell us we all have the same father. And we love each other because our hearts know suffering and we know those who have gone before us 'have opened a

chapter 1, "The Call of God," taken from Mère Geneviève, *Lettre à mes enfants*, copy, Grandchamp archives.

46. Laufer, "Témoignage," 51–52.

47. Brocher, *La Doctoresse*, 14.

48. [Beaumont], *Lettres*, 1.

49. Russian Orthodox theologian Paul Evdokimov later dedicated his book, *Les ages de la vie spirituelle*, to her.

door that no one can close" and that death has been vanquished
. . . you have opened your arms so wide to me, your heart and
home. I feel I am kneeling in your chapel . . . I hear the prayers
of your hearts like sweet perfume rising to God and I adore the
one you praise with such purity . . . May the Holy Spirit descend
on you in fullness of love, wisdom and faith . . ."[50]

The power of the spiritual retreats she experienced among Catholic friends as well as among her Protestant sisters at St.-Germain-en-Laye had a profound impact on her life, an impact she wished to share with her friends in Switzerland.

Marguerite de Beaumont (1895–1986)

Born into a wealthy Genevan family, Marguerite was baptized at the Cathedral where John Calvin once preached. Sara, their maid, frequently told the children Bible stories and when an aunt died she told them the parable of the grain of wheat which fell to the ground and died so that it might be fruitful.[51] Marguerite remembered the story and it became part of her calling to community life at Grandchamp.

At the age of twenty she was not content to "stay near her mother doing embroidery" but wanted to "make something of her life."[52] Attracted by the ideas of Dr. Champendal, she enrolled (1916) at *Bon Secours* to learn nursing. She was graduated in 1918 and was accepted at the military hospital in Paris.[53] In 1919 she returned to Geneva where she lived with her mother and continued nurse's training. In 1925 Marguerite heard Toyohiko Kagawa speak in Geneva.[54] She had read his books and found his story of living and ministering in the slums very moving. In 1926 she opened a home care service which lasted until 1928.

That year she and Geneviève Micheli went together to Assisi where they prayed the Beatitudes together, a practice of the *Veilleurs*. They shared a love for Franciscan spirituality with its love of beauty and deep caring

---

50. Micheli to Mère de Wavrechin, May 16, 1939. In [Beaumont], *Lettres*, 63–64.

51. Beaumont, *Du Grain*, 23–29.

52. Ibid., 41.

53. Ibid., 44, 46. She summarized her experience in an article for the *Bon Secours* newsletter: "The Ten Commandments of the Christian Nurse."

54. Kagawa was discipled through the Japan Evangelistic Band, and pursuant to that Holiness ethic became an activist for social justice. On Kagawa, see Simon, *A Seed Shall Serve*; Schildgen, *Toyohiko Kagawa*.

for humanity.[55] Though Geneviève left Geneva to be with her daughters at school in Paris, they corresponded regularly to share their spiritual reading, experiences, and challenges as well as their prayers for one another.[56]

Marguerite found the liturgical poverty of her church in Geneva quite striking in comparison with the Catholic liturgical traditions of both Paris and Collonges, where her family summered. Christmas Eve 1932 she recalled,

> I wanted to celebrate the birth of the Lord . . . I found the doors of the cathedral locked. So I made up my mind to go into the Catholic church . . . the doors were wide open for the midnight mass, the church was brightly lit, the crowd of faithful prayed with devotion and joy.[57]

She wrote about this experience to the leaders of the Reformed Church in Geneva, asking that a Christmas Eve service be held in future. In 1932 she published her first book designed to help Protestants prepare for Christmas, a book of daily scripture readings for Advent.[58] After two years of requesting the Company of Pastors for permission, she was allowed (1934) to organize, with others, a concert in the cathedral for Christmas Eve. There was standing room only; one by one all the Protestant churches in Geneva began to hold Christmas Eve services.[59]

Three women—three trajectories that met, influenced by the precocious feminism of Dr. Marguerite Champendal, the *Réveil* values of the *Fédé*, and especially by the spirituality and ecumenism of Pastor Wilfred Monod. The relationships established as young women remained strong for the rest of their lives. They were united by the durability of the spiritual vision they formulated for women, and their shared tenacity to concretize that spirituality. The structures could grow, supported by their sisters, the *Dames de Morges*, and the Bovet family, two overlapping subsets of Swiss *Réveil* Christianity that provided support and space at Grandchamp.

---

55. Meroz, "Liminaire," 8.

56. Collected and edited by Sr. Marguerite, preserved in the archives of Grandchamp. See [Beaumont], *Lettres*.

57. Beaumont, *Du Grain*, 62.

58. Beaumont, *Lectures quotidiennes de l'Avent*. In 1934 she developed a similar program on preparation for Easter using the Beatitudes: *Prépare-toi à célébrer Pâques*.

59. Grandchamp, *Marguerite*, 4. Grandchamp archives.

Silent Retreats: A New Development for the *Dames de Morges*

After fifteen years of active participation in the *Dames de Morges*, and perhaps after reading Antoinette Butte's proposal for an annual spiritual retreat in the April issue of *Veillez!*[60] Geneviève Micheli suggested to Hélène Laufer that they plan such a retreat. In May 1930 she suggested a small gathering of *Morgiennes* to discuss the possibility; small because the idea of spiritual retreat was so easily misunderstood by Protestants. A committee of six, *Les Responsables* (the leaders), was formed to make plans for such a retreat: Geneviève, Hélène, Amy Bovet and three friends, Mesdames Exchaquet, Lenoir, and Rossier. Aware of her friend Marguerite de Beaumont's spiritual sensitivity, Genevieve invited her to help in the planning: "I sense that the preparation for this retreat can make a significant contribution to our lives. I like to feel that you are with us and carry these preparations in your heart."[61]

Geneviève's goal was to persuade them "to choose a program that poses no intellectual problem, but one on love—the love of God for us, our love for those dear to us, and our love for him. There will be a great deal of silence and few human words."[62] By January, 1931, she reported to Marguerite, "We have all accepted the idea of the Retreat with all it implies of silence, personal surrender and preparation in prayer. They like the program on love where there will be no intellectual research but rather surrender, contemplation and prayer."[63]

The first *Retraite de Grandchamp* was held September 22–26, 1931, in the library of Félix Bovet, a space offered by Mathilde Bovet, a *Morgienne*. The invitation clarified that *La Retraite* was for women between forty and sixty-five and would consist of "Days of silence and recollection lived with Christ."[64] Its theme was God's love as revealed to humankind throughout the ages, as revealed in Christ, and through his death. Afterward Geneviève said of the Retreat, "I experienced in the library, in the 'upper room,' some of the most beautiful hours of my life and it now seems to me that all of life is marvelously beautiful and rich with possibilities for joy."[65] In October Geneviève, still reflecting on that first Retreat, reported to Marguerite that she had discussed it with fellow *Veilleur* Antoinette Butte at St.-Germain-en-Laye,

60. Butte, "Projet de Retraite," 12–13.
61. Micheli to Beaumont, October 8, 1930. In [Beaumont], *Lettres*, 14.
62. Micheli to Beaumont, December 1930. In [Beaumont], *Lettres*, 16; Westphal, "In Thanks," 1. See Beaumont, *Du Grain*, 51 for Marguerite's recollections.
63. Micheli to Beaumont, January 13, 1931. In [Beaumont], *Lettres*, 16.
64. Retreats, 1931. Grandchamp archives.
65. Micheli to Beaumont September 20, 1930. In [Beaumont], *Lettres*, 20.

"In the little chapel, so poorly and luminously Franciscan . . . On Sunday the *Veilleurs* met there—a true spiritual community."[66]

Geneviève and Marguerite, along with the *Responsables*, including Amy Bovet, continued to plan and host the *Retraites de Grandchamp* for many years. The facilities at Grandchamp were made available each time by Mathilde Bovet. Themes included: "God is Light" (1932), and "The Kingdom of God is within you" (1933).[67] Geneviève insisted on "Very few words, much silence and prayer and contemplation of Christ."[68] That year she asked Marguerite to speak on St. Francis of Assisi: "It would be so wonderful to have our Retreat introduced by St. Francis—for we want it to be at once very simple, fervent, humble and joyful—bathed in the Franciscan spirit."[69] Geneviève wanted the worship simpler, with more silent meditation:

> I see first love, then surrender—the opposite of what you write to me. For me God reveals himself first to the soul and makes himself loved. This is the first step and it is dazzling and wonderful, this free gift, this grace, this joy—then comes surrender, through love—for once we love, we see all our impurities, we thirst for sanctification, we cannot advance in relationship with God without surrender. And then, all that we give up, all our sufferings, all our nights, lead to new joys, new consolations, new light. I cannot see Christ otherwise, or his teaching. I also see St. Francis this way; and all my personal religious experience has been this way. I cannot believe in all this self-deprivation before having known the love and the joy of the gift. I would like this *Retraite* to be full of Franciscan simplicity, purity, love, that it may shine a new light on our daily lives so that they will become radiant: our hearts purified, prayerful, loving—the kingdom of God within us. This is how it is for me, finding that joy, that love; looking inside myself to find God—and to see him so close to us—this is the secret of a radiant life—becoming more human, more compassionate, more tender toward others as Christ was.[70]

This is a common theme in Geneviève's letters to Marguerite who often saw the sacrificial side of the Christian life before she saw the centrality and transforming power of God's overwhelming love for each individual. Because of her life-changing experience just after her husband's death,

---

66. Micheli to Beaumont, October 21, 1931. In [Beaumont], *Lettres*, 20.
67. Retreats, 1932, 1933. Grandchamp archives.
68. Micheli to Beaumont, January 9, 1933. In [Beaumont], *Lettres*, 23.
69. Micheli to Beaumont, June 14, 1933. In [Beaumont], *Lettres*, 26.
70. Micheli to Beaumont, June 26, 1933. In [Beaumont], *Lettres*, 27.

Geneviève always saw the love of God and the revelation of that love to the individual human heart as the starting point.

During the 1933 Retreat, the Beatitudes were prayed each day at noon, a spiritual disciplines of the *Veilleurs*. The meditations were supported by other Scripture readings and quotes from spiritual writers such as Vinet, Heinrich Suso, Joseph Gratry, Catherine of Siena, Bernard de Clairvaux, Pierre Nicole, Blaise Pascal and Wilfred Monod, chosen by Geneviève. Readings were followed by silence or music.[71] After the retreat Geneviève wrote "I sense that the living spring of love at Grandchamp was so powerful that to the extent that we remember it each day, we will be renewed. I feel that I am walking down a new path, heading with wonder toward new joys."[72]

The Retreat House at Grandchamp: The Genesis of a Presence

The popularity of the silent retreats at Grandchamp revealed "a thirst for spiritual experience such that the question was posed rather quickly of a permanent place for retreats,"[73] at a center that might minister more broadly to the churches as a source for renewal "in a context of silence, recollection and prayer."[74] The *Morgiennes* began to consider the implications and logistics of such an institution. Early in 1934 Max Dominicé,[75] a young pastor in Geneva, approached Marguerite on this matter.

Marguerite struggled with the idea of directing such a center. Geneviève was more positive: "I think it's a necessity to respond to the needs for silence and the interior life."[76] She had already begun to hope that they could create a center "where human silence calls out for the creative word of God."[77] "I've been praying for you and with Wilfred Monod as well, about this desire for a Retreat House."[78] October 11, 1934, they went together to the next Retreat planning session, Marguerite's first meeting with the *Responsables*.[79]

71. Notebooks of *Morgienne* Yvonne Martin, 1933. Retreats. Grandchamp archives.
72. Micheli to Beaumont, October 25, 1933. In [Beaumont], *Lettres*, 30.
73. Meroz, "Liminaire," 9.
74. Beaumont, *Du grain*, 81.
75. Max Dominicé (1901–1975), a nephew by marriage of Geneviève Micheli, became (1959) General Secretary of the National Church of Geneva. See: Fatio, "Dominicé, Max."
76. Micheli to Beaumont, June 11, 1934. In [Beaumont], *Lettres*, 30–31.
77. Micheli, "*Silence dans nos vies*," 2.
78. Micheli to Beaumont, July 17, 1934. In [Beaumont], *Lettres*, 32.
79. [Beaumont], *Lettres*, 41, note 1.

Amy Bovet reported, "The house called the 'Hospital' at Grandchamp is now closed . . . Several people have already asked about renting it. But my husband [Pierre] would like very much for it to become a house for spiritual retreats, open all year. He asked me to speak to you about it." Marguerite, feeling called by God, gave Amy Bovet a provisional "yes."

In the midst of the negotiations necessary for this larger project, the *Responsables* continued to plan retreats, and to expand the networks invited. In 1934 the theme was "God is Spirit," and for the first time women not belonging to *Morges* were invited. In 1935, a Retreat was planned for those with arduous ministries, rather than for *Morgiennes*. "We can no longer keep this treasure for ourselves, we feel peoples' need, their expectancy, which God calls us to respond to."[80] After this retreat Geneviève wrote that she felt Grandchamp was "holy ground."[81]

Finally, in November 1935, Marguerite felt assured that God was calling her to ministry in a permanent Retreat House at Grandchamp, in the "Hospital."[82] Yvonne Martin, a *Morgienne*, wrote, "Wonderful answer to prayer: the opening of the Retreat House which Sister Marguerite will direct, for which we all feel responsible, for it is certainly the fruit of our Retreats."[83] In early December, 1935, Marguerite visited the "Hospital." She was accompanied by Marc, manager of the farm, son of Pierre and Amy Bovet, who took her back to the farm house where a long-time servant of the Bovet family, Marguerite Bossert (later Sister Marthe) agreed to join the project. Since 1931 Marthe had helped prepare rooms for the silent retreats of the *Morgiennes* and had participated in them.[84] Geneviève wrote joyfully that she was ". . . feeling this Retreat House to be a grace and the fulfillment of our Retreats, seeing our group support you, giving and receiving—all of this gives me deep peace."[85]

Marguerite corresponded with Wilfred Monod, seeking his counsel for the Retreat House and its daily discipline, hoping her fellow *Veilleurs* would gain from such a spiritual communion.[86] She suggested Marthe join the *Veilleurs*, which she did. *Veillez!* described the Retreat House at Grandchamp as, "a patiently conceived project, developed over the course of the

---

80. Notebooks of *Morgienne* Yvonne Martin, 1935. Retreats. Grandchamp archives.
81. Micheli to Beaumont, June 18, 1935. In [Beaumont], *Lettres*, 37.
82. Beaumont, *Du Grain*, 85.
83. Notebooks of *Morgienne* Yvonne Martin, 1936. Retreats. Grandchamp archives.
84. Beaumont, *Du Grain*, 86.
85. Micheli to Beaumont, Nov–Dec, 1935. In [Beaumont], *Lettres*, 41.
86. Gaulué, "Vers un monastère réel," 142.

last few years by a series of spiritual retreats, the House for silence and prayer in a favorable setting will be directed by a *Veilleuse*."[87]

A new era began. On March 3, 1936, the two Marguerites took up residence in the former "Hospital" of Grandchamp which was still being remodeled to host retreats. At the consecration, Pastor Marc Du Pasquier presided at Communion and preached on "The Houses Where Jesus Entered."[88] After recitation of the Beatitudes and a meal of loaves and fishes, Marguerite read the biblical text of the multiplication of the loaves and fishes by Jesus (John 6:1–14).[89]

Marthe confessed, some years later, "Our life as two began. I was happy, but our very different personalities led to some friction and a few difficulties. The first year was a little hard because there weren't many people; the House was not well known and the most frequent visitors were *Veilleurs*." Their first retreatant was Sister Alice Vernet[90] who arrived on April 1, 1936.

"It is wonderful to think of April 1 when the Retreat House will begin to live its deep life," wrote Geneviève, urging Marguerite to temper her desire to achieve perfection. "Wait for the seed to germinate . . . do not push yourself too hastily . . . Let God work and his inspiration fill you."[91] Geneviève thought Marguerite's idea of silence shared in the Oxford Group style for one worship gathering was good, but felt that they had not yet reached the full potential of their silent retreats.[92] Another letter joyfully informed Marguerite that Pastor Marc Du Pasquier had agreed to lead a retreat.[93] Their dreams were beginning to take shape.

The ninth *Retraite de Grandchamp* (1936) crossed class lines for the first time: "working class" women were invited. Twenty-four participated. Amy Bovet spoke to them of Félix Bovet, her father-in-law, whose life had been devoted to God through prayer. Yvonne closed the evening with a talk on silence and recollection. Lunch was taken in silence, after the recitation of the Beatitudes. In the afternoon there was rest, silence, and walks by the lake. The evening discussion on personal devotions was led by Yvonne, attempting to be sensitive to the tight scheduling needs of working women.[94]

87. "A Retreat House in Switzerland," 16.
88. Beaumont, *Du grain*, 88.
89. Ibid., 88–89.
90. Daughter of an evangelist and sister of Montricher co-founder Sophie Vernet. She spoke at Vaumarcus girl's camps and in their notice in the Neuchâtel newspaper *Feuille d'Avis* (July 12, 1926), 2, was referred to as "sister."
91. Micheli to Beaumont, March 31, 1936. In [Beaumont], *Lettres*, 43.
92. Micheli to Beaumont, April 25, 1936. In [Beaumont], *Lettres*, 45.
93. Micheli to Beaumont, July 1, 1936. In [Beaumont], *Lettres*, 46.
94. Notebooks of *Morgienne* Yvonne Martin, 1936. Grandchamp archives.

Marthe wrote that their principal activity was still the Retreats planned by the *Dames de Morges*. Since a name for the house had not been chosen, it was simply called *La Retraite*. She was thankful that these brought their "Spiritual Mother, Madame Micheli, the inspirer of the Retreats. We confide in her, and Sister Marguerite consults with her and together they give everything into God's hands, for without God we can do nothing (John 15:5)."[95]

In July 1937, the *Morgiennes* provided a second *Retraite de Grandchamp* for working women, drawing more participants than the first. Their twelfth retreat, its theme was "Apart from me you can do nothing (John 15:5)."

In 1938, the theme was "The Living Christ." Marguerite had been ill all winter but came back to Grandchamp in April. She and Geneviève prayed together, in silence. "Suddenly came a feeling through my whole being like dew on arid ground . . . and I felt healed."[96] Geneviève wrote later, "I leave Grandchamp with my heart overflowing with gratitude for having found so much strength and joy there. Christ is there and it is good to feel you there close to him who wants to heal you and call you anew into his service."[97]

Yvonne Martin noted that those participating at their Retreats increasingly represented the diversity of Swiss Protestantism: "There were several members of the Oxford Group, one Pentecostal, and *Veilleurs* . . ."[98] In 1938 the *Morgiennes* hosted a third retreat for "working women." Geneviève took Marguerite's report to their mentors, Wilfred and Dorina Monod. "I read to them from your letter and then we knelt and prayed with ardent hearts."[99] Yvonne Martin remembered the retreat as: "a miracle of the love of God."[100] Geneviève assured Marguerite of her prayers for Grandchamp: "I praised God with you for the wheat, and prayed for the seed and the sewer, and for all the souls who are at Grandchamp, who have been and will be there."[101] The last retreat of 1938 was for the young women catechumens of Genevan pastor Jean de Saussure (1899–1977), who would be an important influence on the development of the Community of Grandchamp and its chaplain (1945–1954).[102]

---

95. Bossert, *Cahier de Sr. Marthe*, 9. Grandchamp archives.

96. Beaumont, *Du grain*, 97.

97. Micheli to Beaumont, Saturday, April 1938. In [Beaumont], *Lettres*, 53.

98. Notebooks of Yvonne Martin, 1938. Retreats. Grandchamp archives.

99. Micheli to Beaumont, Jeudi, July 1938. In [Beaumont], *Lettres*, 54.

100. Notebooks of Yvonne Martin, 1938. Retreats. Grandchamp archives,

101. Micheli to Beaumont, Lundi, July 1938, in [Beaumont], *Lettres*, 54–55.

102. Notebooks of Yvonne Martin, 1938. Retreats. Grandchamp archives. In an interview, Minke de Vries stated that Jean de Saussure, like many male supporters eventually tried to direct, rather than be available to, Grandchamp and so the relationship

The success of the Retreat House which drew more women each year required more infrastructure and information. Space was added;[103] gardens were tended.[104] Marguerite made notebooks, with practical information and an essay on silent retreats. Every year they learned more about hosting retreatants. "We had to learn from experience that without him we can do nothing. It is necessary to place each soul who enters into God's care . . . Each guest should be welcomed as Jesus himself, that is, in his name."[105]

By February of 1939, Europe was at war.[106] The *Responsables*, having grown in number from the original six to eleven, wrote a letter about the retreats that demonstrated their awareness:

> The gravity of the present hour makes us feel our Christian duty and the need to receive a new spirit. This year again, Grandchamp "refuge of peace, prayer and contemplation" will open its doors to all who are thirsty for spiritual renewal and wish to strengthen their prayer life. Several retreats are planned allowing for four days of silence and recollection . . . The theme will be "Behold I make all things new (Rev 21:5)."

The letter was signed by the eleven *Responsables*, using, for the first time, their first name initials rather than the traditional "Madame," followed by their husbands' full names; a step toward independence for women just catching a glimpse of its powers. In all preceding years Geneviève had signed Mdm. Léopold Micheli. Now she felt free to be G. Micheli and the *Responsables* followed suit.[107] The response to the invitation was dramatic. There

---

became less close (Minke de Vries, interview with Nancy Gower, November 19, 2012). "Grandchamp Jalons." Unpublished document, Grandchamp archives, 1.

103. Sr. Marthe wrote, "No one will ever know all that there was to put together and all that we succeeded in doing with very little—this is another of Marguerite's gifts . . ." (Bossert, *Cahier de Sr. Marthe*, 15).

104. Sr. Marthe wrote, "Again the fall arrived too soon and before the winter freeze we needed to prepare the garden path, plant tulips and pansies, divide plants that had grown too large, clean up the lawns so that in the early spring all the little flowers can come out and welcome us home" (ibid., 11–13).

105. Ibid., 13.

106. Micheli to Beaumont, 20 October 1938. In [Beaumont], *Lettres*, 58: "How good it is to feel that our Retreat House is there, a refuge of peace and a source of strength. . . . Here in Paris the evacuation has thrown everything into chaos . . . I feel ever more profoundly that we must ask for the Holy Spirit. For we need a new spirit. The hour is so grave that only the Spirit of God can save the world. I feel that our work for the 1939 retreats must be a call, that prayer, that faith. I'd like the retreats for the *Veilleurs* and mothers to also reflect the call for the Holy Spirit."

107. Letter from the *Responsables*, October 2, 1939. New to the *Responsables* are the names M. Berguer, J. Rumpf, N. Soutter, C. Weber and M. de Beaumont.

were more individual guests than ever and the four planned retreats drew large numbers. So many women signed up for the May retreat that they had to divide them into two separate weeks of May.[108] Two retreats were added for July.[109] The crush of guests made the offer of assistance by retreatant, Mrs. Rubin, most welcome. She helped Marthe with the housekeeping and cooking. For the closed months, December to February, Marguerite rented for them a "charming little lodging."[110] During those months Mrs. Rubin[111] and Marthe repaired the bedding, musing together about turning their little "Beguinage"[112] into a shelter for the elderly and lonely. They made aprons as well "which I would not wear for long, though I didn't suspect it then," wrote Marthe.[113] The next year aprons were replaced by the blue habits of the Community of Grandchamp!

Marguerite was feeling the weight of responsibility at Grandchamp with ever-increasing numbers of guests. She loved it but was uncertain of God's guidance. In February 1939 she and Geneviève visited the Sisters of Pomeyrol who affirmed, "Yes, life in community can be good!" Next they visited, Mother Elisabeth de Wavrechin prioress of the Sisters of Sainte-Françoise-Romaine. Praying in the chapel before the service, Marguerite had the vision of the grains of wheat which marks the beginning of the transformation of the Retreat House at Grandchamp into the Community of Grandchamp.[114]

Pastor Jean de Saussure asked Marguerite if she had ever thought of being consecrated for her ministry at Grandchamp.[115] She and Geneviève decided it was a good idea, but that they should proceed cautiously to preserve their independence. In December Geneviève wrote saying that after much reflection and prayer she believed this should be done in the spirit of the *Veilleurs*: "We should remain faithful to our community, to our discipline." She advised asking Wilfred Monod to officiate so that the church of Geneva would not make decisions for them, but rather "he who guides and inspires us in such an evangelical and pure spirit. I don't want the pastors to discuss us so that we leave our silence and anonymous service and become

---

108. The first afternoon of each of the May retreats was given to a teaching on intercessory prayer. Retreats, 1939.

109. Retreats, 1939. Grandchamp archives.

110. Ibid., 18.

111. Mrs. Rubin joined the *Veilleurs*. She left Grandchamp in 1941.

112. House for lay religious women popular in the twelfth to fourteenth century.

113. Bossert, *Cahier de Sr. Marthe*, 19.

114. For full text of this vision, see Minke, chap. 1, *The Great Field (Grand Champ) of the World*. From Beaumont, *Du Grain*, 101–3.

115. Micheli to Beaumont, December 3, 1939. In [Beaumont], *Lettres*, 65 note 2.

celebrities. I see so clearly our path in fidelity to the *Veilleurs*; I would like to see us remain intimately connected."[116]

These women were undoubtedly given space by the Reformed Church because they were from the privileged classes, the Retreat House was not a convent, and because it was at the Grandchamp of the Bovets that the silent retreats were held. The Bovet traditions of undertaking ministries of all kinds and their involvement in intellectual inquiry on the cutting edge without asking permission, or forgiveness, from the Reformed Church extended back for more than a century. The women claimed that tradition!

The Community of Grandchamp

Major changes took place in early 1940. While Marguerite de Beaumont, in close consultation with Geneviève Micheli, continued to serve as the director of the Retreat House, she also took steps toward establishing a community. Marthe remembered the transition: "The first event of our fifth year [1940] at Grandchamp was the arrival of our third sister, Irène."[117] Marthe had spent time in retreat that winter and felt God was asking her to give herself "even more fully to him and to truly work for him without reserve . . . I accepted and obeyed and an immense peace descended and joy filled my heart. Then Sister Marguerite began working to form the community. . . . Our blue uniforms were its first mark."[118]

Irène Burnat, a pastor's daughter, consulted with her pastor, Jean de Saussure in the fall of 1938, asking his advice on how and where to live a life of total consecration to God. "He spoke to me of these early Retreats at Grandchamp, of this search for a way to be more attentive to God, more prayerful, more available to do God's will, of the Retreat House just opened for individual retreats . . . it seemed to him in line with what I was seeking."[119] She spent time at Grandchamp. "Right away I relished the warm welcome, the peace, the joy which reigned in the house. It was very Franciscan, with a quality of love and liberty which was unknown to me before then."[120] The notion of a sense of the presence of God was new to her and touched her deeply. In January 1940, she arrived at Grandchamp confirming to Marguerite that God was indeed calling her to join them in community life. Marguerite immediately communicated Irène's intention to Geneviève who

116. Ibid., 65.
117. Bossert, *Cahier de Sr. Marthe*, 19–20.
118. Ibid., 21.
119. Beaumont, *Du Grain*, 104.
120. Ibid.

answered, "It is so moving to think of this little community which is forming, of this seed sewn which sends up its first green shoot."[121]

Geneviève advised Marguerite and Irène to visit Pomeyrol to learn more about the Protestant women's coenobitic community. Jean de Saussure urged Marguerite to visit the Abbé Paul Couturier, whom he knew from the inter-confessional dialogue at La Trappe des Dombes.[122] The Abbé agreed to meet and Geneviève encouraged Marguerite:

> The letter from the Abbé Couturier overwhelmed me. Yes, you should meet, for this is God's answer and you will be working for God's reign by living this union which is the sign of a new era . . . I see possibilities and openings for you which are God's will. May you be completely open and humbly ready! I carry you in my heart.[123]

Marguerite met with the Abbé Couturier on February 22, 1940 and wrote of both visits to Geneviève who replied,

> Thank you for writing so fully . . . of all that touches on the inner soul of Grandchamp. What a beautiful harvest you have made and I believe, like last year, you will return to Grandchamp renewed, your heart full of hope and joy, new relationships, and more intense prayer . . . This meeting with the Abbé Couturier must have been wonderful. I wrote to him and he replied with exceptionally profound thoughts on unity . . . I would like us to address this issue at our retreats and win many over. I can no longer think it possible to say, "Hallowed be thy name" without suffering from the disunity (of the church) and asking for the grace to desire unity.[124]

Irène recalled that they learned much about the blessings and difficulties of life in community from Antoinette Butte and the other sisters. On the way back to Switzerland she met with the Abbé Couturier, who confirmed her vocation to community life and prayer for the unity of the church.[125]

Geneviève also visited the Abbé. "My stop in Lyon is a red letter day in my life . . . an admirable clarity on what love in unity ought to be and

---

121. Micheli to Beaumont, September 29, 1938. In [Beaumont], *Lettres*, 57.

122. Gaulué, "Vers un monastère réel," 144. The Group des Dombes was founded by the Abbé Paul Couturier (1881–1953), a Catholic priest with a passion for ecumenical dialogue, in 1937 and is still the most influential ecumenical francophone dialogue. Minke, "L'Abbé Couturier," 121.

123. Micheli to Beaumont, February 8, 1940. In [Beaumont], *Lettres*, 68.

124. Micheli to Beaumont, February 28, 1940. In [Beaumont], *Lettres*, 68–69.

125. Beaumont, *Du grain*, 106.

adoration which is the basis of unity . . . I think, love and pray differently—you will thank God for it!"[126] She found him wise and inspiring, seeing in his methods a way to work for the unity of the church. The meeting reinforced her conviction that the unity of the church was an issue that needed to be addressed at their Retreats.

The Abbé Couturier responded that he would like to see Grandchamp develop as a place "for spreading the word that our divisions cause suffering to our Lord Jesus Christ, as much as it can be . . . reaching the heart of each retreatant, that his prayer for unity (John 17:20–21) might become that of each one—may Grandchamp become an ecumenical spiritual center." Later he expressed joy at the formation of Protestant communities concerned for the unity of the church: "Grandchamp, Roche-Dieu (Bièvres),[127] Pomeyrol . . . What gifts! What prospects!"[128]

Noémi Soutter, a *Responsable*, wrote out her greeting to the May retreatants. It is a powerful reflection on their sense of the spiritual roots of their community in the Grandchamp of the Bovets, and of its place in the new spirit of unity, the Abbé Couturier's universal prayer of Christians for Christian unity, and the ecumenical movement:

> It is God we seek at Grandchamp. It is in God that we gather in this library where many of us have experienced unforgettable times which have marked our souls with the seal of eternity. We encounter here the whole Bovet family who founded the orphanage, the "Hospital," which is now the Retreat house . . . especially we find here the admirable person of Félix Bovet. One cannot enter here, which was formerly called the Upper Room, without feeling enveloped again by this great soul who many of us know by way of his beautiful letters.[129] If in many ways Grandchamp reminds us of Port Royal, it is perhaps because of him who loved it so much. The three words engraved on his tombstone are "God is Love," which sum up his whole life, and extend all the way to us. The love of God in Christ creates unity among all souls, those of the past whose presence we sense, and those of today. Now it seems that the walls of this room widen and fall away. We are here with all Christians of all places and times. If there is one thing striking and joy giving in this dark hour it is the unity of the church. In spite of all appearances of

126. Micheli to Beaumont, April 23, 1940. In [Beaumont], *Lettres*, 75.

127. Retreat house similar to Grandchamp where Genevieve went on retreat in May 1940.

128. Couturier to Beaumont, May 9, 1940. In [Beaumont], *Lettres*, 71.

129. Bovet, *Lettres De Grandchamp*.

division, today it is rising up like an immense cathedral which is being built up in the invisible on the ruins and wounds of this world. It is out of prayer, sacrifice, consecration and fervent intercession that unity is made. And coming from every part of the world without exception souls are joined to one another in the living Christ. Our retreats are one of the stones building up this edifice.[130]

Five Retreats took place in 1940, all with the theme "Thy will be done on earth as it is in heaven." In addition, there were retreats planned for the *Veilleurs*, for working women, and two for mothers, drawing on Saint Cyran and Mère Angelique, two leaders of the Port Royal movement, the Huguenots, Paul Rabaut, Saint Monica and Nicholas de Flue, patron saint of Switzerland.[131]

"I am happy to sense the retreat house full and carry you in my prayers for this life where God speaks to hearts... this should be your only prayer— then God's work will be done... The retreat house must be the place where God is listened to."[132] More retreats at Grandchamp were good, Geneviève thought, if those responsible "always keep in mind the original rule of slow and silent germination; nothing hasty or organized as palavers, reunions, or meetings. This must be repeated often and we should refuse to lend the house unless this is understood. Be diligent... Be firm on this, please."[133]

Early in 1941, Marguerite wrote a Rule for the community of three. Geneviève advised a few changes and the sisters began to use it. Marthe found it a summary of the Gospel, "This Rule we must read often so that it can become our prayer."[134] She also wrote of another new step for the little community: "Sister Marguerite wanted us to join her in making a vow of poverty so that we could better help many more retreatants who come to nourish their souls and meet the only one who can fill all their needs."[135]

---

130. Retreats, 1940, " Retraite de Pentecôte Mai 40." Grandchamp archives.

131. Letter to retreatants: "By inviting you once again to Grandchamp, we sense that we are responding to the needs felt by many, but especially that we are obeying the call of God, more pressing than ever. From God alone comes our help. During these days of silence, intercession and recollection, we will be in constant communion with the suffering of the world. Together we will seek to know what God expects of us" (Retreats, 1940).

132. Micheli to Beaumont, August 6, 1940. In [Beaumont], *Lettres*, 79.

133. Micheli to Beaumont, November 6, 1940. In [Beaumont], *Lettres*, 81.

134. Bossert, *Cahier de Sr. Marthe*, 26.

135. Ibid., 27.

Grandchamp was becoming more than a Retreat House. By early 1941, it was a religious community with an ecumenical mission, a retreat ministry for a broad constituency, and a "Rule," as well as monastic habits of blue.

Grandchamp, Catalyst in the Development of Taizé

During 1940, the Retreat House began to attract young people searching for spirituality.[136] Among these young people was Roger Schutz (1915–2005) who was himself in the process of founding a community. Marguerite wrote,

> In the spring of 1940 there was a knock on the door. I found before me a young man . . . Roger. He felt called to form a community of young men. He had just heard that we were starting a community and wanted to spend a few days with us in prayer. I gave him a cell and we took care to be very quiet during his stay. Later that year, in August, he found the village of Taizé where he would found the community.[137]

That summer Jean de Saussure showed Geneviève the daily liturgy composed by *Église et Liturgie*, a group of Swiss pastors concerned for the renewal of worship in their Reformed churches. The three sisters began to use it in place of the prayer book of the *Veilleurs*.[138] At an *Église et Liturgie* retreat, August 1940, Max Thurian[139] also discovered the initial typed version (1936) of the group's divine office. He made a copy for himself, by hand.[140] In November 1940, the sisters hosted Jean de Saussure's theology students, including Max. The Abbé Couturier wrote that he was praying for them:

> Whoever helps his brother to welcome the Spirit of God works for Christian unity. May all of these dear young men leave Grandchamp with the wound of our divisions in their hearts

---

136. Ibid., 22.

137. Beaumont, *Du grain*, 115. A letter in the Grandchamp archives, from Roger to Marguerite seems to indicate otherwise: Roger wrote, "If I put off coming to Grandchamp until autumn 1940, it was that I feared being too strongly influenced" (Roger to Marguerite, June 25, 1941, 1).

138. Gaulué, "Vers un monastère réel," 149. Monod, *Livre de Prière*. The huge manuscript was developed earlier and served as a base for the quarterly publication of the *Veilleurs, Veillez!*

139. Future co-founder of the Community of Taize.

140. Bardet, *Un combat*, 88, 167; Gaulué, "Vers un monastère réel," 150.

and the spiritual fire of prayer for unity. May they all be ardent workers for unity in being first fervent soul guides."[141]

In this letter he enclosed a prayer guide for the three sisters to follow, in union with his small group of twenty members, which he called "a Catholic cell of the Invisible Monastery of prayer for Christian unity... Nothing is more important than prayer... which puts us on a quest for truth ever more eagerly sought and welcomed... all of our divergent doctrines will melt in the fire of our adoration."[142]

Just after the retreat, Jean de Saussure wrote his thanks to the Abbé for his prayers, noting that he had read excerpts of the Abbé's letters to the students. One of the young men, Max Thurian, received his calling during this retreat:

> At the Retreat House at Grandchamp I was very clearly given the form of my future ministry. After making contact with this community of women... I realized that God was also calling me... to create a spiritual retreat house for men, where, alone or with brothers, I would exercise the ministry of prayer and the cure of souls, while pursuing theological, liturgical, and spiritual work with a view to publication.[143]

Marguerite had already begun correspondence with Roger Schutz. In November she forwarded to Geneviève his prospectus for a community of Christian intellectuals, published in the *Federation News Sheet* in November 1940. Geneviève replied,

> I think that the idea of M. Schutz is good and believe it viable and certainly the will of God, for community is necessary in the struggle against the assaults of evil. His project appears to me superficial (especially what he writes on prayer), but he will gain in depth for the guiding principle is right. He has not yet the experience but the inspiration is there.[144]

In this prospectus there was nothing about coenobitic community or ecumenism.

> We are aiming at action among intellectuals who have left college, parallel to that of the *Fédé* among students. We wish our

---

141. Micheli to Beaumont, November 2, 1940. In [Beaumont], *Lettres*, 72.
142. Ibid., 72–73.
143. Gaulué, "Vers un monastère réel," 151.
144. Micheli to Beaumont, November 6, 1940. In [Beaumont], *Lettres*, 80–81; Gaulué, "Vers un monastère réel," 152.

movement to correspond to a well-organized "post-*Fédé*" and we hope to be able to work in harmony with the *Fédé*. This community in *Suisse Romande* (French-speaking Switzerland) is very conscious of the situation among French intellectuals and has decided to come to their aid. It wishes, therefore, to found in this country a retreat house to be the center of its activity.[145]

It was probably Roger's visit with the Abbé Couturier in early March, 1941, that turned him in the direction of prayer for Christian unity, and his experience of Grandchamp that turned him toward the idea of coenobitic community. The Abbé wrote to Marguerite about Roger's visit: "Mr. Schutz was here. A part of my dream is coming true. It is among my Protestant brothers that a real monastery for prayer for Christian unity is beginning . . . we agreed that I will go to Taizé March 31 to say mass in the church."[146]

In December 1940 Roger wrote to Marguerite, opening with an apology for not keeping her up to date on his own undertaking at Taizé. "It is not that I have forgotten Grandchamp. On the contrary, I think daily of your House and the experiences I had there. What you have told me of it has already helped and strengthened me in certain convictions."[147] These convictions almost certainly related to the permanent residential coenobitic community and a discipline of common prayer which the three sisters were living at the time of his fall visit. His question about accepting men into the Grandchamp community[148] shows that by December 1940 he had begun thinking of coenobitic community, in part due to his experiences at Grandchamp.

Later that December, Roger moved into the house he had purchased in the village of Taizé. There he began his practice of daily prayer and hospitality to those fleeing the Nazi occupation of France. At the same time he reflected carefully and prayerfully on the form his proposed community should take. Experiences at Grandchamp and his meeting with the Abbé influenced his thinking. By late 1941 he had completed a pamphlet which

---

145. [Schutz], "Switzerland," 4. Five rules of spiritual direction were proposed for this community of intellectuals: Schutz wrote, "1. Reserve in your day some period so that work and rest may center in reading, and particularly Bible reading, in self-recollection, prayer and meditation. 2. Let the compassion and joy of the Gospel penetrate your soul. 3. Aim continually at greater simplification of your personal life. 4. Try always to maintain interior silence. 5. Remember that you are the member of a community and are no longer working in isolation" ("Switzerland," 4).

146. Couturier to Beaumont, March 3, 1941, in [Beaumont], *Lettres*, 73.

147. Letter R. Schutz to Sœur Marguerite, December 26, 1940. Grandchamp archives.

148. Ibid.

communicated his developing ideas on life in community. In it are found a summary of the earlier five rules of his prospectus. This summary became a permanent part of the Rule of Taizé and of Grandchamp. The motto was: "Pray and work that Christ may reign." The three rules were: (1) "Let work and rest be filled with the Word of God," (2) "Keep inner silence that you may dwell in Christ," and (3) "Be filled with the spirit of the Beatitudes: joy, simplicity, mercy." This last, he wrote in a footnote, was reworded "in order to be in solidarity with the *Veilleurs* with the hope of connecting ourselves at one point with a tradition which, while quite new, is answering a present need in the church."[149] It was printed that fall with the help of the Abbé Couturier and distributed among Roger's friends, including his friends at Grandchamp.[150]

During the winter 1940–1941, the Retreat House at Grandchamp was kept open. "This way the retreats could continue . . . We even had guests in December."[151] One of these, February 6, was for six theology students. The Abbé Couturier had written to Marguerite asking her to let them know that he was praying for them. She conveyed his message and retreatant Max Thurian, revealing his ecumenical progress, wrote their thanks to the Abbé saying that they were "happy to be able to unite [themselves] with the Catholic Church in intercession."[152]

In all, there were twelve Retreats planned by the *Responsables* that year, 1941. Seven of these were on the theme "The call of God." In the letter of invitation Genevieve wrote, "In the present disarray the retreats take on greater meaning. They must become for us a source of living water . . . We don't go to Grandchamp to forget the distress of the world, but to commune more deeply with it by carrying that distress to God in prayer together."[153] Retreats were also hosted for *Veilleurs*, deaconesses, the *Bon Secours*, *Église et Liturgie*, one for men organized by Jean de Saussure, and a planning retreat for the *Responsables*.[154] The Abbé Couturier sent materials for the universal prayer of Christians for Christian unity, including his vision for an Invisible Monastery, the gathering of all those throughout the world whose hearts and minds turned together in Christ to pray with him that all Christians might be one, that the world might believe.[155]

---

149. Schutz, *Communauté de Cluny*, 10.
150. Laplane, *Frère Roger*, 122.
151. Bossert, *Cahier de Sr. Marthe*, 23.
152. Gaulué, "Vers un monastère réel," 153–54.
153. Grandchamp archives, Retreats, 1941.
154. Ibid.
155. Couturier, *Œcuménisme spirituel*, 159.

In January, 1942 Max Thurian once again came to Grandchamp on retreat. There he picked up Roger's pamphlet and found it astonishingly similar to his own thinking: "Ah, so someone else is thinking of this too."[156] In it he found the Abbé Couturier's vision for forming a community which would "keep the image of the torn body of Christ before the eyes of all believers in order to be a ferment of disquiet for those who consider normal the division of the universal Church."[157] It indicated that Roger and his seminary friends had "looked at Christian traditions of community. The attempt to form a community living in the world, a community where each member was joined together by his faith in Christ and his adhesion to certain rules, that was the call which for some of us became irresistible."[158]

As the first ministry of the community, Roger explained that retreats were to be offered in the homes of those who "have benefited from a true retreat," for those who have experienced the value of silence to offer the same opportunity to others, by teaching them "the need for being silent together at times, a silence which is centered on *"l'unique recherche."*[159] It indicated that "Houses dedicated as gathering and retreat centers are planned. One of these has been opened in France: the Maison de Cluny."[160] His footnote was revealing: "We are often asked the question: are you going to create in this House a permanent community? This is as yet too burning a question to be answered more precisely at this time."[161] It seems odd that he did not mention Pomeyrol here, which had been conducting exactly this type of retreat for members of *Les Veilleurs* and others since 1929;[162] or the house at Grandchamp, where retreats of this description had been offered since 1936 and where the three sisters had welcomed him just the year before. He had copies of the pamphlet placed at Grandchamp, knowing that those interested in silent retreats and community life would find it there.

The pamphlet ended with these revealing words:

---

156. Max Thurian quoted in Paupert, *Taizé et l'Église de demain*, 59.

157. Schutz, *Communauté de Cluny*, 17.

158. Ibid., 3. Schutz wrote, "For publication of their intellectual work, it proposed the formation of groups according to the diverse disciplines, with "a director of studies to assure continuity in study, establish good relations between members, through regular correspondence ... the scheduling of meetings for study together, the publication of articles" (*Communauté de Cluny*, 14).

159. In quotes in Schutz, *Communauté de Cluny*, this phrase is from the teaching of the Abbesses of Port Royal and refers to seeking God alone. See Carr, *Voix des Abbesses*, 360.

160. Schutz, *Communauté de Cluny*, 17.

161. Ibid.

162. Butte, *Semences*, 178.

> In the darkest periods of the Middle Ages, when great upheavals were shaking humanity, men united with the same desire for silence, retreat, consecration, in order to better serve the reign of their Lord, and by this service to help many. And we do not believe it pretentious to desire, in our own time, to make a similar effort in a framework adapted to our modern twentieth century.[163]

These highlights from Roger's pamphlet, so attractive to Max Thurian, show to what an extent Roger had been influenced by the sisters of Grandchamp and by their friend and spiritual mentor, the Abbé Couturier. As soon as Max returned to Geneva he set out to find its author. Max wrote later, "After an evening of conversation, I had the absolute certainty that God had long been preparing me for this encounter. We agreed at every point and . . . decided to put our plans into action as soon as possible: the creation of a resident community . . ."[164]

After a three day visit to the Trappe des Dombes, Roger Schutz wrote to his mentors: to the Abbé, "After being with these men of God, the monks of Dombes, I realize that their monastic lifestyle helps us better understand the great gospel ideals;"[165] and to Marguerite,

> We urgently need to understand better the Catholic communities . . . I am working, like never before, on the question of monasticism. The Rule of St. Benedict seems to me to be a goldmine of incredible richness. We would have a great deal to gain from this study, and already it is guiding us in practical ways.[166]

Max Thurian, his friend Pierre Souvairan, and Roger Schutz met at Grandchamp May 9–10, 1942 to exchange ideas with the sisters and to meet Geneviève Micheli.[167] Returning to Geneva, the three moved into an apartment owned by one of their families, to start practicing their ideas on community and prayer. Roger continued to write Marguerite about his developing ideas and Max did as well. The three sisters were experiencing the difficulties of balancing a life of prayer with a very busy schedule of retreats. After two years of friendship and correspondence, he gave Marguerite his first word of advice, marking the beginning of the role reversal which would characterize relations between the communities of Grandchamp and

---

163. Schutz, *Communauté de Cluny*, 18.
164. Gaulué, "Vers un monastère réel," 155.
165. Laplane, *Frère Roger*, 127.
166. R. Schutz to Sœur Marguerite, March 16, 1942. Grandchamp archives.
167. Laplane, *Frère Roger*, 128.

Taizé. "If the Lord, sovereign of our lives and vocations, has called you to the ministry which falls to you at Grandchamp, he will himself supply all the natural qualities you lack: 'When I am weak, then I am strong' (2 Cor 12:10)."[168]

Still, as the Community of Grandchamp developed, the *Responsables* continued to plan and lead Retreats. For 1942 seventeen were scheduled. There was a retreat for the *Fédé*, a Bible study led by Willem Visser't Hooft and Suzanne de Dietrich, and a retreat for pastors. Seven silent retreats were planned for the *Dames de Morges* and all who had come to love the *Retraites de Grandchamp*.[169] Retreats were planned for working women, deaconesses, the *Veilleurs*, the pastors of *Église et Liturgie*, and the last one for the *Responsables* themselves.

In October Roger wrote to Marguerite that they would be spending the winter in Geneva where he and Max and Pierre would be living as the Community of Cluny, his chosen name, and praying regularly at the cathedral. The offices of *Église et Liturgie* had been used by the three sisters at Grandchamp for their common prayer since mid-1940, and by Roger in his first solitary days in Taizé, from late 1940–1942. Now they were used by the fledgling Community of Cluny (Taizé) during its Geneva days, 1942–1944, in the Cathedral of St. Peter where Roger's sister Geneviève accompanied on the organ.[170] This liturgy was finally published in 1943 as *Office divin de l'Église universelle (Divine Office of the Universal Church)*. Its author, Richard Paquier, noted that the new interest in communal living within the Reformed Church necessitated a daily office, to serve the need for "an order of prayer, collective and daily, inspired by the tradition of the universal Church."[171] Sisters Marguerite and Irène joined the brothers at the cathedral for prayers for the two months of winter during each of those years. Geneviève enjoyed Marguerite's description:

> Thank you for telling me so well all that concerns the "brothers." How dear they are to me and how much more beautiful to recite the office while imagining them on their knees in St. Peter's cathedral praying in the same way—this really is a cell of the Invisible Monastery . . . and it surpasses Grandchamp and Cluny. There is something infinite about it which connects me

---

168. R. Schutz to Sœur Marguerite, May 12, 1942, 4. Grandchamp archives.

169. The themes, established by Geneviève, were "Jesus Christ and the Church," "The Community of Believers," "The Christian as a Sentinel," "Mother Church," "The Christian as a witness in the Church," and finally, "The Power of the Holy Spirit."

170. Laplane, *Frère Roger*, 137.

171. Paquier, "Avant Propos," 11.

with my husband, La Doctoresse, and eternity in an extraordinary way.[172]

Geneviève invited Roger Schutz to lead the May 1943 retreat for the two fledgling communities. It was to be on the "Incarnation, at three levels: for the individual, Mary receiving the Messiah; for the community, the presence of Christ in prayer and work; and the church in which Christ is incarnate, bringing him to the world."[173] He replied,

> We have great hopes that this retreat will be rich for our two communities, for each of us. By spending days such as this may we become more accessible to the action of the Holy Spirit, more receptive to the Word of the Lord. May each of us prepare to better receive the One who wishes to remain in us and whose mysterious presence is the only source of power, of an authentically Christian life, of total consecration. Christ cannot be incarnate in the community except by this adherence of each member to the One who is our Lord and Savior.[174]

Knowing the struggles of the sisters to build a community while conducting dozens of retreats, creating a suitable Rule, and establishing some hierarchy of authority, Roger and Max had discussed and agreed on a solution: "We envision a ministry like that of a mother superior exercised by Madame Micheli whom you consider as your spiritual mother, with you becoming her assistant in the case that you cannot accept for yourself the responsibility of Mother."[175]

The Community of Grandchamp Welcomes Its First Prioress

Through all of the beginning years of the development of the Retreat House at Grandchamp and then the Community of Grandchamp, Geneviève Micheli had been a constant spiritual guide, consultant, speaker, retreat master, frequent visitor and even substitute during illnesses. Finally, in 1943, the three sisters felt such great need of a Mother for their struggling attempts at community life, that they asked her to join them permanently. Geneviève wrote to Marguerite that she had not yet sensed the call to form a community within Protestantism.[176] In April she wrote again, "I am praying for

---

172. Micheli to Beaumont, November 8, 1942. In [Beaumont], *Lettres*, 88.
173. Micheli to Beaumont, March 1, 1943. In [Beaumont], *Lettres*, 94.
174. Roger Schutz to Micheli, March 23, 1943. In [Beaumont], *Lettres*, 96.
175. R. Schutz to Sœur Marguerite, May 12, 1942. Grandchamp archives,
176. Micheli to Beaumont, March 18, 1943. In [Beaumont], *Lettres*, 96.

you and I think that if God asks you to take on the authority of Mother [of the community], God will give you the wisdom and love. And if it is I who should come, the obstacles will disappear."[177]

In consultation with her pastor, Edouard Mauris,[178] she made two recommendations to Marguerite regarding an "official consecration" for the three sisters: she felt it was premature in the spring of 1943 and when it did take place it should not be in a church, which would need to be consulted on all of the delicate questions of vocation and community, but by Pastor Mauris, and it should begin as commitments which could lead to a consecration.[179] Once again, Geneviève resisted institutional pressures likely to come from too close an association with the Reformed Church.

Alone in her "hermitage" in the mountains above St. Moritz, Geneviève put her own teachings into practice, waiting in silence before God for confirmation of such a calling. This she received in February 1944. Sister Marthe wrote with joy of her coming:

> Retreats succeed one another, numerous and beneficial, rich in blessing. She organizes the work so that each sister has her share in the pain and joy of it, and that all goes along peacefully . . . Silence is kept strictly and this was where we often faltered . . . Madame Micheli has become our sister or our Mother. As for me, I prefer to call her Mother.[180]

That year another sister joined the community as well, Évangéline Lenoir. She and Geneviève Micheli arrived at Grandchamp just in time for the celebration of the eighth anniversary of the founding of the Retreat House.

> Here it is the eighteenth of March and we are five instead of three, and our friends, the *Responsables*, are our guests: Mrs. Martin, Mrs. Exchaquet, Miss Soutter, Mrs. and Miss de Rougemont . . . and Marc Du Pasquier, faithful to our requests, for it was he who consecrated the House . . . We all re-consecrated ourselves to God for this new year.[181]

Lessons of community life were learned all along the way. The next year, 1945, saw the entry of one more sister, a *Veilleur*, Marguerite Schneider.[182]

---

177. Micheli to Beaumont, beginning of April, 1943. In [Beaumont], *Lettres*, 97.

178. E. Mauris was a member of *Église et Liturgie*.

179. Micheli to Beaumont, June 8, 1943. In [Beaumont], *Lettres*, 98. Wilfred Monod, Geneviève's earlier choice to lead the consecration, died in 1943.

180. Beaumont, *Du grain*, 126.

181. Bossert, *Cahier de Sr. Marthe*, [34-35].

182. Ibid., 38.

Béatrice, who had come to help with Retreats in 1944, also asked to become a sister. Marguerite de Beaumont summarized the new reality:

> Sister Geneviève, with her big heart, quick mind, motherly nature, wide horizons, is not content to direct a few sisters on their road to life in community. She is still the leader of the *Responsables*. She is present at every retreat and assists with all of the Bible studies. She gives special importance to conversations with the pastors before and during the retreats. As for me, I am responsible for the welcome and guidance of the individual retreatants. I am Geneviève's assistant and replace her during her absences.[183]

The war ended and the sisters began the immense task of forgiving, and helping others to forgive, its perpetrators. When praying the Beatitudes, "Blessed are the peace makers" took on new meaning.[184]

Sisters Laurent and Beatrice joined the original five in 1945, soon followed by three others. "Soon ten sisters!" wrote Marthe, planning for space to lodge them.[185] March 19, 1946 they celebrated the tenth anniversary of the dedication of the Retreat House.[186] A few months later, in July 1946 the community celebrated the Moravian heritage of Grandchamp by attending as a community the annual dinner and celebration for the Moravian Church, at Montmirail.[187] In 1948 a clear separation was established between the members of the resident community, the sisters, and the *Responsables* who continued to plan retreats. The community joined the Federation of Protestant Churches of Switzerland (FEPS) as an independent ministry.[188]

In 1952 Geneviève visited an Anglican community and returned to Grandchamp convinced that it was time for consecration. Pastor de Saussure and Brother Roger were present when the first six sisters made their lifelong commitments and Geneviève was consecrated as Mother.[189] That year they adopted the Rule of Taizé as their Rule, after eight years of using Roger's brief rule. An agreement was made with Taizé and then Pomeyrol (1953), for unity of witness, mutual support and solidarity among the three communities who all shared the same vocation and Rule.[190]

---

183. Beaumont, *Du grain*, 126–27.
184. Bossert, *Cahier de Sr. Marthe*, [45].
185. Ibid., [49].
186. Retreats. Grandchamp archives.
187. Bossert, *Cahier de Sr. Marthe*, [59].
188. "Mère Geneviève, Geneviève de Lacroix: 1883–1961," 1. Grandchamp archives. In 1954 the *Responsables* would become the Third Order of Grandchamp.
189. Laplane, *Frère Roger*, 190.
190. "Grandchamp: Jalons, " 1. Grandchamp archives.

By the time Minke de Vries visited Grandchamp in 1955,[191] there were more than a dozen sisters and a handful of novices, with ministries well beyond the village, a "daughter-house" at Sonnenhof, near Basel, Switzerland, for German speakers and small groups of sisters in Algiers, Saint-Ouen, a working-class neighborhood of Paris, Jerusalem, and Lebanon, living their vocation to prayer and service in areas of distress, hoping to bring the loving and healing presence of Christ to all.

Conclusion

The journey of these Swiss Protestant women, from holding retreats for women of the privileged classes to the establishment of the Community of Grandchamp, was a long and patient one. Their quest led them to transcend the established Swiss values for women: they broke with mores of class, the role of women in religion, the roles of women in service and medicine, and the role of women in reformed Christianity, establishing financial and ecclesiastical independence. This was not a project that they took on unaware of the women's issues. As *Morgienne* Geneviève Westphal explained, "In the nineteenth century . . . a new culture developed which put women's work on a pedestal and idealized the wife-mother-housekeeper. Not only was the woman to take care of the house, she must be devoted to it body and soul." It was a paradigm imposed on all levels of society, and remained the norm until the 1950s. As such, a woman "was deprived of political rights as well as intellectual and economic independence . . . By the inactivity of the spouse, the privileged classes found a way to affirm their social position."[192]

The search for God and the search for space for women in the realms of society, church and the mind went hand in hand. The women, finding meaning and experiences of God in their evolving community, quickly focused their efforts on both increasing the number of individuals from different social classes in the project, and on institutionalizing a Protestant women's religious community to perpetuate that vision. It is out of this expanding and concretizing vision that the attention to ecumenism, the discussions with scholars from all confessions, and the ventures into inter-faith conversation are to be understood. It is clear that the narrative of Minke de Vries and the present reality of the Community of Grandchamp are congruent with their past in the *Dames de Morges*!

---

191. Cornuz, *Soeur Minke*, 45.
192. Westphal, *Nos fondatrices*, 26

THE AUTHOR

Minke de Vries (1929–2013)

BORN TO A DEVOUT Dutch Reformed mother and a convert from Mennonite to Reformed father, Minke de Vries grew up in a world where religion was important.[1] Her father had used skillfully the opportunities provided by Dutch mobilization during World War I to leave carpentry and to become a construction engineer. Her mother was a teacher and joined the Oxford Group movement of Frank Buchman,[2] which Minke thought improved the family's home life.

When the Germans invaded the Netherlands on May 10, 1940, Minke was only a young girl. World War II, the terror of German occupation and the growing deprivations had a definitive impact on her life and on all the Dutch.[3] When food shortages made life tenuous, the family escaped, or so they thought, to the Island of Texel, to the farm of her maternal grandparents. They arrived just in time for the famous uprising of the Georgian troops against the Germans. It became a terrible battle: 565 Georgians, about 800 Germans, and 120 Texel islanders were killed.[4] At some point, the family farm burned as well. The hatred of the Dutch against the Germans was a feature of Minke's life.

After the war, Minke studied at the University of Leiden, without great enthusiasm. Searching for her way in life, she became involved with the Salvation Army, whose ministry and spirituality she admired. At one point, in her searching for a place in life, she considered joining. Through

---

1. All of the information in this section, except as noted, comes from two source: (1) the published interview of Cornuz, *Soeur Minke de Grandchamp*; and, (2) an interview of Minke de Vries with the author, November 2012.

2. On the Oxford Group, see Clark, *The Oxford Group*; Grensted. *What Is the Oxford Group?*

3. Zee, *The Hunger Winter*.

4. Reeuwijk, *Opstand der Georgiërs, Sondermeldung Texel*.

her mother, she had contact with a Christian "healing movement" and participated in "revivalistic efforts" in Leiden and The Hague. Her searching led her to De Hezenberg, a center inspired by the German Lutheran healing evangelist Johann Christoph Blumhardt (1805–1880) of Bad Boll. She was also reading Karl Barth (1886–1968) and the Dutch theologian Kornelis Heiko Miskotte (1894–1976).

Through a friend, Minke found her way to the Community of Grandchamp, first as a visitor. Enraptured by what she saw, she returned and began the process which ended with her profession in 1962. Eager to have a positive influence in areas of trouble in the world, she served in "fraternities," small outposts of the community, in Paris where she worked in a factory, in Algeria, and in Lebanon.

In 1966, Sister Minke was elected assistant to the community's second Prioress, Mother Marie Bonna-Bornand, who had succeeded Geneviève Micheli, the first Mother of the Community of Grandchamp. In 1970 Sister Minke became its third Prioress. In 1999 she stepped down due to illness and was succeeded by Sister Pierrette Guinchard who had served as Minke's assistant for several years.

The Fruits of Grace is her story and that of the community! Sister Minke treasured the history of her community, some aspects of which she discusses in detail, others which she does not. She was well aware that the Community of Grandchamp was the project of a family and of a group of women who were testing the social and religious limits for Protestant women in early to mid-twentieth century Switzerland. They were making a place for themselves in a country where they could not yet vote[5] or serve as clergy or professors of religion. She joined a community that had dared much and had managed to maintain its independence. As its leader she joyfully seized the baton and continued the race.

---

5. 1971 for national elections; after 1991, all elections.

The Fruits of Grace

The Ecumenical Experience of the
Community of Grandchamp

Sister Minke de Vries

Introduction

THIS BOOK WAS WRITTEN to preserve a small part of the history of the church; not a scholarly work, without literary or even spiritual pretensions, it is simply a witness to Life. As such, it contains all of these layers of understanding and others even more personal. The act of writing it is an act of faith, my testimony that God is at work everywhere and at all times.

In 2004 I was invited to contribute to the ecumenical roundtable of Milan. I said "yes" and found myself in the company of two pillars of spiritual theology and ecumenism: Monsignor Georges Khodr, bishop of the Orthodox Patriarchate of Antioch in Lebanon, and Dom André Louf, a French Cistercian monk. Both of them, without knowing it of course, had been very influential in my life. I was very moved to be there with them.

I was there to share my perspective on "the spiritual journey and the birth of religious communities within Protestantism—the fruit of a renewal in spirituality and of ecumenical openness." Following my contribution, the publisher Paoline of Milan asked me to write a book on this topic. The theme was to be "the ecumenical experience of the Community of Grandchamp." Again, I said "yes," without knowing I was setting out on an adventure well beyond my capabilities.

In the first place, at age seventy-seven, my physical energy is limited. And the writing of a book is a whole new learning experience, invigorating but demanding. Then there is the theme: it is a perilous exercise to write as a sister of Grandchamp and former prioress (1970–1999), about my own community. It is only possible by keeping this essential thought in mind: the community is not an end in itself. What is important to grasp is what the Spirit is impressing upon the church.

Writing this book just seven years after handing off leadership of Grandchamp to another sister, I feel a little like I've arrived at the summit of a small Mount Horeb;[1] the joy of a look back, the joy of sensing the outpouring of Life there. What an extraordinary experience it has been to see gathered together all the wealth of my experiences since coming to Grandchamp. Some connections between events, encounters, and aspirations of the moment, which I barely suspected at the time, now appear with clarity. I've been given the gift of a long-range perspective on things we experienced from day to day through many years.

At first, I didn't know where to start. I wrote parts of the story as I was inspired, as the liturgical calendar or requests from outside the community brought them to mind. Later I was greatly helped by Marie-Laure Ivanov, an Antiochian Orthodox friend of the community and a trained writer, without whose help this book would never have been seen the light of day. She arranged the texts, gathering and drawing inspiration from other writing I had done for conferences and retreats when I was prioress. She also collected testimonies. Most importantly, she encouraged me in the birthing process.

The writing of this book carries traces of this entire editorial process. It is part of a movement that extends from the beginnings of the community through persons and events (chapter 1), continues by sharing what shapes the community (chapter 2), which opens onto our solidarity with this world (chapter 3), and gives other sisters and friends a chance to bear witness to what connects us all in our otherness (chapter 4). To illustrate our close relationship with the world, I sought these ecumenical—in the larger sense—perspectives. I wanted to reveal the backdrop that is the context of our ecumenical vocation of prayer and reconciliation. The first person, "I," is used as a way of highlighting my personal and unique experiences as a Christian, invited to follow Christ to the fullest. I use "we" as a sister of Grandchamp taking part in community life, a reality all the more intensely lived as long-time prioress. This "we" does not make the community responsible for my words, but rather indicates the way I see the Spirit working through our community. This perspective relies on some very concrete points in our history and our experience of community life, of the Mystery we carry, but always setting it within a larger reality—that of the ecumenical movement and of the recent history of the church and the world. I should point out another particularity of this book: its first edition was not in the original language, French, but in Italian as translated by the publisher, Paoline.

The Spirit sent us people, first of all our sisters, and helped us to discover many other brothers and sisters. So many were sent to us along the

---

1 Deut 4:15; 5:2.

way. We were surrounded by the well wishes of people imbued with the wisdom of God, among them Brother François of Taizé, Rosette Genton, Frau Vera, and others who are filled with the foolishness of God (1 Cor 1:25): I think especially of our brother Jean Goss, and of many others. All look to the future. They love the church and take her challenges to heart.

I would also like to express here my gratitude to Sister Gianfranca of Paoline, who had the courage to suggest that I write this book; to Father Enzo Bianchi of Bose, Father Franz Müller, O.P., and Sister Lorraine Caza, CND, for their encouragement; to Gottfried Hammann, Hans-Ruedi Weber, Father Michel Froidure, O.P., and so many others for their helpful comments; and, to Colette Joray, Fernand Trabaud, and Father Matthias of Bose for their attentive editing. I am also grateful for the kind hospitality of the Abbey of Maigrauge, the Monasteries of Eygalières and Bose, and the Oltramare families, and especially the attentive and prayerful support of my sisters throughout the writing of this work.

I am in the evening of my life. Little by little, I have become overwhelmed with gratitude for all that has been given me. I know how insignificant we are in this ecumenical experiment that we try to live each day. And yet God needed our "yes" to get us started in spite of our limitations, and to remain open with the same openness that characterized Mother Geneviève and our first sisters.

And so I have come to a place of inner rejoicing in discovering the extraordinary fruitfulness of the experience of this community. I am so grateful for it and ardently desire to share it, first with my sisters, but also beyond, with those whom God wishes to strengthen in their call to a living ecumenism. This is the hope that fills me. In witness to his grace, I know that truly, *when the world is troubled . . . God acts!*

Sister Minke

2008

CHAPTER 1

In the Beginning

God asks everything of us, but above all God gives us everything. And I see God in the center . . . as the one who loves.

I see first of all, Love, and then surrender. For me, God reveals himself first to the heart and makes himself loved. That is the first dazzling, marvelous step, that free gift, that grace, that joy.

Then comes surrender, through Love—for once we love, we see all of our impurities, we thirst for sanctification, we cannot move forward into divine union without baring ourselves before God . . . And then all that we surrender in our lives, all of our sorrows, all of our nights, end in new joys, new consolations, new light.

MOTHER GENEVIÈVE, 1933[1]

When the World Is Troubled and in Distress . . . God Acts

God and the church need witnesses who live their faith openly, showing by their whole existence that God is—and that God acts. The love of God and God's compassion burn brightly in Christ and in his witnesses. They

---

1. Micheli, *Message de Sœur Geneviève Micheli*, 9.

experience his prayer; he breathes his passion into praying communities so that they commit themselves, because of him and of the Gospel, that his love may be shared and do good, spreading everywhere its capacity for healing.

This "acting" of God is present in every era of history. How has God acted in the twentieth century? And particularly in the churches of the Reformation? What sign does God wish to give by way of the birth and ecumenical experience of the Community of Grandchamp, a little cell of the church to which I belong? What can we understand of this project of God's in order to better live it out in the here and now in each of our communities?

This "acting" of God greatly surpasses us. Along with other communities, the Community of Grandchamp, "community of monastic inspiration, of prayer, of reconciliation, and of ecumenical vocation," planted itself in ground within the church already cultivated by the ecumenical movement which had began a century earlier. This took place at a precise moment in history.

"When the world is troubled and in distress—and it is today—God acts!"[2] Mother Geneviève, one of the originators, along with a few sisters, of the Community of Grandchamp, spoke these words in 1948, shortly after the disaster of World War II. Auschwitz, Hiroshima, and the gulags were somber reminders of how far crimes against humanity can go when they are organized. How all of this resonates still today, alas! Trouble continues to distress our world, and is found within us as well. An unregulated free market, driven by globalization, is but one example that has already led to many destructive, deadly results—not only on the human level, but also on the level of the whole creation. Worn out by abuse, God's creation no longer just sighs, but groans. How then can we be a sign of hope, of free and creative joy?

In beginning her message entitled "Witness of a Community of Prayer," her heart full of the book of Jeremiah, Mother Geneviève situated the Community of Grandchamp and the renewal of religious community life in the churches of the Reformation within salvation history. She saw that their existence plays a part in God's project for the church and the world of today. They are truly the work of the Spirit. This woman, widowed very young and the mother of three children, knew what she was talking about. For neither she herself, nor any of the other women, had ever dreamed of founding a community at Grandchamp. No Protestant pastor had thought of it either. There was too much resistance to "anything that seems Catholic." The community is the product of a series of "yeses"—sometimes given painfully—to spiritual needs that gradually made themselves felt and became

2. Ibid., 25.

evident to those concerned about this new call, to those around them, and to their own church. At the same time, the Holy Spirit raised up other new communities within all parts of the church, all over Europe.

The new religious communities born into the Protestant churches were greatly inspired and encouraged by the little book by Dietrich Bonhoeffer entitled *Life Together*,[3] the fruit of an experience of community life in a seminary he founded for future pastors of the Confessing Church in Germany. He wrote the book in one draft after the Nazi regime closed the seminary. He had based this community life on the Gospel, and was also inspired by what he experienced in the Anglican monastic Community of the Resurrection[4] in 1935, while he was serving as a pastor in London.

Those who commit themselves to these communities discover a life of prayer with a strong communal emphasis, sharing all of their material and spiritual goods, joys and sorrows. They find that God is present and active to the very end, for God is the beginning and the end of all things! Many times each day, the community gathers to express this in common praise, to strengthen itself through listening, prayer, meditation, and study of the Bible. Together they bring the world to God, to Christ, to whom they belong with all that they are. They intercede, standing in the gap between God and humanity, on behalf of all the voiceless for whom they would be the voice. They seek with all their hearts that God who is love be loved in them,[5] and among them. Thus these communities become places of hope: "See how they love one another!" (Acts 2:42). They are oases of a simple and warm welcome, a sign of the coming kingdom, which is here already, and wherever two or three are gathered in his name.

This description greatly resembles the life of the first communities in the Acts of the Apostles (2:42-47; 4:32-35). It's true: each community enjoys a time of grace at the beginning. Those who live in community experience this deeply: then comes the time of storms, apprenticeship in fraternal life, the validation of a life built on the rock and not on the sand![6]

Among these communities, is our Community of Grandchamp. To this day, faithfully praying together at common prayer, we renew daily, by the gift of our life, the experience of the moment of offering which is at the heart of the Eucharist. At the words of the minister, "Let us pray together as we offer the thanks of the whole church," we respond together with all

---

3. Dietrich Bonhoeffer, *Gemeinsames Leben*, 1939. French translation, *De la vie communautaire*, 1947. English translation, *Life Together*, 1954.
4. The Brothers of Mirfield, England.
5. John 3:16-17.
6. Matt 7:24-27.

faithful Christians, not in words, but by our lives radically given "for the glory of God and the salvation of the world."

As our Rule says, I give my life in a two-fold movement: offered to God and in solidarity with the world. This is the primary meaning of our lives consecrated to following in the footsteps of our only high priest, Jesus Christ (Heb 5:1–10). We are called to live this life in the church and for the world.

At Grandchamp, the link between community life and a vocation to unity is profound. In a letter written to the Abbé Paul Couturier[7] in the early days of the community, Sister Irène, one of the first three sisters, helps us understand this in speaking of daily life among the sisters:

> The Evil One is par excellence the one who divides . . . The Evil One gives us the idea that it is impossible to understand one another, that we will never manage it, that one cannot get along without mutual understanding, and so what's the use? . . . In Christ, a communion, a companionship of souls has been established for those who live as Christians, that is to say, at the foot of the cross . . . and looking around, one is often astonished to find another who was thought to be very "far off" suddenly so close, at the same level, loved with the same love, at Jesus' feet.

Her letter is a cry of love for the church: "The thought of the great re-memberment [of the Body of Christ] is a daily one, and vital to us."[8]

Signs in the Church

The Protestant communities born into this milieu in the twentieth century are there first of all as a sign within their own churches, wounded by the war as much as by their intellectualist and individualistic approach. The communities quickly became a source of inspiration for Christians of other churches. The impact of the Community of Taizé,[9] their Rule and the writings of

---

7. Paul Couturier (1881–1953) was a French Catholic priest, an early Catholic ecumenist, the founder of the inter-confessional Week of Prayer for Christian Unity in 1935 and in 1937 the francophone ecumenical dialogue group, Groupe des Dombes. See footnote 48. For more on Paul Couturier see Villain, *L'Abbé Couturier*.

8. Sister Irène, Letter to the Abbé Paul Couturier, 1941, archives of the Groupe des Dombes.

9. Taizé has now become an ecumenical community of Catholic brothers as well as Protestant brothers from various denominations. See appendix: "Several Communities Introduce Themselves."

Brother Roger Schutz[10] is well known. The participation of Brothers Roger Schutz and Max Thurian at the Second Vatican Council, where they were invited as ecumenical observers, helped to raise their profile.

Catholic communities were inspired by the new Protestant communities. Our Protestant communities greatly benefited from the welcome of Catholic, Anglican, and, later, Orthodox communities. At Grandchamp we had everything to learn in living our call to a consecrated[11] life inspired by the monastic traditions.

Later I will mention the Reformed roots of the Rule of Taizé, the Rule by which we live, having made some minor adaptations to it to suit our situation. This Rule aims to be a simple commentary on the Gospel. It is strongly influenced by Benedictine life in its common praise and by Franciscan fraternal life in its stress on simplicity. In writing it, Brother Roger was also inspired by the Little Brothers and Sisters of Jesus, founded in 1933 by René Voillaume. Part of that community's form of life influenced that of the communities who live by the Rule of Taizé; from the 1950s on, the "brothers on mission" of Taizé went to live in small fraternities outside of Taizé.[12] And we, the sisters of Grandchamp, at that time very close to them, sent a small group of sisters to live in Algeria. Other missions followed. How much our communities owe to the generosity of welcome and the simplicity of sharing of brothers and sisters of other traditions!

Yes, across the whole church God acted during this troubled period. In the Catholic Church, God acted by way of communities and fraternities, a new ecclesial form. A seed that fell on good soil at the beginning of the twentieth century, Charles de Foucauld,[13] beatified in 2005, hoped so much for companions to live his call with him. His apparent failure yielded a hundredfold in the new form of monastic life which has germinated everywhere. Certainly there will always be monks of the desert, living apart from society, and theirs is a vital presence. But everywhere in the world,

---

10. Roger Schutz (1915–2005) was a Swiss Protestant pastor and the founder of the Community of Taizé.

11. Every baptized person is consecrated to Christ. Profession is a recommitment to our baptism through the radical gift of our lives.

12. Fraternity has become a technical term referring to a small group of sisters or brothers sent out from the mother community to represent the community in a difficult or needy area and immerse themselves in its daily challenges. The term is also used among the Little Sisters and Little Brothers of Jesus. It could be defined as a fellowship group with a mission.

13. A French Catholic priest who lived among the Tuareg in the Sahara in Algeria. His writings inspired the founding of the Little Brothers of Jesus among other religious congregations.

others are living consecrated lives "in the heart of the masses," in the words of Father Voillaume.

In the aftermath of World War II there was a blossoming of new forms of spiritual and social commitment. God acted through both clergy and laypeople. Some felt called to involve themselves even more in the life of the world; this was the era of the worker priest, a movement born in France in 1941. In renouncing their privileged position, these priests lived a true immersion among ordinary people, most often non-Christians, and were strengthened in their own commitment to God. Although Rome unfortunately put an end to this movement in 1954, the Second Vatican Council rushed to permit it anew and to encourage it. This led to an increase in the number of priests integrated into the world of the working class, and into the fields of health care and addiction rehabilitation.

God acted again and again after the council. The audacious inspiration of Pope John XXIII to invite observers from other traditions had a far-reaching impact. Members of each tradition had the opportunity to discover the differences between them, but also the amazing similarities. Through meetings and conversations, the Community of Grandchamp became aware that it shared the same concern: how to communicate Christ to this changing world, how to pass on the Gospel, how to make the church credible and transparent so that the Good News might comfort, heal, and renew all. The council helped us discover a true reciprocity and an already fruitful communion among the people of God.

What a gift that the intuition of great witnesses belonging to different traditions could come to light with such clarity at the time of the council, and be welcomed into the heart of the church; what a gift that communities raised up and prepared by the Spirit were ready to receive this prophetic intuition, this word of a new day, in order to embody it and become witnessing communities. What a gift that the unstinting prayer and work of the great witness of unity, the Abbé Paul Couturier, was being answered and bearing fruit!

What a grace to take to heart, together, the prayer of Christ, addressed to his Father on the eve of his passion: "Father, that they may be one . . ." (John 17:21).

Today the task is to continue faithfully without growing weary. Yes, this is also my profession of faith: when the world is troubled and in distress—and it is today—God acts!

The Great Field (*Grand Champ*) of the World

I pray in silence, kneeling in the convent chapel,[14] next to Geneviève.

The crowd is there, hungry, waiting for the Bread of Life. Jesus says to me, "give them to eat," and he holds out to me a grain of wheat.

"Lord, what use is a grain of wheat feed such a crowd?" Jesus says to me, "Throw your grain into the earth, cover it and then wait and hope!"

I threw my grain into the earth and waited, in the midst of the hungry crowd. At the appointed time my grain of wheat had produced a hundred more grains. I brought them to Jesus and said to him,

"Lord, here, my grain of wheat has produced one hundred others, but what will I do with a hundred grains of wheat to feed this multitude?" Jesus replied, "Dig a furrow, and throw in your hundred grains, wait and hope!"

I dug the furrow, sowed the hundred grains of wheat and waited in hope, surrounded by the crowd who cried out in hunger. The following year each grain produced a hundred more; I brought to Christ ten thousand grains of wheat and said to him,

"Lord, here, the hundred grains of wheat have each produced a hundred more, but what are ten thousand grains of wheat to feed this large crowd?" Jesus said to me, "Work my field and sow it with the ten thousand grains of wheat. Wait and hope!"

I worked my field, sowed the ten thousand grains of wheat and waited in hope. At harvest time each grain

---

14. The Monastery of Sainte-Françoise-Romaine, in Cormeilles-en-Parisis, founded in 1924 by Mother Marie-Élisabeth of Wavrechin.

produced a hundred others. And I wore myself out in cultivating this great field [grand champ] all alone.

When the harvest was gathered I said to Christ, "Lord, I have gathered a million grains of wheat from my field. The crowd is crying out and dying of hunger. What shall I do?"

Jesus answers: "Do not say, 'I have gathered from my field, for the field is mine.' My field is as big as the earth and you are but one worker. I will send other workers to work with you the part of my field which I have entrusted to you. Together you will labor in my field. You will sow there half of the harvest, and with the rest you will feed the crowd."[15]

VISION OF SISTER MARGUERITE

When I came for the first time to Grandchamp, like others I was struck by the sign placed at the entrance to the village: "Dead end Street." A few years later, arriving by bicycle to begin my postulancy, I stopped for a moment, rather moved: "Dead end?" I had left behind me in Holland everything that had made up my life until then: my family and friends. Everything—and for good! There was no turning back. I was totally available to whatever was to come.

So what meaning did that sign have for me? Why this "Dead end street?" A warning? I was truly ready to jump into the unknown with all the generosity of my heart, of my youth. Had not the Lord told me to follow him, leaving everything behind, to live from now on in this "lost corner" of Switzerland with sisters I barely knew?

Within a few days the reality of community life, all that I discovered of the routine nature of such a life, had shaken me. It was not easy, this monotonous work, without particular interest. The prayer, yes, but standing, kneeling, all at the same time, these synchronized movements, like in the army? These sisters . . . Why had I come here? Why in the world? Hoping for what?

---

15. Beaumont, *Du grain à l'épi*, 101. Vision—later discerned to be her call to common life at Grandchamp.

A word from Mother Geneviève oriented me toward my deepest desire, re-centered me, and has not ceased to inspire me ever since: "*nur Christus!*" She spoke the word in German, for I did not yet know French very well. "Christ alone!"

Even today this word still resonates within me and urges me forward, or more accurately now, with age, pushes me deeper. Like the apostle Paul, "everything which I considered gain, I now consider as loss because of Christ . . . I press on that I may lay hold of Christ for I have been laid hold of by him" (Phil 3:8; 12b).

It was a "Dead end street" for my little ego, so easily self-absorbed; a dead end for so many things left behind. But I knew this: I had come here and have stayed to follow Christ, preferring nothing to him[16] and his will for my life; to let his love penetrate every fiber of my being. His compassion, is not only for me but for every human being in the whole world, to be transformed by him. Just a few months ago the "Dead end street" sign was removed . . . perhaps a new sign!

How can I describe this place that I love? Grandchamp is a little hamlet at the foot of the Jura Mountains on the bank of the river Areuse, on the plain of the same name. To the quiet pastures and wheat fields of the first spiritual retreats held here have been added—for the discerning ear—the vague background hum of the freeway and, especially at certain times of day, with a west wind, the sound of small aircraft from a nearby airport. So this haven of peace, far from city life, has not escaped the nuisances of our era. Perhaps it is so that our ties to the world may remain daily in the hearts of our sisters and of my own heart, not only by way of the beauty of creation, but also via this noisy thorn in the flesh!

Grandchamp: a few large old renovated houses and three fountains, one in the middle of the courtyard surrounded by the houses. A vast and rather tall stone and wood barn, formerly used for drying muslin, dominates the site. It has become a large chapel that we call *L'Arche* (the Ark), on the second floor, and on the ground floor there are guest rooms. In the large courtyard mingle sisters, village inhabitants, and walkers, often accompanied by their four-legged companions. The monastic cloister is primarily interior, even if certain spaces are reserved for the sole use of our community.

The houses we live in, of stone with great wooden shutters, were built in the eighteenth century for manufacturing Indian muslin, an industry that flourished in this area for more than a hundred years. At the beginning of the nineteenth century the Bovet family acquired this hamlet.[17] After the

---

16. Benedict, *Holy Rule*, chapter 4.
17. Rougemont, *La geste des Bovet de Grandchamp*, 3.

decline of the muslin industry, the village became a center of the *Reveil*,[18] with a certain influence inspired by the first deaconess house, at Kaiserswerth, in Germany. It was a place of prayer and service to neighbor; an orphanage, a hospital, a school—but also a place of theological research and conversation centered on Félix Bovet, professor of theology, renowned as well as suspected because of his prophetic ecumenical openness; an avant-garde European scholar of the Old Testament and of Judaism.

The community has its roots in the spiritual retreats organized at Grandchamp starting in 1931. In this hamlet, already infused with prayer, love, and care for others, a small group of French-speaking Swiss women[19] held an initial retreat, at the invitation of Amy Bovet, one of the participants. This type of retreat had never before been experienced in the region's Protestant churches of that era! Nearing the age of 50, their children at college, these women were seeking to deepen their spiritual lives: "Why not try to organize a retreat in the way the Catholics do?"

They had all been in the habit of intimate sharing with each other on important subjects such as education and emotional growth. A retreat, however, is something altogether different. They quickly realized that a retreat does not consist in days of spiritual conversation, but in a journeying with God where God alone is to be listened to. "That implies silence, a renunciation of subjective desires, an intense preparation in prayer, a humble listening for the will of God, surrender. God must be the retreat Master!"[20]

In preparing for their retreat planning meetings, each woman spent time in silence, listening and meditating on the Word. Then, after listening attentively to one another, they continued to seek the will of God concerning the theme, the flow of the retreat, and other details. The first fruit of this interior and communal attitude was a retreat on love in 1931. An important renewal in the spirituality of the Reformed churches of French-speaking Switzerland issued from that retreat, a renewal which then spread well beyond the area. The Community of Grandchamp has its roots in this movement.

The retreats multiplied. After a few years the need for a permanent presence of prayer to accompany these retreats and to welcome persons

---

18. Movement called the *Reveil*: a period of renewal within the churches of the Reformation characterized by a call to an active Christian life of personal prayer, Bible study, social ministry and evangelism, in the 19th century, beginning in francophone Europe.

19. Les Dames de Morges, an association of women founded in 1913 by Hélène Laufer Gautier.

20. Micheli, "Lettre au groupe des responsables des retraites, " (Letter to retreat planners) partially printed in [Beaumont], *Lettres*, 116.

desiring to spend a few days in silence became evident. Marguerite de Beaumont, an unmarried nurse who sometimes collaborated in planning these retreat days, giving short introductory talks, was invited by a pastor, Max Dominicé, and then by the retreat day steering committee[21] to take this permanent position at Grandchamp. Never having considered such a possibility—she had planned to stay with her aging mother—she finally answered "yes."

From "Yes"... to "Yes"...

In March 1936, Marguerite rented a house at Grandchamp that was for sale. Already several potential buyers had visited the house, but Pierre Bovet, Amy's husband, preferred to rent the house to Marguerite. She gave the name Amandier (almond tree) to this former hospital, an allusion to the prophecy of Jeremiah, as a promise: the word in Hebrew, *Shéqed*, means both almond tree (Amandier) and watchman (*Veilleur*).[22] To Jeremiah, God had said, "What do you see, Jeremiah?" I replied, "I see an almond branch." Then the Lord said, "You see correctly, for I watch over my Word to accomplish it" (Jer 1:11–12).

A young woman, a former resident of the orphanage of Grandchamp, helped with the housekeeping. After a time, this other Marguerite, who later became Sister Marthe, offered to serve without pay, "since we pray and live together for the Lord." She described what she felt: "If one offers oneself, one should give without holding back, one's goods, clothing, houses, family, friends, and he will give us infinitely more than we have given up for him."[23]

And there we have it . . . the nucleus of a community, born without it having been sought. Guided by Jean de Saussure,[24] a pastor in Geneva, a third person who would later become Sister Irène asked to join them. At first Sister Marguerite refused her request: "that would complicate things . . ." But could she resist the plan of God? By her "yes" to life in community, a "yes" not obvious to her at first, Sister Marguerite made it possible for our great field of Grandchamp to welcome the seeds sown for an adventure of

---

21. Translator's note: The steering committee of women, "Les responsables," part of the larger women's association, Les Dames de Morges, who planned and made possible the silent retreats at Grandchamp, starting in 1931.

22. *Les Veilleurs*, a liturgical renewal group, was important for the development of Grandchamp as well as Taizé.

23. Beaumont, *Du Grain à l'Épi*, 106.

24. Close friend of the Abbé Couturier, active member of the Groupe des Dombes, chaplain of the Community of Grandchamp from 1950 to 1955, and organizer of the first "Ecumenical Sessions" (1950–) with Mother Geneviève.

faith. Following the vision she received at vespers with the sisters of Sainte-Françoise-Romaine in Cormeilles-en-Parisis, near Paris, she had asked their mother superior, Mother Marie-Élisabeth of Wavrechin:

> "Mother, what is a community?"
>
> "Community is this: where two or three are gathered in my Name, I am in their midst."
>
> Her second question was "How does one know if one is called to live in community?"
>
> "It's when one can say whole heartedly, 'Thy will be done'... It is always to keep one's ego in the presence of God."
>
> "From that moment," explained Sister Marguerite, "I knew that God was calling me to live in community, and from then on, I never doubted my vocation for a moment. Note that I say a call to the common life—and not a call to found a community. I have neither the calling nor the gifts of a founder."[25]

Sister Marguerite again asked counsel of Geneviève Micheli, her close friend in spiritual matters since the late 1920s, and the key person among the leaders who organized and planned the silent retreats at Grandchamp. Geneviève was glad to hear of her desire for a communal life. She suggested that Marguerite, along with Sister Irène, attend a workshop on community life, its blessings and its difficulties, hosted by the sisters of Pomeyrol.[26] Afterward, the Abbé Paul Couturier confirmed Marguerite in her call to community life, and to prayer for the unity of the church. She concluded: "We begin life as three, full of joy, of good will, but with no experience. No rule, no book of common prayer, no precedent within Protestantism. All is to be created, all is to be lived." Irène arrived at the beginning of 1940. The community took life!

Here, in a letter addressed to Sister Marguerite, is Irene's testimony as to what she discovered at Grandchamp at the time of her initial welcome:

> I was seeking a way to live a life fully consecrated to Christ, more attentive to God, more prayerful, more available to do His will... Right away I experienced a warm welcome, peace, joy ... It was very Franciscan, with a quality of love and of liberty I had not known until then. When I think about it, I realize that I owe you a great debt of gratitude for this notion of the presence

---

25. Beaumont, *Du Grain à l'Épi*, 103.

26. Community of Protestant women founded by Antoinette Butte in 1929 for the purpose of providing a permanent venue for silent retreats.

of God. Only with the Little Sisters of Jesus, some time later, did I find this presence. I, who had been focused for so long on the tragedy of the human condition, the inability of Christians themselves to remedy this situation; I, who did not want to throw myself into the social or medical solutions because they are only palliatives that do not reach the roots of evil; I discovered the source of a life worth living, a life worth communicating . . . You had (already) understood that the Lord was asking you to enlarge your tent.[27]

But nothing happens automatically. Sister Marguerite, realizing that she was not gifted for the responsibilities she was taking on, called on Geneviève to come to Grandchamp as Mother of the budding community there.

Once again the "yes" was slow to come. Living in her chalet in the mountains since 1940, Geneviève had planned to remain there for the rest of her days as a sort of hermit. For her, the beauty and solitude of the mountains were the perfect surroundings for the life of prayer she was living. From time to time she shared this life with guests for whom she was a spiritual guide, and kept up an extensive correspondence with those who counted on her for guidance. She struggled against the invitation, reluctant to leave the mountaintop. But God disrupted her plans and brought her down to the plains. By March 1944, her "yes" was total and unconditional. Thanks to her, our community was able to come into being, to grow, and to establish itself.

Monastic Inspiration within the Churches of the Reformation

We give you thanks, O Lord,
To you who have saved us

You call us to follow you,
Here we are, to do your will,
Our lives belong to you.

But Lord,
You know our weakness,
And our faults are not hidden from you,
Pardon and purify!

---

27. Beaumont, *Du Grain à l'Epi*, 104.

Give us the grace to remain in your love,
To love one another in you.

We ask you for your Holy Spirit
That He may give us life,
That your Word may light our way,
And that we may let ourselves be guided by you in all things,
To faithfully obey you,
To serve you with joy,
Abandon ourselves to you in our suffering,
Live in prayer
And dwell in unity,
That your name may be hallowed.

PRAYER OF OFFERING OF THE COMMUNITY
Written by Sister Marguerite de Beaumont,
1940–1941

Before this coming together of Protestant women for a common life inspired by monasticism, before Sister Marguerite was inspired to write this prayer, the churches of the Reformation were already several centuries old. We need to immerse ourselves for a moment in the world of the Reformation, to recognize the Spirit at work there, then and now. We also need to understand and rejoice in the amazing novelty, and at the same time the continuity, of a monastic-style community coming to life within these churches born of the Reformation.

The Reformers, especially Luther, knew that a form of community life could be considered for certain persons, but that the decision to belong to such a community must be made with total freedom of conscience. The Reformers were therefore not *a priori* against a life set apart for the Lord, especially as they recognized the capacity of such places for biblical and liturgical formation. However, for them, the people of God could not be divided into classes, some higher than others, more meritorious, more consecrated than the others, by the simple fact, for example, of their state of celibacy or of their ministry. The reference is clear: by his or her baptism, each man and each woman has been set apart and consecrated to Christ by the Holy Spirit.

The events of the Reformation happened at a time similar to our own: an era of great change and upheaval. One of the greatest differences between Catholic and Reformation theologians was on the doctrine of justification by faith. An important advance on the road to unity was made on October

31,[28] 1999, at Augsburg, when the Catholic Church and the Lutheran World Federation signed an accord on this contentious point.[29]

In the sixteenth century, as insecurity increased, reactionary thinking was exacerbated and the rejection of all that was "other" led to a great deal of bitterness and hatred. The wars of religion, which today we might rather call confessional wars, took place in this troubled era. This did not prevent the Spirit from working. Building on the concept of justification by faith, the Reformers gave fresh theological value to marriage and to the responsibility of each believer, of each layperson—the priesthood of all believers. They called family households to be true households of light, as in Judaism—little churches within the church (Luther and Bucer[30])—living henceforth by faith in Christ alone, trying to put the Word into practice in daily life. Many families put their lives in danger during the persecutions because they wanted to remain faithful to their beliefs: in Bible reading in their own language, Bible study, and singing hymns and psalms each day in family worship and, on Sundays, in church. This intense practice of the faith within the family community replaced what Catholics had practiced in the convents.

The ministry of the pastor took on great importance for the spiritual support of these families by explicating the Word of God, leading the worship service, and administering the sacraments. In regions where the Reform was in the minority, during periods of persecution, these men of God were often itinerants, visiting gatherings in homes or in forests (in the "Desert"),[31] risking their lives for the love of Christ.

A life set apart for the Lord is a mystery of faith and a response to a growing sense of call to belong to God alone and to his kingdom, as an eschatological sign of that kingdom which is to come (1 Cor 7). But among Protestants, this call had to remain hidden for hundreds of years, though it did not disappear totally. During the torment of the persecution of the Huguenots in France after the revocation of the Edict of Nantes (1685), one Marie Durand,[32] imprisoned for thirty-seven years in the Tour de Con-

---

28. Anniversary date of Luther's theses nailed on the door of the Church of the Castle of Wittenberg, October 31, 1517.

29. Augsburg, town of the Holy Roman Empire. In 1530 the Lutherans presented to the Assembly (Diet) of rulers their first confession of faith, called since then the Augsburg Confession.

30. Martin Bucer (1491–1551) was a Reformer in Strasbourg.

31. Figure of speech indicating and describing the deprivations of persecuted Christians of the Cévennes, a region in the South of France especially persecuted by Catholics after the Edict of Nantes was repealed.

32. Gamonnet, *Lettres de Marie Durand (1715–1776)*.

stance, lived, without knowing it, like a monk, entirely consecrated to the Lord. From God she drew the strength to resist and to encourage the other women imprisoned with her, who remained faithful to their beliefs.

In countries where the Reformation could take root and give birth to official churches, for centuries, small groups formed, usually around some remarkable teacher, sometimes a pastor, to live a life of prayer and intense piety. Some of these teachers remained celibate for the Lord. This happened most notably during the period of Pietism, a spiritual movement that appeared in reaction to an overly intellectualizing theology from the seventeenth to the nineteenth century. In Germany, for example, a monastic-style community of eight celibate men gathered around Gerhard Tersteegen (1697–1769) in the Pilgrims' Hut. In Herrnhut, founded by Count Nicolas Zinzendorf (1700–1760), celibate women and men lived in "different choirs." By their prayer they participated actively in the great adventure of mission in what would later become the Moravian Church.[33]

Call to Life in Community

To speak of the birth of religious communities within Protestantism is to emphasize the work of the Spirit in history. In every era God acts through the decisions of more or less enlightened men and women. God leaves them free, and sometimes intervenes and reorients the course of history in answering calls for help (Moses, Gandhi, John XXIII, Suzanne de Dietrich,[34] Bonhoeffer, Martin Luther King Jr., etc.), or God intervenes through the persons or groups who are listening and available to do his will. It does not happen at just any moment in time, but "in the fullness of time" (Gal 4:4), at the *kairos* moment, often during times of great suffering.

Not until a time of great misery in society at the beginning of the nineteenth century did the deaconess movement appear. This idea was born in the heart of a German Lutheran pastor, Theodore Fliedner (1800–1864), founder of Protestant deaconess movement. Celibate women chose, for love of the Lord, to consecrate themselves entirely to the service of those in distress. Fliedner himself was impressed by the work of the Lazarists. Soon other deaconess houses were founded elsewhere in Germany and in the Netherlands, Switzerland, and France (Paris, Strasbourg), as well as in Scandinavia. The deaconesses were wholly dedicated to the service of their brothers and sisters, sustained by their life of prayer in community, and firmly directed by their pastor-director (and his wife) or by a sister-director

33. Beyreuther, *Zinzendorf.*
34. Weber, *The Courage to Live.*

and a pastor. They were and still are a great blessing both within Europe and overseas. Their worldwide organization is called *Diakonia* and is comparable to the International Union of Superiors General (UISG), a worldwide association of Catholic religious orders.

In 1971, the World Council of Churches organized an important meeting for representatives of both Protestant deaconesses and Catholic religious at the Ecumenical Institute of Bossey, Switzerland. Continuing in the ecumenical impulse of these years, a delegation of deaconesses was invited to the UISG assembly, and vice versa, during the annual meeting of *Diakonia*. Already oriented toward an ecumenical perspective, the rapprochement between these sisters and deaconesses has evolved naturally since then. Indeed, these communities have their origins in the same inspiration to serve. Today they all face the same difficulties when it comes to their future—notably a lack of vocations—in a world that has changed, where the social dimension has become more and more secularized.

The deaconesses have had to liberate themselves from their organizational model, usually patriarchal, inherited from the time of their founding. Some are still struggling. Currently, the deaconesses who emphasize true community life of prayer and service, inspired by monasticism, are places of influence. The sisters of Reuilly[35] in France illustrate this reality. Perhaps they were able to evolve in this more contemplative direction thanks to the communitarian vision of their foundress, Sister Caroline, a woman who understood intuitively the importance of community.

In 1979, the Sisters of Strasbourg[36] founded a community of prayer at Hohrodberg in Alsace, with support from the sisters of Pomeyrol. This led to a renewal in the mother house.

In Switzerland, the evolution of the deaconess community at Riehen (Kommunität Diakonissenhaus Riehen, near Basel) is remarkable. These deaconesses have detached themselves from their hospital and now offer hospitality, retreats, and catechism classes while living an intense life of prayer, community, and sharing. They supported the small Reformed religious communities that have formed in German-speaking Switzerland.

---

35. The Community of the Deaconesses of Reuilly, founded in Paris in 1844 by Caroline Malvesin and Antoine Vermeil grew out of the *Reveil*, a movement of spiritual renewal and missionary zeal. See: Messie, *Les Diaconesses de Reuilly*; and Lagny, *Le Reveil de 1830*.

36. Founded (1842) during the *Reveil* in Strasbourg by Lutheran pastor François Haerter (1797–1874), this community of deaconesses was originally called Servants of the Poor. They were teachers and home nurses, ran day-nurseries, soup-kitchens, and eventually the Mulhouse municipal hospital.

In the Anglican Communion,[37] monastic and active religious communities were founded thanks to the Oxford Movement, a catholicizing renewal movement. This spiritual renewal took place at the beginning of the nineteenth century. It would be more correct to speak of a restoration, since these communities took existing Catholic communities as their model—including their monastic garb. However, their spirituality is rooted in the Anglican tradition. After World War II these communities were in crisis, as were the deaconesses. Several of them were able to renew themselves and open up to their era. Some Sisters of Whitby, for example, went to live in the inner city.

In the twentieth century, the Holy Spirit also raised up religious communities on the Continent, among the churches of the Reformation. It is amazing to see how these communities were born more or less independently of each other and then grew up side by side, often experiencing a "mutual encouragement," as the apostle Paul puts it (Rom 1:12).

The communities of Pomeyrol and Grandchamp originated before World War II. The Community of Taizé and the Sisters of Darmstadt began during the war; after the war, the Brothers and Sisters of Imshausen, the sisters of Casteller Ring in Schwanberg, *Communität Christusbruderschaft* in Selbitz, *Ordo Pacis*, the Sisters and Brothers of Gnadenthal, and many others began in Lutheran Germany and in Scandinavia. Some of these have already disappeared; so many kernels of wheat fallen into the earth . . .[38]

The astonishing birth of a "more monastic" religious life in our churches was unquestionably accelerated by the upheavals within all of the churches as well as in society, upheavals due to the horrors of war. Many men and women, moved by the Holy Spirit, realized the importance of encountering the "other," carrying in their hearts the call to reconciliation. The ecumenical movement awakened a renewal—notably through the ecumenical Bible studies of Suzanne de Dietrich. This woman who inspired a very down-to-earth, practical spirituality, made the life experiences of people in the Bible accessible. She was also instrumental in making the ecumenical liturgy *Venite Adoremus* widely available in the early days of the ecumenical movement. Her work is an example of the biblical and liturgical renewal that prepared the ground in which these communities could take root. In 1927, at the time of the first assembly of Faith and Order, in Lausanne, several local Reformed pastors had the opportunity of encountering Lutherans, Anglicans, and Orthodox. Together, these pastors founded *Église et Liturgie*,

---

37. Presided over by the Archbishop of Canterbury, the Anglican Communion includes churches on five continents.

38. Allusion to John 12:24.

a group that worked together on liturgical renewal within the Reformed churches of French-speaking Switzerland.

They began work on a little book of daily prayer, *L'Office Divin*, modeled on the Anglican prayer book, with the addition of Lutheran, Anglican, Catholic, and even Orthodox prayers. From the time of its publication in 1943, it became our book of prayer as well as that of the Brothers of Taizé. It was the foundation of what has become the *Office of Taizé*, called now the *Louange des Jours*.[39] The rediscovery of praying the Liturgy of the Hours in the Protestant world turned out to be crucial for the communities of prayer born within the churches of the Reformation, since a religious community without a liturgical text is at risk of going in circles in a prayer life that is overly subjective.

Wilfred Monod, one of the pioneers of the ecumenical movement, and his son Théodore, the well-known scholar of the Sahara, made another very important contribution. In 1923 they founded the Third Order of the Watchers[40] (*Tiers-Ordre des Veilleurs*) within the Reformed Church of France, inspired by the model of the Franciscan Third Order.[41] Wilfred Monod spoke of this initiative at Stockholm in 1925 during an ecumenical meeting,[42] and tried to attract others to this manner of living the Gospel. His rule was to recite the Beatitudes each day at noon and try to live them daily, underlining three aspects: joy, simplicity, and mercy. He also offered a lectionary of prayers for each day and encouraged regular attendance at Sunday worship. Another "third order" moved by a desire for liturgical renewal, especially eucharistic, appeared in the Lutheran churches of Germany and France: the Brothers of St. Michael (*Evangelische Michaelsbruderschaft*), founded in 1931.

Our earliest sisters were members of the *Veilleurs*. Today, our closeness to the *Veilleurs* is seen in a common desire for renewal in the faith life of Christians. The Third Order of the Watchers enjoyed a period of deep spiritual renewal under the leadership of Daniel Bourguet, a Reformed monk trained at the Cistercian abbey of Les Dombes, France. Brother Roger also knew the *Veilleurs* very well and wished to express his connection with them in his third Rule: "Be filled with the spirit of the Beatitudes: joy, simplicity, and mercy." This fit well with his own inner orientation, which was wholly inspired by the Gospel. This spirit remains what unites Grandchamp's extended spiritual family, including our Third Order of Unity, and Servants of Unity, as well as all who sense a deep communion with us. The sisters of

---

39. Taizé, *Louange des Jours*.
40. Neh 4:9; Matt 26:41.
41. For several years it has been called the Fraternité des Veilleurs.
42. Meeting of "Life and Work" (Archbishop Nathan Söderblom was president).

the Community of Grandchamp reaffirm this each morning as a send-off for the day.

Presence to the World: First Steps

Pray and work that He (Christ) may reign.

Throughout your day
let work and rest be quickened by the Word of God.

Maintain interior silence in all things
in order to dwell in Christ.

Become filled with the spirit of the Beatitudes:
joy, simplicity, mercy.[43]

FROM THE *RULE OF TAIZÉ*

Adopted by our sisters at the time of the first professions in 1952, the *Rule of Taizé*[44] lays down clear principles for life in community, stressing the blessings of forgiveness both given and received, with the idea of constantly beginning again. Reconciliation is at the very heart of the Rule.

What can I say of this Rule? It is prophetic, inspired. It keeps just the right balance between presence to God and presence to the world: "open yourself to all that is human and you will see any vain notion of fleeing the world disappear." It unites seeking God and the unity of the church, as well as compassion toward all human beings, especially the most disadvantaged. "Love the dispossessed, all those who, living amid man's injustice, thirst after justice. Jesus had a particular concern for them. Have no fear of being disturbed by them."[45] Our first response to this love for the least of these,[46] was to send out sisters in small fraternities . . . which makes us like the Little Brothers and Sisters of Jesus, a Catholic religious order. These were our first

---

43. From Br. Roger's first written expression of the Rule, Schutz, *Communauté de Cluny*, 4–10.

44. First published version of the *Rule of Taizé* (1953), modified many times. First English translation, 1961.

45. *Rule of Taizé* (1953). Citation from Communauté de Taizé, *Rule of Taizé in French and in English* (1961), 15.

46. Matt 25:40.

steps of a very concrete fellowship with the world. This new style of expression of the vocation for communal life fits well with the aspirations of the younger sisters who are now joining the Community of Grandchamp.

In 1954, two years after the first life commitments at Grandchamp, other horizons opened and the community intensified its retreat ministry. Until then, our sisters lived in the French-speaking area of Switzerland, and in Paris. We were already receiving German-speaking guests and Swiss German members of the Third Order of Unity. The latter fervently desired a presence in their region. Grandchamp is located near the linguistic and cultural border between French- and German-speaking Switzerland. This location prepared us, without our knowing it, for our first step toward discovering the "other"; a first step toward reconciliation! Two francophone sisters moved into a house suitable for offering spiritual retreats, the Sonnenhof, where they were soon joined by a German-speaking postulant. By going to the Sonnenhof, near Basel, the Sisters lived out a sort of exile and the community as a whole discovered, in offering hospitality to German and Dutch women, the full weight of the consequences of the war in the hearts of these two peoples.

Other sisters went to Algeria, at that time still a French colony. Sister Marguerite arrived at the beginning of November 1954, just as the war for liberation was beginning. In spite of the precarious political situation, the sisters did not give up on the project of establishing a fraternity there. Two sisters joined her and together they established themselves first in a slum in Sainte-Corinne, then at the Cité Dessolier (Maison-Carré), and finally in Oued Ouchaia (Hussein Dey). Our sisters experienced life in community among the poorest people during the war years, which were filled with misery and violence. Their presence touched the whole community, especially Mother Geneviève as a Frenchwoman, from a military family. It was a shock to her to hear from our sisters of some of the actions of the French soldiers. The daily reality of acts of torture perpetrated by her countrymen was unbearable to her. Her conscience was deeply affected. No longer could she put all of the blame on one side; the Nazis, the Germans, "the others," were no longer the only ones who could do evil in her eyes. No, that reality is found in the heart of every man and every woman. This new awareness, at first individual, gradually spread throughout the community. It took time. A similar crisis of conscience came later for the Dutch sisters with regard to Indonesia, which also fought for its independence.

Other fraternities opened in the following years, and each time our sisters immersed themselves in a world of great difficulty for the least of these: for example, in a working-class neighborhood in Paris (Saint-Ouen) and in Lebanon. My time in the factory, when I was a young sister, as well as my visits to our various fraternities, gave me a solid grasp of the conditions of the poorest among us and how precious they are to Christ, who is love sent to us from the heart of our God. God who sees our distress became incarnate in Jesus and in turn looked on the multitude with compassion (Mark 6:34). Those first years of presence, with my sisters, in the midst of the least of these[47] prepared me for my task as mistress of novices, and then for the ministry of prioress. Confronted daily by the struggles of the poor, I was stripped of many prejudices and opened to other human realities. It was also during those years, because of ties of friendship developed with Catholic and Orthodox women religious doing similar ministry, that division among Christians became insufferable to me.

Remembering these first steps, these small adventures in open fellowship, I am moved by and grateful for the ties woven together with brothers and sisters of other traditions. In Algeria, we were welcomed immediately by the Little Sisters of Jesus into their fraternity of adoration for our days of retreat, by the Soeurs Blanches (Sœurs missionnaires de Notre-Dame d'Afrique), and at Lebanese Orthodox monasteries, newly founded because of a renewal of faith among young Orthodox Christians. In Saint-Ouen we were close to the Institut Saint-Serge (Orthodox), warmly welcomed at the Sainte-Françoise Romaine monastery (Catholic sisters of Bec-Hellouin) and the Deaconesses of Reuilly (Protestant), and in Israel, near Tel Aviv, by a small Anglican parish.

Taizé, Pomeyrol . . .

When we began the adventure of fraternities in Algeria because of the call from the Brothers of Taizé, it was thanks to the many ties that already existed between our two communities. We both grew from the same soil of the Swiss Reformed Church, prepared by the ecumenical movement then emerging everywhere, be it through groups like the inter-confessional Conversations of the *Groupe des Dombes*,[48] or the work of remarkable personalities, among whom were Catholics like Dom Lambert Beauduin,

---

47. Matt 25:40.

48. A group of twenty Roman-Catholic and twenty Protestant theologians that has met regularly since 1937 in a monastery near Lyon, France, founded by the Abbé Paul Couturier. See Clifford, *The Groupe des Dombes*.

OSB[49] and Yves Congar, OP;[50] Anglicans such as Lord Halifax[51] and Father Geoffrey Curtis;[52] or Protestants such as Wilfred Monod, Suzanne de Dietrich,[53] Marc Boegner,[54] Willem Visser 't Hooft,[55] and so many others! The Holy Spirit strengthened the roots of our two communities in the same soil: the Third Order of Watchers (*Veilleurs*), Dietrich Bonhoeffer, and the Abbé Paul Couturier, among others. All of us had a similar passion for unity, a reconciled church and a more brotherly and just world. We all desired the visible unity of the church and still long for it, each one according to the grace and charism given us.

In 1940 during World War II, Roger Schutz began, at first alone, to live a life of prayer at Taizé. Near the line of demarcation, he offered hospitality to those fleeing for their lives, including Jews, and soon had to leave France himself, near the end of 1942. He moved to Geneva, where he began a communal life with other young men (1942–1944). Near the end of this same period, Geneviève Micheli accepted our invitation to become the prioress of Grandchamp (1944). In a letter addressed toward the end of 1940 to Sister Marguerite, we can already see her benevolent view of what was beginning to happen at Grandchamp and Taizé:

> And I think that for you, as for M. Schutz, the best is to simply listen to the teachings of the Master, obey, await the Holy Spirit, then be witnesses ... we must believe in this renewal which will take place right here in our somber darkness. I think the idea of M. Schutz is beautiful and I believe it is viable and certainly the

---

49. Dom Lambert Beauduin (1873–1960), a Belgian monk who founded the monastery now known as Chevetogne Abbey in 1925, was one of the important figures of the early Liturgical Movement in the Roman Catholic Church and a leader for Christian unity.

50. Yves Congar (1904–1995) was a French Dominican priest and early Roman Catholic ecumenist.

51. Edward Frederick Lindley Wood, 1st Earl of Halifax (1881 –1959) was an Anglican layman who initiated the Anglican/Roman Catholic conversations on unity with Abbé Fernand Portal, a Catholic priest.

52. Priest of the Community of the Resurrection, Mirfield, an Anglican religious community for men in England. He wrote a biography of the Abbé Paul Couturier.

53. Suzanne de Dietrich (1891–1981) was an Alsatian Protestant woman theologian, a leader in the ecumenical movement and the World Student Christian Federation and a friend of the founders of both Taizé and Grandchamp.

54. Marc Boegner (1881–1970) was an influential pastor in the Reformed Church of France, the principal voice for French Protestant Christians during World War II and a leader in the ecumenical movement.

55. Willem Visser 't Hooft (1900–1985) was involved in the Dutch student Christian movement and became the first secretary general of the World Council of Churches in 1948.

will of God, for community is necessary in order to fight against the assaults of evil. His project . . . will deepen, for its principle is right. He does not yet have experience, but the inspiration is there—so I would have confidence in it.[56]

Filled with this confidence, the two communities began to establish ties. At the beginning, between 1942 and 1944, the first sisters lived in Geneva during the winter months and prayed the Office with the earliest brothers at the Cathedral of St. Peter. In the spring of 1943 Geneviève Micheli invited Brother Roger to lead a retreat at Grandchamp on the theme of "The Incarnation." He accepted with joy. After the war, these ties were strengthened, as were those with the Sisters of Pomeyrol,[57] whom Geneviève had known since 1931, when they were offering retreats at Saint-Germain-en-Laye, France. Like Geneviève, Antoinette Butte[58] belonged to the *Veilleurs*. Their closeness in spirituality explains why, in 1939, Mother Geneviève urged Sister Marguerite to meet with the Saint-Germain-en-Laye retreat team. Soon after, when the team was forced to leave the Paris region and to gather at Pomeyrol in the south of France, Antoinette Butte invited Sister Marguerite and Sister Irène to participate in her teaching on community life. Geneviève Micheli also encouraged this contact: "You are right to go there; you must not remain alone, but rather join together with others in order to experience the power of unity."[59]

From 1953 on, our three French-speaking communities, Grandchamp, Pomeyrol, and Taizé, expressed in writing their "common vocation to the service of Christ and the unity of their witness within the churches of the Reformation and the world" via the same Rule (of Taizé), the same Office, with variations, the teaching of the brothers of Taizé, and frequent visits and mutual assistance between sisters.

But ten years later, this closeness became impossible. Each of the women's communities needed to respect its own context and ecclesial identity and individual charisms, there in the place where they had been planted. After a time of mourning and a rather long separation, for years now we have been experiencing a true visitation of the Spirit between us, recognizing with simple joy the work of the Spirit in each community.

---

56. Micheli, Letter to Soeur Marguerite, November 6, 1940, in [Beaumont], *Lettres*, 68.

57. Protestant community of women in Provence.

58. Antoinette Butte (1898–1986); founder of the Sisters of Pomeyrol, as well as the French Federation of Girl Scouts (Fédération française des éclaireuses).

59. Micheli, Letter to Sister Marguerite 1939, in [Beaumont], *Lettres*, 66.

The prayer of the Office—*L'Office de Taizé*—remains foundational to our life of common prayer at Grandchamp. The Rule puts this prayer in perspective: "The prayer of the Office is in the communion of saints. But to make real this communion with the faithful throughout the ages, we must give ourselves up to fervent intercession for humankind and for the church."[60] On the topic of this office, I should mention, besides the contribution of the group *Église et Liturgie*, all the work of Brother Max Thurian of Taizé, who continued with several brothers to adapt this office to community life; revisions continued until the last edition in 1977. The Brothers of Taizé long ago ceased to use this office. They have replaced it with a more adaptable form, introducing a long silence after the reading of the Word, as well as the famous Taizé chants—done in a musical form called *ostinati*—which invites one toward the experience of interiority (prayerfulness). This evolution is well adapted to their particular ministry, which is oriented toward youth groups. At Grandchamp, we seek to adapt the language of the Office, and introduce necessary modifications while keeping its evangelical simplicity. Our desire is to make sure that the liturgy remains life-giving and simple, a source of living water for all who come to our community.

Growing up together as brothers and sisters, the communities of Taizé and Grandchamp have known both sunshine and storm, each having the responsibility to adjust to its own community's call. We have become aware that the part of field—the gift of community—entrusted to our care by the Lord is different for the brothers of Taizé and for us. This learning happened gradually as events shaped our way forward.

The brothers continue to support our community by sharing their lives, their teaching, and their dynamic liturgy. What would have become of Grandchamp after the death of Mother Geneviève in 1961 without the loving and effective help of Brother Roger and his brothers? It is he who called, on two occasions, a council of the sisters. In June 1961, the sisters elected Mother Marie as prioress. A sixty-seven-year-old widow, she was among the first sisters to commit their lives to the community. Thanks to her faith, courage, and mother's heart, many of our sisters found her easy to approach. Another woman, Rosette Genton,[61] took care of the growth of the community during that period of vulnerability. The unity of the church was of great importance to her, and she had belonged to the Third Order of Unity from its beginning. She attended the councils during this sensitive period and long afterwards, a sign of her exceptional closeness to the community.

---

60. Communauté de Taizé, *The Rule of Taizé* (1961), 17, 18.

61. Rosette Genton worked with Mother Geneviève to create the Servants of Unity. See chapter 4.

She was close to Mother Geneviève and Mother Marie, and as a theologian taught the community about the Desert Fathers and the beginnings of monasticism. I cannot remember this period without mentioning Father Gibbard, one of those who put their gifts at the service of Grandchamp. An Anglican of the Community of St. John the Evangelist, he strengthened us in our monastic calling. When he came to Grandchamp, he also trained pastors in retreat ministry.

In 1963, Brother Roger asked Sisters Marguerite and Gilberte to come to Taizé. A fraternity remained there until 1990. With Geneviève, the sister of Brother Roger, and other women, Sister Renée had already lived there for some years, helping the brothers to raise the orphans they took in just after World War II. During the 1960s, Sister Renée and others also helped with the ever-growing hospitality needs of Taizé, and all of us attended the inauguration of the Church of Reconciliation in August 1962.

In 1966, Brother Roger invited us to Taizé for our annual council. We discussed the themes of "authority and responsibility," "common growth," and "autonomy and solidarity," among others. With Brother Roger's consent, the sisters elected me as assistant to Mother Marie with "authority to make decisions," with the expectation that I would succeed her, as Mother Geneviève had suggested. I was then thirty-seven and also took on the responsibilities of mistress of novices for the following year. After accompanying us closely for many years, Brother Roger urged us henceforth to enter a new stage and to take steps forward on our own—which turned out to be a prophetic word.

So we really needed to rediscover the depths of our own roots and find a renewed balance between our presence in the world (fraternities) and the original mission, that of offering silent retreats (at Grandchamp and the Sonnenhof). In 1969, we therefore needed to call back our younger sisters in order to consolidate the community at Grandchamp. They left their various areas of service, including Taizé. The Sisters of Saint-André, who were already on site and more available than we were, took over the hospitality ministry at Taizé. With these sisters also a profound tie of fellowship and friendship developed, thanks to Mother Claire and *Kaire*,[62] and to the young people they have sent to us.

We still maintain a regular and profound relationship with Taizé through Brother François and Brother Pierre-Yves, especially through their teachings and retreats given at Grandchamp. Taizé remains for us a resource for renewal. But we have also opened ourselves to movements that came to us at Grandchamp: the ecumenical and spiritual inspirations of the World

---

62. A fellowship of communities—see chapter 3, "From Visitations to Visitations."

Council of Churches, the Bossey Institute, the charismatic renewal, Judaism, peace and reconciliation movements, Gospel nonviolence, feminist theology, and recently a program for "evangelization of the interior life."[63]

In the 1980s we made explicit the intuition of the *Rule of Taizé*: "presence to God, presence to the world." Inspired by the Gospel of Mark (6:30–44), we formulated this double call which orients our life: "Come apart, seek his face, let yourself meet God in solitude and silence, disarmed and unified by his love" (Ps 27:8; Mark 6:31). And "enlarge the space of your tent[64] . . . of your heart, do not be afraid of being disturbed by those He will send to you, do not hold back!"—a reflection of that tension we all live between time alone with God and presence in solidarity with God's world.

The violent death of Brother Roger in 2005[65] was a shock for me, as for all our sisters—and for many within and outside of the church. From the time of my installation as prioress on July 22, 1970, I went to Taizé accompanied by a sister at least twice a year to talk with Brother François and Brother Roger. When Sister Pierrette became prioress in 1999, she kept up the same regular visits. Our young sisters continue to go to Taizé each year, where they are also welcomed by the Sisters of Saint-André.

For a colloquium in Lyon in 2002, I wrote of our relations with the brothers of Taizé that our unity with them had progressed from a visible unity—passing by way of a crisis of growth at the end of the 1960s—to an almost deeper unity that manifests communion in Christ, with great respect for our very real differences. It is like a parable: a true communion in Christ while respecting differences is a reciprocal stimulation toward the kingdom where God will be all in all, "a spiritual emulation," as the Abbé Paul Couturier would say.

I am so grateful for having been able to experience this deep communion that I sensed at that time. I remember, as though it were yesterday, my time at Taizé, two days after the birth into heaven of Brother Roger, on August 16, 2005. I went there with one of our sisters and two pastors, to pray near his body. Arriving on the hill, what peace! It was time for noon prayer, the church was full, and Brother François greeted us. "God can only give love . . . our God is tenderness." This refrain touched me profoundly, as it did all of the young people who were there, as a balm and also as a call. As if the violence of Brother Roger's death and all that had gone into his life were nothing but goodness; his face and his whole body were radiant

---

63. A program developed by Simone Pacot of Bethasda entitled Évangélisation des profondeurs. See Pacot, *L'Évangélisation des profondeurs*; *Reviens à la vie!*; *Ose la vie nouvelle!*

64. Allusion to Isa 54:2.

65. During the evening prayer service he was attacked by a woman with a knife.

with this goodness. Thus the witness became entirely transparent. By his blood, a flood of mercy had inundated humanity, first the brothers and all the young people assembled there on the hill, and then all those who kept filing through the church.

A few days later, many of us, along with our prioress, attended his burial. One year later, almost to the day, Brother Alois, now prior of Taizé, came for the first time to Grandchamp, with Brother Richard. What a joy to share the offices together, to recognize one another, so similar and yet so different, as sisters and brothers. Brother Alois wanted to make a pilgrimage to the place of Brother Roger's childhood. In Provence, the village of his birth, about 20 kilometers from Grandchamp, the countryside appeared to us in an intense and peaceful light. How dazzling was the splendor of the countryside which marked his childhood. How moving it was to experience these moments with the prior and prioress of our two communities, who carry today the ministry of communion, as the luminous beauty of the creation whispered to us the presence of Brother Roger, also a witness . . . beyond the visible.

Through the Prayers of an Apostle of Unity: Abbé Paul Couturier[66]

. . . May it come, O Christ, that day which is your will! The day that since the Last Supper, you have not ceased to pray for; that day on which we will have but one mind . . . your mind: unity in the faith of your one and only church. That day will come, when our sufferings because of our separation will have made us suffer enough . . . and that the flame of our love for you will have become bright enough, and ardent enough the fire and light of the same Spirit, that in response to our love for you, already at work, you will send us . . . your Spirit, the Spirit of your Father.

On that day will be the great restoration and the great scandal will cease.

Until that day, your name: Father is scarcely hallowed

---

66. This chapter is a revision of my talk at the Lyon colloquium in November 2002: Centre Unité Chrétien ed., *L'œcuménisme spirituel de L'Abbé Couturier*, 119–30.

on earth . . . but on that day, it will be.

"Father, hallowed be your name . . ." Amen! Amen!

"Hallowed be Your Name,"
Abbé Paul Couturier (1940)[67]

This adventure of an ever more open communion, which our community desires to live, is the first growth of seeds sown in Christ. One of these seeds sown was Paul Couturier. This man of prayer dared to go outside the camp[68]—while remaining intensely loyal—in order to meet Christ in his humiliation (Heb 13:12–13). Following him in his *kenosis*, Couturier was able to reach out to the humble of our earth, as well as the humble of our churches.

During his visit to the Monastery of Unity[69] at Amay-sur-Meuse in 1933, he became a Benedictine oblate. There he received the inspiration that would orient his entire life: the vision of a spiritual ecumenism consecrated to the unity of all Christians "as Christ wills, and by the means that he wills."[70] Filled with the prayer of Christ, he was impelled to meet others who were not of his camp, in humility. Don't all of our churches need to be converted by letting themselves be filled with the supplication of Christ "that all may be one . . . that the world may believe" (John 17:21)? All need to discover the love of the Father, especially those most humble and distressed in our time.

The influence of the Abbé Paul Couturier spread thanks to Cardinal Gerlier and the whole "Lyonnaise team":[71] the Jesuit Center of La Fourvière, the Abbé Monchanin, and pastor Roland de Pury. In Paris, the Dominican Center Istina of Father Dumont was created, and enriched through frequent contact with Russian Orthodox immigrants. Other people and places contributed to the new ecumenical impulse.

---

67. Text cited by Mother Geneviève. The prayer of consecration of the sisters of Grandchamp ends with these words: "to remain in unity in order that your name be hallowed."

68. He was Roman Catholic but reached out to those outside the Catholic Church.

69. Founded by Dom Lambert Beauduin, this monastery is currently located at Chevetogne, Belgium.

70. Murray, *Receptive Ecumenism*, 409.

71. Fouilloux, *La pensée catholique française*.

Though in delicate health, the Abbé Paul Couturier never stopped reaching out to others, without any feeling of his own superiority. He created strong bonds of trust with those he encountered and maintained these through his visits. His messages affirmed those who agreed with his ecumenical vision. A large inter-confessional network of prayer resulted, in Lyon, England, Switzerland, and elsewhere, laying the groundwork for the birth of ecumenical communities and, I believe, Vatican II, truly unimaginable in that era.

> Currently dispersed, a group of Catholics form a veritable "Invisible Monastery"[72] of unity. And I'm not including a multitude of monks and nuns who have made of their religious consecration a heartfelt gesture in support of, and as a sign of, prayer for Christian unity. All the faithful who do the same—I know of Anglicans in large numbers—and I know of some Protestants . . . all together, they form an invisible cohort, a great Invisible Monastery of unity.[73]

I became aware of the importance of the link between the Abbé Paul Couturier and the Community of Grandchamp while preparing my lecture for the colloquium in Lyon marking the fiftieth anniversary of his death. Quietly, the spiritual ecumenism of the Abbé Couturier worked itself into our community in a profound way, but without our being aware of its author. We quite simply forgot the one to whom we owe so much for having directed us onto this path; at least we, the sisters who came along a bit later forgot. The Abbé Couturier was a true *starets*[74] for our first sisters, a *starets* whose prayer continues to support the community in the communion of saints, both in heaven and here on earth.

Beginning in February 1940, our sisters were in regular contact with the Abbé Couturier. Mother Geneviève, then still Geneviève Micheli, met him for the first time in April, in Lyon. She wrote to sister Marguerite about this meeting:

> My stop in Lyon is a great day in my life and for my personal inner life . . . an admirable clarity on what love in unity ought to be, and adoration which is the basis of unity. I think, love, and pray differently—you will thank God for it . . . and the Abbé

---

72. Phrase and concept popularized by Paul Couturier.
73. [Beaumont], *Lettres*, 71–73.
74. Venerated adviser and teacher in the Russian Orthodox tradition. Brother Emile of Taizé used this expression to describe the role of the Abbé Couturier in his presentation at the colloquium: Les actes du Colloque. See Centre Unité Chrétien, *L'œcuménisme spirituel*, 189–99.

Couturier with Wilfred Monod are united in my soul as my spiritual guides. From this conversation has emerged a vision of the manner in which to work for unity, and the retreat at Bièvres manifested a new spirit . . . The pages written for us by the Abbé Couturier on "Hallowed be Thy Name," which I will send you, are admirable . . . it is truly the dawn of a new day, the certainty of evil vanquished, and Saturday evening my heart sang "Thy kingdom come" in total fullness.[75]

And so a friendship in Christ was forged, profound and definitive, between the Abbé and Geneviève Micheli. It was the same for the other sisters. Two months earlier, Sisters Irène and Marguerite had been welcomed by the Abbé Couturier in Lyon; it was a deeply moving encounter. Sister Marguerite wrote to him afterward: "This Saturday, as we do each Saturday, we will pray for the church; join with us sometimes in spirit in your Saturday evening intercession for the church of Christ and that he himself may unite us all together in his love which breaks down every barrier."

L'Abbé Couturier took a spiritual interest in all that happened at Grandchamp. The retreat programs were sent to him during the early years and he prayed over them. When Geneviève Micheli returned to Switzerland, she asked for his prayers:

> I write to ask you to send me your daily prayer list as you do it at Grandchamp—we are forming here in the mountains a little prayer cell of the "Invisible Monastery." I have recruited two of my nieces, both French, one Catholic, ardently and profoundly so . . . I have converted her to unity—the other is Protestant . . . and also won over to the idea of unity. We will be spending the winter together and would love there to be a tangible link between us, like a secret flame which unites our hearts—you will help us with your beautiful prayer requests for each month.[76]

And the Abbé, in his letters to the sisters, to Sister Marguerite in particular, speaks of what he senses as the vocation of Grandchamp, which remains today the heart of our ecumenical engagement:[77]

May 22, 1940

---

75. Letter Geneviève Micheli to Marguerite de Beaumont, April 23, 1940. Partially printed in [Beaumont], *Lettres*, 75.

76. Archives of the Groupe des Dombes.

77. Letters from Paul Couturier to the sisters at Grandchamp in [Beaumont], *Lettres*, 71–73.

These times are distressing. Others have lived in such times. They are also a time of hope, renewed faith, and the love our faith inspires. These are God's times. His glory, the manifestation of his glory, carries us through. His ways are not ours. Could we not hope that these trials may draw Christians closer to one another, inspire prayers for the unity of Christians, and extraordinary self-sacrifices in both numbers and the manner in which they are offered? Into your hands, Lord, we commend our spirits.

Through these somber days, the quiet spaces of peaceful silence at Grandchamp and Roche-Dieu give rest and delight to my soul. Blessed places where those who work for Christian unity are formed and reformed, where souls purified by the suffering and the prayer of Christ can enter into prayer, or better, be filled with Christ praying within them the entirety of his prayers to the Father.

August 18, 1940

To know that Grandchamp has become a fervent home of spiritual emulation,[78] a center of prayer for that "Christian unity" Christ asked of his Father so that many may come there to pray and leave with peace of mind, enlightened and aware of that suffering which Christ revealed in his prayer . . . what joy . . .

God is calling you to a profound work for unity. If he calls you to raise up a movement of contemplative life within Protestantism . . . may He be a thousand times blessed! Visible unity is coming.

September 13, 1940

I sense that the Invisible Monastery of Christian unity is growing in its Protestant branch where Grandchamp is a strong bough.

September 24, 1940

I pray often for the Invisible Monastery and for one of its most beautiful centers, Grandchamp. I even sense that the first real Monastery of Christian Unity, such as I have imagined it, will be Protestant.

November 2, 1940

---

78. Defined by Paul Couturier as "a true communion in Christ while respecting differences is a reciprocal stimulation toward the kingdom."

I pray and ask for prayers for the important upcoming retreat for theology students. Whoever helps his brother to welcome the Spirit of God is working for Christian unity. May all of these dear young men leave Grandchamp with the wound of the separations between Christians in their hearts and the spiritual flame of prayer for unity alive within them.

Utopia or reality? Several times the Abbé Couturier mentions the Invisible Monastery of Christian Unity. In this he incorporates Orthodox thought—explained by Paul Evdokimov[79] in his book *Les ages de la vie spirituelle* (dedicated to Mother Geneviève as a sign of communion). In this book he develops the idea of "interior monasticism" through the eyes of the Fathers:

> "When Christ," says St. John Chrysostom, "orders us to follow the narrow path, he addresses himself to all. The monastics and the layperson must attain the same heights." We can see indeed that there exists only one spirituality for all without distinction in its demands, whether of the bishop, monk, or lay person, and this is the nature of monastic spirituality. Now, this has been shaped by lay-monastics, which gives to the term "lay" the maximal spiritual and ecclesial meaning . . . When the Fathers spoke, they addressed all the members of the church, the mystical body, without any distinction between clergy and laity. They spoke to the universal priesthood. Our contemporary pluralism: different theologies for the episcopate, the clergy, monastics, and the laity, unknown at the time of the Fathers, would be incomprehensible to them.[80]

In the spring of 1941, Sister Marguerite asked the Abbé Couturier to contribute to her plans for a retreat called "An Introduction to Prayer," saying to him, "We know so little of prayer." He proposed as a title "To Breathe is Life for the Body, to Pray, Life for the Soul." And concluded, "You, who pray, let my little prayer mingle with yours, and be enriched by it. Remember often that I am just a beggar at the door of your souls."[81]

Thanking him, Sister Marguerite, as head of the little community, wrote,

---

79. Paul Evdokimov was born in St. Petersburg, Russia in 1901. Settled in Paris by 1923, he completed his theological studies at St. Sergius Orthodox Theological Institute in Paris where he also taught. He was among the founding members of the Russian Christian Student Movement and was an observer at the Second Vatican Council.

80. Evdokimov, *Ages of the Spiritual Life*, 137–38.

81. Paul Couturier, *Un aspect cosmique de la prière*. Mimeographed text, Archives of Grandchamp.

> My work consists of choosing, grouping, and tying together in a bouquet all of these beautiful sprigs, so diverse. And I am struck by how God reveals himself to each soul according to its needs. We so often want to unify rather than unite. It is best to love and pray rather than judge, and little by little many will open themselves to this idea of achieving unity by joining together rather than by unification. Thank you for praying for this retreat and especially for asking that we, the sisters of Grandchamp, may receive the gift of the life of prayer without which our life here has no reason for being . . . [82]

In a letter written to the Abbé Couturier during this same period, Sister Irène described how much the fraternal life, fraternal love, is the privileged ascetic path to attain the unity of Christians. After recalling how the evil one can intrude to bring division, and affirming her conviction that "we can love one another without necessarily understanding one another," she went on to say,

> We are born to rejoice in God and to love one another with the same love Christ has for us. Most of us know it, but there is our ego to cope with . . . Yes, it is necessary to pray at all times and with all of our hearts, "Jesus Christ, our only rest is in you who loves us all with the same love" . . . May your grace intervene! Reunite your body by your own power! I have suffered from this division among Christians who profoundly wound one another, with Catholic friends and relatives who seem to be going in a different direction, leaving us forever. And each time, I've realized that it is humans who divide, that God only unites, always.
>
> And if, when going "in a different direction," we truly find God, we find each other . . . [83]

If these words are now familiar to many of us who pray for unity, in the 1940s they were prophetic!

After this time of intense exchange of letters, came the time of the desert. The war stopped the postal service. The Abbé Couturier even spent part of 1944 in prison, arrested by the Gestapo. Fellowship had to live in their hearts, hidden with Christ in God. As Father Curtis wrote in his book on Paul Couturier, "the close friendship with the brothers of Taizé and the sisters of Grandchamp deepened through the shadows of the war. This was

---

82. Vries, "L'accompagnement spirituelle," 127.

83. Sister Irène, Letter to the Abbé Couturier, 1941, Archives of the Groupe des Dombes.

very important for their evolution . . . toward a more universal comprehension of the Christian faith."[84]

The Call of God . . . the Commitments

. . . You recognized and respected them, loved and never despised them as women. You spoke to them of the Kingdom.

. . . You take upon yourself the tears of women, those of Rachel, and those of all the mothers of the world, those of Mary, the Mother of Sorrows.

You will take them into your death so that our tears may make an opening and become the very place where we encounter you, the Risen One.

JESUS MEETS THE WOMEN OF JERUSALEM

Meditation at the Ninth Station of
the Cross At the Colosseum (1995)[85]

Our community was born out of silent retreats given at Grandchamp. But the story of the life of Geneviève Micheli, the source of her calling, reveals our calling as well. So what is the mystery, in its original meaning, that this woman carried and that makes our community what we are? What is this total "yes" that we in our turn answer to that call, the radical actualizing of our baptism? What is the essence of the call now blooming on a small part of the great field of God, within the churches of the Reformation?

Mother Geneviève was born to a non-practicing Catholic father and a Reformed Alsatian mother. One could say that she reconciled the two churches in her own flesh. She was baptized Protestant. She married the son of a Reformed family of Geneva, Léopold Micheli.

Three children were born to them as a young couple. But daily life was sometimes difficult because Léopold went through periods of severe

---

84. Curtis, *Paul Couturier and Unity in Christ*.
85. Vries, *Chemin de Croix*.

depression. The visit of a French pastor, Georges Boissonnas,[86] helped them to grasp deeply the reality of Christ living within each person. They experienced this reality in a way that resulted in the full deliverance of Léopold from his depressions. Geneviève saw in this healing the irrefutable proof of the strength of Life to be drawn from the living Christ. Some time later, the family went on holiday, during which the accidental death of Leopold Micheli turned Geneviève's life upside down.

> Wednesday morning June 21, Léopold arrived . . . He had decided to fully enjoy his holiday. I had rarely seen him so well and so happy. In addition, our holiday site enchanted him, and barely ready, we rushed down to the beach; the children were so happy to see him again.

The next day, the current was strong and Léopold drowned after rescuing two swimmers. His body was thrown up on the beach several hours later. Geneviève Micheli, a widow at age twenty-seven, with three young children wrote in her journal,

> As though in a nightmare, I sent telegrams, then returned to the little room where all had been prepared by unknown, but truly loving, hands. Léopold rested there. That is the right word. He rested there with an admirable expression of peace and serenity. His beautiful hands were joined and his dear face was so young and beautiful. There was no trace of suffering or struggle on his face, and looking at him, I could not despair. In spite of myself, peace descended into my soul and a great sense of respect: my beloved was there, and yet so far away . . . And the hours passed, alone with Léopold and my Bible. In the night I lay down beside him, but I did not sleep; I kept vigil next to his motionless body, hearing the storm outside, the sinister howling of the wind so strong that it seemed it would blow the house away. And my only feeling was: he is no longer in the sea, beaten by the waves; my dear one has found shelter.

> It was then that I began reading, reading the whole ending of the Gospel of John. I even asked pastor Georges Boissonnas to read some verses more loudly, when it seemed to me that read in a low voice, they did not make sense. And another night came, a new night of watching and praying in the little bed above his, a night spent in prayer, in silence. And in the morning it seemed to me that through anguish, shortcomings, and distress, peace had entered into my heart and I knew with certainty that God was

---

86. Boissonnas, *Expériences d'un évangéliste*.

helping me. On Léopold's bed were strewn pink geraniums and all the flowers given by the good people of the neighborhood.

And the peaceful, beautiful service took place . . . I do not recall what Georges said, but each word came from God, and they were words of assurance and of love, and I felt Léopold close to me, but a transfigured Léopold, luminous, living a better life, understanding everything, loving completely, delivered from all limitations and of all obstacles . . . Now I could go back to Geneva, alone; God had conquered death; there was no more fear, nor anguish, there was nothing but the great love of God.[87]

The ordeal of her husband's violent death, and the solitude that followed, made very real the evangelical experience they had had in Geneva some months earlier. Now it was in her own flesh that she received the grace to live in the presence of the Risen One. The experience of that presence even into the depths of her human despair became the foundation of her life of faith, her grounding forever in the reality of Christ who died and was raised again.

How her beautiful text "God asks everything of us, but above all he gives us everything" reflects this reality at once agonizing and life-giving: "I see first of all, love, and afterwards surrender."[88] One cannot follow Christ on his path of renunciation, in the gift he gives of himself to the very end, except by being immersed in love, that love which flows from the heart of the Trinity. First one must know oneself loved, accepted, forgiven, "crowned with love and tenderness" (Ps 103). We must accept this grace, this joy, and let it saturate every fiber of our being. The Father loves us: "You are my beloved son, my beloved daughter; into you I have poured out all my love."

"Then comes surrender, through love," continues Mother Geneviève. In the merciful gaze of Christ, we can lay ourselves bare in all our fragility, with our limitations, our weaknesses, our sins. And we can gradually let Christ separate us from all that is not truly ourselves, and receive from him our true image, raised from the dead with him. We must learn to die to all that is motivated by our egocentric self, our "old self" (Rom 6:6) which weighs down our actions and our relationships; a journey of purification and peacemaking when we keep silence within.

Here we approach the mystery of the Lord's touch on Geneviève Micheli in the early hours of her widowhood. Through her, God acted. During those early years, the retreatants experienced silence—many for the first time. Silence and an inner listening for the Word of God are at the heart of

---

87. Mère Geneviève, *Lettre à mes enfants*, copy, archives Grandchamp.
88. Micheli, *Message*, Grandchamp, 9.

the spirituality born at Grandchamp for the churches of the Reformation and for the one church.

For Sister Marguerite and so many others, Geneviève Micheli is a precious guide on the path to which Christ himself initiated her:

> Silence is a purification. When will we make up our minds to die so that we might live? And death is a silence. We must silence all the discordant, prideful, arrogant, hateful, bitter voices, the controlling will . . . "unless a grain of wheat falls to the ground and dies" . . . silence is like the grain of wheat planted in the ground. Happy is he, happy is she who, having given her heart and soul to God, pays no attention to what God does in him, in her; who loves without noticing her love, who walks without knowing the way, without minding her progress; who is, in a word, profoundly forgetful of self, and who rests completely in the arms of God as an infant in the arms of her mother.
>
> God is everything, we are nothing. It is God's Spirit, will, life which must fill us; this is the creation of the "new man" . . . obedience is a fruit of this silence.[89]

Death is a silence. Mother Geneviève experienced this great silence during her nights near the body of her husband. These nights made of her something of a monk (from the Greek *monos*—alone), a woman henceforth consecrated to the love of God: "Do we listen in the silence for the final message of the one who has been taken from us? Let us stop our tears and our despair, and see the heavens open for us. Let us accept that there is a greater love which envelops us miraculously with tenderness."

This is the mystery of Holy Saturday, which carries in itself, like the ground in which the grain of wheat is planted or like a woman close to giving birth, the immense hope of the "new man," the "new woman" who will be born.

At the origins of our community are two women, Geneviève Micheli and Marguerite de Beaumont, women in whom the Spirit of God was at work, with no preconceived idea in mind—much less the founding of a community of monastic inspiration within the Reformed Church. The realities experienced in their very flesh by Mary, mother of the Lord, and Elizabeth, mother of John the Baptist, are closer to the reality of the first days of the Community of Grandchamp than any image of building a material edifice.

The first four women—Mother Geneviève, Sister Marguerite, Sister Marthe, and Sister Irène—all very different and yet so similar in their desire to follow Christ and to serve the one church, opened the way for those who

89. Micheli, *Message*, 16.

would follow in their diversity as well as in their fervent desire for unity. Faithfully, for more than sixty years, several times each week, we pray during the Office: "Lord, help Christians to find visible unity again. 'May they be one so that the world may believe'" (John 17:21). This prayer, prayed so many times in community, has emphasized our desire for unity so much that Sister Pierrette, our prioress, was inspired to write a new, deeper form of the same prayer, which we now pray: "Lord, help Christians to manifest the communion which is in you." To live this communion of love and of life which is in God, Father, Son, and Holy Spirit and demonstrate it, bear witness to it.

The Community of Grandchamp today includes more than fifty sisters of various Protestant confessions, nationalities, and cultures that are at times very different (from Asia, Africa, and Europe). This diversity came about little by little. Until 1957, the community was made up of Reformed sisters of French-speaking Switzerland. Then came the first Lutherans, from Germany, a few Methodists from Switzerland and Austria, and our African sisters from the Baptist Church of the Congo. This diversity is characteristic of our community. Indeed, if national and cultural differences are fairly common in apostolic missionary communities, they are more rare in coenobitic communities of monastic inspiration. Our vocation to a daily ecumenism is a treasure and a challenge which touches each of us deeply. Whatever our ecclesial origins, we strive to respect it. Through this diversity we lean into the church of tomorrow, with no less a goal than the kingdom of God. Against the spirit of this world, which would divide and separate, or absorb and merge, we seek to assume ever more fully our different ecclesial and cultural sensibilities instead of denying them. We have chosen to walk in this evangelical, nonviolent way toward Unity. The task before us is immense and requires all of our creative love.

Ecumenism begins among ourselves: in 1952, at the time of the first sisters' professions, all francophone, two Dutch women knocked at the door, as did one Swiss woman who spoke German. In those early days, those of us who were not francophone did everything we could to learn French as quickly as possible and to embrace everything that seemed so strange—we did this with generosity and interest, but sometimes painfully. One part of our being had no space to breathe. This seemed perfectly normal in the thinking of that era. This has changed over time, thanks to visits by our sisters to the Sonnenhof, our spiritual retreat house for German speakers and thanks to experiences in our various fraternities. Then their friends came to Grandchamp: Muslims and Jews. Twenty years later, Asia opened to us through the arrival of Sister Siong, of Chinese origin, born in Indonesia. Our Congolese sisters arrived more recently from that troubled region, opening us to African perspectives. We continue to discover our differences—even between francophone and German-speaking Swiss sisters!

By reaching beyond our individualisms, we would like to become, all together, a leaven of communion, of unity, of reconciliation in Christ's church, in the world: this is our reason for being, for all of us—"to proclaim the Gospel by my very life,"[90] to show together this love of communion that is in God the Father, Son, and Holy Spirit, this compassion which extends even to the laying down of one's life. We understand ourselves ever more fully as a community of the monastic type: silence and solitude are for us essentials for the growth of the seeds of communion sown by our community. We draw from this silence and solitude the impetus for daily engagement in the conciliar process of justice, peace, and creation care, in an evangelical attitude of nonviolence. We are still learning to live in this open communion which we desire to live.

Here Am I, Holy Spirit, Creator of Life

Each one of us, at one moment or another, has been touched by the reality of the love of God in an irresistible way: no two of our stories are alike. Certain sisters at first rather vaguely, still seeking, entered the community with the sincere desire of spending their lives in a spiritual quest. For others, the reality of the love of Christ, love of all loves, entered their lives little by little, while for others this reality surged suddenly into their lives, like an earthquake, interrupting all of their plans.

And so here we are together, because Christ has said to each of us, "You are loved, loved with an incredible love . . . which welcomes you as you are, with all of your gifts and all of your faults, your weaknesses, with all that has wounded you." By this call of Christ to come, follow him, to follow him alongside these sisters whom he has given us—gifts, weaknesses, wounds included, we discover more and more fully the power of our baptism.

Yes, our baptism, the resurrection, and our profession are tightly joined together. During the Easter season we wear our white habits all day long, a reminder of the paschal mystery. It will be the same on the day of our death—of our birth into heaven—we will be wrapped in white in hope of the resurrection, for Christ will take us up with him into his life.

In hindsight I can bear witness to this: my baptism is becoming more and more important as the years pass. When I entered the novitiate, we sang the Easter hymn "All of you who have been baptized into Christ, you have

---

90. Citation of Charles de Foucauld, engraved on his tomb, from his book *Crier l'Évangile*, 21–22.

been clothed with Christ, alleluia!" Before my entrance into the novitiate, I was told, "This ceremony is but a preparation for the day of your profession."

The day of our baptism, the Spirit grafted our lives into Christ, who died and rose again, and we became members of his body, the church. Because of this spiritual reality, we welcome as an immense gift the fact that baptism, received in our respective churches, is today recognized by most of the other churches,[91] an important marker on our path toward visible unity.

Easter—which celebrates the resurrection of Christ from the dead—is at the heart of our life as baptized women, whose lives are radically given, as Sisters of Grandchamp called to live in one community though coming from different confessions with very different spiritualities. Day after day, we experience that the more we are rooted in Christ, the more able we are to unconditionally welcome one another, opening ourselves to Christians of other churches, and to all humanity. Did not Christ, our one true love, journey to the furthest limits of love in giving his life for the unconditional welcome of the other, beyond all our aggression and stubbornness? "Father, forgive them, for they do not know what they are doing" (Luke 23:34).

Yes, profession is the actualization of our baptism. The Holy Spirit confirms what has already been accomplished at our baptism and after our confirmation: "You are the beloved daughter of the Father; your life is henceforth hidden with Christ in God."

This pilgrimage toward the kingdom, following Christ who gathers us by the Holy Spirit, engages us in a journey of the soul, a slow transformation. As signs of this dynamic, our six promises form a whole. They orient, mark out, and inspire our way through the various stages of our life and of the history of the world. The "yes" of Christ upon our life liberates our own "yes."

The first promise, and the point of departure, is "Will you, for the love of Christ, consecrate yourself to him with all your being?" We are called to follow him on his life's path in obedience to the Father, ever more free and loving, nourished by the Word of God and by the spirit of the Rule, to let ourselves be more and more conformed by the Holy Spirit to the image of Christ in us.

Second: "Will you henceforth with your sisters celebrate the newness of life that Christ gives by the Holy Spirit and let the Spirit live in you, among us, in the church, the world, and all creation, fulfilling in this way your service of God in our community?" Our life is possible only by the movement of the Holy Spirit who refreshes and renews the promise of our baptism. The

---

91. Faith and Order, *Baptism, Eucharist and Ministry*, part II, chapter 1.

Spirit enables us to hear the invitation of the risen Christ to choose Life, in a world of death, in all circumstances, by the power of his resurrection.

In Christ, we can live the three monastic vows (obedience, chastity, poverty), a call addressed in fact to all Christians who follow Christ. These three vows echo the three temptations of Christ in the desert at the beginning of his ministry and concern the three fundamental drives of all human beings: the wish to possess more and immediately; the wish to tie others to ourselves; the wish to dominate. These three instinctive drives create the idols and ideologies of our world: money, sex, power—or, according to the prophets, Mammon, Baal, Moloch.

Third: "Will you, renouncing all property and in an attitude ever more disarmed, live with your sisters not only in community of material goods, but also in that of spiritual goods, trying always to share and to be open hearted?" We follow Christ who was poor, and learn little by little to open our hands, to no longer want to keep anything for ourselves, to let ourselves be disencumbered in order to become ever more welcoming and generous.

Fourth: "Will you, in order to give yourself unreservedly to the love of Christ and to be more available to serve him with your sisters, remain celibate in all chastity?" He invites us also to open our hearts to receive his gracious and universal love and to live it with our sisters, as well as with all others.

Fifth: "Will you, so that we may be of one heart and of one mind in the ministry of communion which God entrusts to us, and so that our unity of service may be fully accomplished, adopt the decisions made by the community and expressed by the prioress?" *Koinonia* is a fruit of Pentecost, a gift of the Holy Spirit. A true common life, a coherent witness, is possible only when our innate and subjective individualism opens itself to the direction of the community received together in the light of the Holy Spirit. This life is summed up and given expression by the presider, the prioress.

Sixth: "Will you, always discerning Christ in your sisters, watch over them in good times and bad, in abundance and in want, in suffering and in joy?" This is to accept and welcome our sisters as a gift of God, as the very presence of Christ, and to watch over them to the end, sharing everything. Our faithfulness can become the humble sign of the faithfulness of God, and a true solidarity, the most fruitful witness.[92]

---

92. Adapted from *The Rule of Taizé in French and in English* (1967), 135–39.

CHAPTER 2

The Adventure of Open Communion

Putting Down Ecclesial Roots Far and Near

THE PROTESTANT CHURCHES ARE more diverse even than the many Orthodox churches. As a "community of prayer and reconciliation of monastic inspiration with an ecumenical vocation," it is essential that our community be firmly rooted in the local as well as the universal church. Local roots allow for universal participation. The village of Grandchamp is located in the canton of Neuchâtel. Our community, bringing together sisters of several Protestant churches, is recognized by the Evangelical Reformed Church of Neuchâtel,[1] itself attached to the Federation of Protestant Churches of Switzerland. In this way we are also participants in the World Council of Churches in Geneva.

    Knowing the origins of a Protestant person (Reformed, Lutheran, Mennonite, etc.) does not necessarily mean knowing the style of church she comes from. Many of our sisters are Reformed, but from different countries. Within these countries, as with the different cantons of Switzerland, the tone of these same churches can be different, since each church bears the traces of its history and its political and cultural context. This great diversity of churches highlights the influence of the ecumenical movement on the rapprochement between certain churches throughout the world. Since 1947, for example, a new church has formed in South India by uniting Anglicans, Presbyterians, and Methodists under the leadership of one bishop. Other mergers have taken place since then. During the postwar period, several Free Churches of French-speaking Switzerland, which had separated from the state churches in the nineteenth century, reunited. We are witnessing a

---

1. Église Réformée Évangélique du Canton de Neuchâtel (EREN).

similar movement elsewhere in the world. In Canada, for example, as well as in the Netherlands, where the three largest Protestant churches (two Reformed churches and one Lutheran) have united to become the Protestant Church of the Netherlands.[2] This is the fruit of patient preparation over the past twenty years by a process called "Together on the way." In Europe, the churches of the Reformation have recognized one another's ministry and sacraments since the Concord of Leuenberg, 1973.[3]

We ourselves are living this type of ecumenism within our community of sisters who are Baptists, Methodists, Lutherans, and Reformed. Another distinctive feature opens us to the universality of the church: our integration in the local church depends on our geographical location. In French- and German-speaking Switzerland, our community belongs to Reformed churches; in Algeria, to Methodist and Reformed churches, themselves supported by the local Catholic Church, that try to care for the Protestant Church of Algeria, whose churches are increasingly filled with Indigenous people. In Jerusalem, our Fraternity of Saint Elisabeth is connected to the Lutheran Church.

It is vital that our rootedness in a local church be unambigous. That is why the recognition of the Community of Grandchamp by the Evangelical Reformed Church of Neuchâtel (EREN) in 1987 was a cause of so much joy. In the 1960s, this church designated Pastor Robert Cand, former president of the Synod, to be our liaison with the local synod and to be available for celebrations, spiritual direction, confessions, and so on. For eucharistic celebrations, the community depends on pastors in the region. At our invitation, these pastors come to preside at our eucharistic celebrations, which is a learning experience for all, and keeps us from being self-sufficient; we need our local church, and the church can count on us and our regular prayer. This reciprocity is at the very heart of our call to unity.

Recall that in the Reformed churches, authority is with the synod, whereas on the global level, the churches are organized in alliances or federations. In this context, as a community of monastic inspiration with an ecumenical vocation, with members from several different churches of the Reformation, we felt the need to establish a board of reference. It is composed of two sisters, one of them the prioress, and five external members, Protestant and Catholic, including our chaplain, a religious sister and a monk. This board of reference keeps a fraternal eye on the community and can be consulted when the need arises. In this way our community shows its desire for interdependence with the church rather than self-sufficiency.

---

2. Protestantse Kerk in Nederland (PKN).
3. Birmelé, "Concorde de Leuenberg," 253.

As for our local involvement, for the first thirty years, the sisters participated in Sunday services in the local parishes. At that time, eucharistic celebrations were rare. Grandchamp was the exception! Each Thursday night, the Lord's Supper was celebrated in our chapel with a local pastor.

As our hospitality increased, we felt the need to celebrate our own Eucharist on Sundays and feast days, before breakfast. On special occasions, one or another of our sisters still attends local Sunday services . . . and our African sisters participate from time to time in the services organized by the African Christian community in Neuchâtel, sometimes bringing other sisters with them. In this way we keep in touch with the realities of life around us.

On the topic of our liturgy, Pastor Bruno Burki, for many years professor of liturgy at the Catholic Faculty of Theology of Fribourg, wrote:

> By their responsiveness to the expectation of a Eucharistic spirituality, the Community of Grandchamp has served a felt need among pastors and faithful members of the Protestant Churches, who, in this generation, have discovered the essential place of the Eucharist in the life of a Christian community. The movement toward celebrating the Lord's Supper every Sunday in Protestantism in this country has been greatly supported by Grandchamp.[4]

In 1962, the Brothers of Taizé published *Liturgies pascales*, which proposed, among other things, an Easter sunrise liturgy. The following year we introduced it, always mindful that liturgy forms our faith. This important celebration has gradually spread in the region and also in other Protestant parishes of French-speaking Switzerland.

On the local front, our ties with the Faculty of Theology of Neuchâtel[5] have been strong, and a number of sisters have taken courses there. From the 1950s to the early 1980s, this faculty was renowned in Europe and beyond for its openness to ecumenism.[6] At that time this was rare! A wonderful reciprocity developed when Mother Geneviève introduced ecumenical sessions, and students from the faculty were given time off from classes to participate.

Ties with the local church are also very concrete. Sisters have been members of the parish council of our church (EREN) in the nearby town

---

4. Burki, "Liturgie et communauté monastique," 9–13.

5. Closed June 2015.

6. A personal relationship developed with Professors Philippe Menoud, Jean-Jacques von Allmen, and Jean-Louis Leuba. Each one in his own manner had a particular tie to Mother Geneviève and the Community of Grandchamp.

of Boudry. We welcome leaders of the local parishes and are often asked to help with spiritual renewal or ecumenical initiatives taken by these churches. Finally, one of our sisters is a delegate to the Synod of EREN.

We remain in relationship with the Federation of Protestant Churches of Switzerland (FEPS). When we were threatened by the construction of a small airport next door (on the Areuse plain), the Federation supported us in our opposition. Unfortunately, in vain! On a happier note, we received an invitation through the Federation to participate in the welcoming of Pope John Paul II to Kehrsatz, Switzerland, in 1984. Our ties with the FEPS were enhanced when the Federation created an office to maintain contact with Protestant religious communities of celibate men and women (including deaconesses), and mixed communities.

Rooted In the Same Ecumenical Dynamic

The beginnings of the World Council of Churches and Grandchamp are rooted in the same ecumenical dynamic. The message of Jeremiah, "When the world is troubled . . . God acts," was seen in the "yes" of a few Christians whom God has made great witnesses, even prophets, of rapprochement. It happened between individuals in the youth movements (YMCA/YWCA),[7] among students in the World Student Christian Federation,[8] then among those engaged in mission and social action who were from different church backgrounds—Protestants and Anglicans. Their eyes were opened by seeing the great suffering, such as poverty and alcohol abuse, in the countries where they worked and in the inner cities of "Christian" countries. They had become aware of just how scandalous it was that different branches of the church should be competing with each other in areas where there was such great need for a word of liberation, of true compassion, and a word of Gospel. In 1910, the World Missionary Conference, took place in Edinburgh, with John Mott, an American Methodist, and Charles Brent, an Episcopalian Bishop serving in the Philippines. The final message of the Mission Conference was this: "The aim of all missionary work is to plant in each non-Christian nation one undivided church of Christ."[9]

A network of relationships developed through these international and inter-confessional contacts. In this context it was a great shock to many, at the time of World War I, to find themselves in opposing camps. In 1920, as the Spirit continued to blow, the Ecumenical Patriarch (the leader of most

7. Young Men's/Women's Christian Association.
8. WSCF, also known as the Fédé by francophones.
9. Fernand-Laurent, *Que tous soient un . . . en Sommes Nous Proches?*

Orthodox churches) wrote a letter to the various churches to encourage fellowship, *koinonia*, among Christians. Between the wars more and more individuals, church leaders, and youth movements met together with a view to renewing the churches and working toward peace and openness. Roger Schutz, who would become Brother Roger of Taizé, participated in an international ecumenical gathering of youth at Amsterdam in August 1939.[10]

All of these occasions were opportunities for the participants to deepen their faith, to open themselves to other expressions of the liturgy and to be stimulated by a renewed reading of the Bible and study of their own church's spirituality. Each one was moved by the prayer of Christ "that they may be one that the world may believe" (John 17:21). The ecumenical meetings that followed, including with the Orthodox, allowed the participants to form relationships of friendship and solidarity across borders. Even the Second World War did not destroy this powerful experience in the communion of saints on earth. These friendships were a source of great consolation amid all the desolation despair. Dietrich Bonhoeffer, for example, experienced this solidarity among Christians during his resistance, imprisonment, and execution by the Nazis. He was greatly supported by his friendship with the Anglican Bishop Bell and the Reformed ecumenist Visser 't Hooft. Before his execution he gave an Anglican fellow prisoner, Payne Best, a message for Bishop Bell: "Tell him, for me, that this is the end, but also the beginning. With him I believe in our universal brotherhood which must supersede all nationalistic interests and that our victory is certain."[11]

The World Council of Churches (WCC) was founded in Amsterdam in 1948, with some participants still wounded by the war. Unfortunately, the Catholic Church was not one of the participants. The war had delayed this event by ten years! In fact, since 1939 Dr. Visser 't Hooft, appointed Secretary of a preparatory office, had been living in Geneva; he kept up as many international connections as possible, preparing for the postwar era. In 1946 he was able to rent the Chateau of Bossey, near Geneva (now the Ecumenical Institute of Bossey), and made it a place for meetings, ecumenical formation, and reconciliation. Participants from the various churches of the world can meet there for a few weeks or even longer.

After the war, one of our Dutch sisters had already participated in a meeting for "workers in the church." Grandchamp's relations with the WCC

---

10. World Conference of Christian Youth, Amsterdam, 1939, organized by the Joint Youth Commission of the World Alliance for International Friendship through the Churches, The Universal Christian Council for Life and Work, The Youth Group Committee of the Faith and Order Movement, and The International Missionary Council.

11. Bethge, *Dietrich Bonhoeffer*, 847–48.

far surpass those facilitated by our institutional membership through the Evangelical Reformed Church of Neuchâtel (EREN). The Community of Grandchamp has always been close to the WCC, especially through the Ecumenical Sessions of Grandchamp to prepare for the Week of Prayer for Christian Unity (1950-1965). Often Mother Geneviève and Pastor Jean de Saussure, later Professor Leuba, invited WCC leaders as speakers. Nothing was a given in this era, and Catholic theologians could not always come. However, Father Jerome Hamer O.P. did participate in 1956, as did Dom Olivier Rousseau of Chevetogne. Later it became easier to obtain permission from the Catholic authorities to attend such meetings. In addition to Orthodox theologians like Paul Evdokimov and Leon Zander,[12] and theological faculty members from French-speaking Swiss universities, a number of theologians came to us from the Bossey Institute. These sessions helped to develop an effective ecumenical network. Suzanne de Dietrich, for example, chose to begin her retirement at Grandchamp in 1954. Our sisters had the privilege of welcoming her, studying the Bible with her, and meeting friends of hers from around the world. In addition to her presence at Bossey, she was recognized for her outstanding ability to hold together currents of the ecumenical movement as diverse as the youth ministries of the YMCA and WSCF, missions, Faith and Order, Life and Work, and the liturgical renewal.

The fruit of this friendship is the special relationship we have with her spiritual son Hans-Ruedi Weber. He was for many years head of the Biblical department of the World Council of Churches, and as such our ties were strengthened at the end of the 1970s. From 1980 to 1985 and from 1990 to 1994, sisters participated in the Graduate School of the Bossey Institute, a semester of studies organized for pastors, priests, and theology students. Our sisters were responsible for preparing the evening praise service and were a presence of prayer, listening, and friendship. In 1981, a group of theologians from the WCC came to Grandchamp to work on the preparations for the 6th Assembly in Vancouver, Canada.

From the beginning, Grandchamp has supported the WCC with prayer, grateful for all the work of reconciliation among Christians accomplished there. We are attentive to its inner workings. For example, at the Harare Assembly in Zimbabwe in 1998, the WCC went through a crisis; the Orthodox Churches called into question their participation, discouraged because the Protestants had more influence in decision making. This crisis was settled at the Porto Alegre Assembly in Brazil in 2006. At times like this, we intensify our prayers for the WCC, without losing hope, for knowing the

---

12. Russian Orthodox Theologian who taught at St. Sergius Orthodox Theological Institute in Paris and was present at the first two sessions of Vatican II.

history of our own community shows us that God is watching over the work begun in them. If the forces of darkness are at work to destroy and separate what should be united, these forces cannot conquer the church of God and the work of the Holy Spirit. Thus the birthing of a universal communion of the churches and Christian confessions is already experienced in part in the WCC, a communion of churches in a world divided by painful fractures of which even the creation is a victim.

In this context, the challenge of the monastic and apostolic communities is highly relevant: how can we be, in the name of Christ and moved by the Spirit, ever more respectful of one another? How can we truly reconcile our many differences within our communities in order to become places of hope for others? One of our sisters participated in the WCC Assembly at Porto Alegre in 2006.[13] She returned with renewed hope, which was infectious.

As prioress, I also had the privilege of participating in several of the Assemblies, each of which was a stage in the development of the WCC. I recall well, for example, the sixth, in Vancouver, in 1983. Sister Fides, of the Community of Imshausen, and I were partly responsible for prayer on the campus. A large delegation from the Pacific Islands was there with us to bear witness to what their people were going through; we were on the shores of the same ocean and far away, on the other side, a people was suffering because of the nuclear tests conducted in their region. The day of their testimony, we were to celebrate together the feast of the Transfiguration and the anniversary of the atomic bomb being dropped on Hiroshima. The theme of the Assembly, "Jesus Christ, Life of the World," encouraged us to accept our responsibility to open up to one another theologically, in our humanity, and spiritually. We, the whole people of God gathered there, must choose life, reach out to others, and make alliances beyond these two weeks, beyond these celebrations under a big tent, expressing all the richness of our differences, beyond the cries of despair as well. Together we became very aware of our joint responsibility for the very survival of the planet. A night of prayer took place on August 6, remembering Hiroshima. It was also a night of solidarity with the Pacific Islanders and South Africans, a night of waiting for Desmond Tutu, who finally received his visa and arrived at midnight! How good it is to feel we are on the same wavelength, in solidarity with God's creation! By our way of life, we try to be active participants in the process of "Justice, Peace and the Integrity of Creation"—a theme taken up once again at the Assembly in Seoul in 1990, in which Catholics participated. At Vancouver I realized more clearly just how much Grandchamp is a small

13. See the testimony of Sister Anne-Emmanuelle in chapter 4.

cell in the universal church; I met many old friends there and established many new connections.

From an ecclesial perspective, the high point of Vancouver was unquestionably the presentation of the Faith and Order document *Baptism, Eucharist and Ministry* (BEM) at a solemn ceremony. This convergence text was developed by Faith and Order, now a commission of the WCC; Faith and Order includes Catholic theologians authorized by their church.[14] Since then, this text has served effectively as a point of reference for many mutual recognition agreements between churches, and it remains a model today.

The Assembly in Canberra in 1991, during the Gulf War, had the theme "Come Holy Spirit, Renew the Whole Creation!" I was asked to speak about monastic spirituality, for since Vancouver, spirituality had become more and more important for the WCC.

On the European level, the Assembly at Basel marked a joyful new stage: for the first time, the Conference of European Churches (KEK),[15] composed of Anglicans, Protestants, and Orthodox, and the Council of [Catholic] European Bishops' Conferences (CCEE),[16] planned a large ecumenical event together. On this occasion, another first occurred: the participation of Christians from the Eastern bloc. A symbolic march was organized around the city of Basel on German, French, and Swiss (Dreiländereck) territory, and all without visas. The borders opened, as a sign of what was to come: a few months later the Berlin wall would fall! The organizers had also chosen "Justice, Peace and the Integrity of Creation" as the theme of the meeting. The second European Assembly, in Graz, Austria, focused on "Reconciliation—Gift of God and Source of New Life." An ecumenical charter was proposed and signed at Strasbourg in 2001 by numerous churches. The charter serves as a reference point for churches and Christians who seek to live this spirit each day in concrete ways. The theme of the third Assembly, at Sibiu in Romania in 2007, was "The Light of Christ Illumines All People."

In this overview of our ecclesial involvement both near and far, I have not spoken of that fundamental reality of the one church which we enjoy: our monastic ties. They are true visitations, which is why I have chosen to speak of them separately in chapter 3. Nevertheless, I would like to mention here our ties with the monasteries of our region. At the beginning of 1980, as prioress, I was invited to take part in meetings of the SDC (Service des

14. Faith and Order, originating at the time of the 1910 Edinburgh World Missionary Conference, is one of the three constitutive organizations that joined together to form the WCC in 1948.

15. Conférence des Églises Chrétiennes/Konferenz Europaischer Kirchen.

16. Conseil des Conférences Episcopales Européennes.

Contemplatives de Suisse Romande)[17] with the Little Sisters of Jesus, like us, un-cloistered contemplatives. These annual meetings brought us very close together, and our relations deepened during the period when I was a member of the committee. The major events marking the life of each community and monastery also brought us together. The concrete result of this is that for some years now, our novices have benefited from a biblical formation within the framework of an inter-novitiate relationship with the SDC. Grandchamp organizes, from time to time, sessions for leaders of monastic communities in Switzerland and France. Thanks to our monastic ties, our sister responsible for novices participates in the meeting of those with the same ministry in their respective orders. These include Cistercians, Benedictines, the Protestant Deaconesses of Reuilly (France), and the ecumenical *Monastero di Bose* (Italy). This very real communion is a rich blessing for all of us. We are so different from one another. Many prejudices have fallen away and we have discovered each other's reality. We all seek to be a living sign of communion and witnesses to the living Christ.

Yes, I firmly believe that in order to be credible in their witness, the Christian churches are called to recover their unity: "That they may be one, Father, that the world may believe that you sent me!" (John 17:21). They are also called to become more and more aware of their responsibility to proclaim the Gospel of Christ together, to glorify God, Father, Son, and Holy Spirit, together, but also together to make the world, which has been entrusted to us, a more habitable place. In the image of what was experienced in a small way at Graz and Porto Alegre, the church united in Christ bears the responsibility of becoming a forum where Christians from different parts of the globe can reflect together in their praise and in their lamentation. We must seek to understand one another on a theological level, but not only on that level. As followers of Christ, our commitment to solidarity compels us to give a voice to the voiceless and, if necessary, to become their voice.

Easter, Feast of Feasts . . . of Unity

> LEADER: *Let us proclaim our faith in the living and true God, Father, Son, and Holy Spirit, the faith of our baptism. We celebrate God our Father who loves us as he loves his Son Jesus Christ. God entrusts into our hands the world which God created in love.*

---

17. A union of contemplative communities in the region of French-speaking Switzerland.

ASSEMBLY: *Lord, you are the source of life.*

LEADER: *We celebrate Jesus the Christ, our Lord, born of Mary into our human condition, who died and rose again in order to give us life.*

Still living among us, He gives us assurance that his light is brighter than the darkest night, that life triumphs over death.

ASSEMBLY: *Lord, you are the source of life.*

LEADER: *We celebrate the Spirit of Holiness which opens to us communion with the Father and the Son, and with one another, which gathers us in the church and pours out upon her every gift. The Spirit of holiness sends us into the world as witnesses of love and of life, as artisans of justice and peace.*

ASSEMBLY: *Lord, you are the source of life.*

LEADER: *We await the day when God will be all in all, day of unending light and the great feast of the kingdom for all peoples.*

ASSEMBLY: *Lord, you are the source of life.*

LEADER: *Will you leave all that leads to death and choose new life in Jesus Christ, promise to live as beloved children of the Father in the life-giving breath of the Spirit who makes us members of one body, the church?*

ASSEMBLY: *Yes, by God's grace.*

PROFESSION OF BAPTISMAL FAITH
Porto Alegre, 9th Assembly of the WCC

"Christ has risen from the dead; by his death he has vanquished death. To those in the tomb he has given life!" sing the Orthodox on Easter morning. It's true, Easter is a fire kindled at the heart of our life, at the heart of our vocation to unity, to communion, to ecumenism.

Easter, the resurrection of Christ, is a home and a hearth of love. The presence of the Risen One burns in us, and burns us. It is the bubbling source, the energy, the power of new life. "He has risen, Christ my hope!" Each of us has discovered it personally. Our whole life, our existence to the very depths, has been turned upside down, reoriented; nothing is as it was before: "Who can separate me from the love of Christ?"[18]

At each new Easter sunrise, the Holy Spirit opens a little wider the ear of our heart. The dimensions of this event, of events are so vast for our life, our community, the church, for personal and collective life, our families, our countries, our churches... Easter compels us to let the Risen One illumine every fiber of our being: toward our interior, that microcosm that each of us is, and toward the exterior, toward the other, the others, toward all humanity and all the creation. Our consciousness expands: I open myself so I can truly see the other. I discover her to be different and yet so much like me—all these others, sisters, brothers, each one loved with a unique love.

And a prayer rises up within me: "May love be beloved by all." From Christ, who conquered darkness and death, we draw the strength to resist the currents of death present in our world and in each of us. Each of our small personal victories, each opening of our hearts to love, has a healing influence on the Body of Christ, which is his church and, beyond the church, on the world. In the risen Christ, I become a being ever more alive, more free, stronger; and at the end of life, he will receive me/us into his glory!

Each Easter experienced intensely helps us to enlarge the tent of our hearts[19] a bit more, to overcome the barriers we have set up between ourselves and others. The risen Christ, his presence in us, is the source of reconciliation within and around us: he is our peace. Not only on Easter, but every day! To live God's today is to open ourselves each morning, at every moment, to the presence of the Risen One. Through a description of the Easter sunrise of 2006, it is a joy to share a bit of the liturgical intensity with which we celebrate year after year.

---

18. A personalization of Rom 8:35.
19. Allusion to Isa 54:2.

Easter Sunrise at Grandchamp

It is 4:30 in the morning; the sky is still dark. It has rained heavily, but the wind has chased away the clouds. Even a few stars are visible. In the entryway of *L'Arche* chapel, pilgrims from nearby and farther away are already gathering. Our retreatants, having come to us from the four corners of the earth, and with us since Wednesday of Holy Week, enter one by one. Together we follow Christ step by step through his passion into his death and resurrection.

The fire begins to burn, as yet slightly hesitant. The sisters arrive; our prioress, Sister Pierrette, carrying the pure white paschal candle. The pastors arrive. Everyone waits in breathless silence, filled with anticipation. The candle is lifted high: "O, You who sleep, awaken! Arise from among the dead. Upon you shall shine the light of Jesus Christ." Brother fire now burns brightly, illumining our faces. The chaplain carves the date on the candle, proclaiming: "Jesus Christ is the same yesterday, today, and forever, the Alpha and the Omega, the First and the Last, the Beginning and the End. To him belongs all of eternity, to him the glory and honor forever and ever. Amen!"

"Light of Christ!" This proclamation pierces the night, opening the heart of this small gathering; from our hearts spring the beginnings of praise: "We give thanks to God!" The light spreads, like a delicate ripple of joy—from one candle to the next we pass it on from person to person, and sometimes several times, for the wind blows—but does not extinguish the flame! Light around us and light within; the fire of his love begins to burn within us.

We climb the stairs and enter the chapel, which is still in darkness: "Light of Christ!" On its stand, the paschal candle seems to dominate *L'Arche* and to be its center. Soon all is illuminated by the flickering candlelight. Near the paschal candle is the baptismal font. It will remain there until Pentecost, a tradition we discovered in the Trappist monastery of Tibhirine in Algeria.[20] This "Light of Christ!" and our response resounds one last time, completing our very first paschal "Alleluia!"

The choir announces, "Christ is risen!" and we all respond in song with the paschal greeting handed down to us from the earliest days of the church: "He is risen indeed! Alleluia!" again and again, with great joy, as the people continue to enter. A sister sings the refrain of the paschal hymn of praise: "We praise you, splendor of the Father, Jesus Son of God!" and we all

---

20. Abbey of Our Lady of Atlas, Trappist monastery founded in 1938, closed in 1996. Seven of its monks were martyred in 1996 by Islamist insurgents during the Algerian civil war.

repeat it. The verses of the paschal praise are derived from the Easter Hymn of Saint John of Damascus (the liturgy of the Orthodox Easter vigil):

> It is Resurrection day! Let the people rejoice in the Passover of the Lord, because it is from death to life, from earth to heaven that Christ our God has brought us, we who sing our joy... Let the heavens rejoice, Let the earth be filled with joy; Let all the world be festive, All the world, visible and invisible, because He is risen, Christ the eternal joy... Jesus has risen from the grave—as he told us. He has given us life eternal—and his great mercy.

The beauty of these hymns engraves their words on our hearts, each year more profoundly, and binds us more closely to the whole church. Several of our sisters have experienced an Easter Vigil with the Orthodox, the culmination of the Great and Holy Week, at Saint Serge in Paris, and in Lebanon with the Melkites, in Jerusalem and in Geneva—but also in Moscow, Zagorsk, and other places. Unforgettable experiences!

In the 1970s we began to integrate some of these elements into our liturgy, for through the liturgical intensity of the Eastern churches, we felt ourselves contemporaries of this great event, the resurrection: "Yesterday I was buried with you O Christ—I awaken today in you, the Risen One!" This reliving of the mystery of the resurrection, which intrigued me in reading Dostoyevsky, I have, and we have, experienced ourselves. The Easter liturgy was and remains for us extraordinary.

After the paschal hymn of praise, we sing again, "Christ is risen! He is risen indeed!" as well as the Easter troparion (hymn) in numerous languages: German, English, Dutch, Russian, Greek, Chinese, and Malagasy; Italian, Swahili, Hebrew, Arabic, etc. Our chapel is in communion with the church all over the world, including the Orthodox Church, which is preparing for Easter as it begins the Great and Holy Week. Several of our sisters also participate in the Easter services at the Romanian Orthodox Church in Neuchâtel, for our relationship of prayer and friendship with them is growing.

Belonging to different peoples, we are truly united in the risen Christ: we sing of it together. Then we follow the Western tradition by the reading from the Prophets. This year (2006) there will not be any baptisms, but we will all renew our baptismal vows: "All you who have been baptized in Christ, you have been clothed in Christ, Alleluia!" This is followed by our profession of faith, inspired this year by the Assembly at Porto Alegre: "It is Easter today and the Resurrection of Jesus proclaims hope for new life. The rocks may tumble, tombs open forever, tears can be banished, fears are not eternal, joy comes for the downhearted, peace touches all heavy hearts."

During the procession with the Book of Gospels, we sing again, "Christ is risen! He is risen indeed!" in several languages. The Gospel is proclaimed, as at Christmas, from near the door—facing the whole world! After the Gospel reading in French, the core of this reading is repeated in every language of the people gathered in *L'Arche* chapel—fifteen languages in all. It is very moving to realize that the Good News has been proclaimed in all the earth by disciples of Christ, and that today, people come from other continents to evangelize old Europe...

After the kiss of peace, "The Peace of the Risen One!" given to all, comes a long procession of offerings. Among others, our Malagasy friend, the wife of one of the pastors, carries a cup to the altar, and the children bring flowers.

By the time we celebrate the Eucharist, the sun has risen. The birds add their singing to the Sanctus—yes, Easter is the celebration of all creation: "Let the heavens rejoice, let the earth celebrate, the whole earth and the entire cosmos, the visible and the invisible, for he is risen, the eternal joy!"

The hours go by, but does time still exist? We receive the Eucharist, Body and Blood of Christ! Like newborns we partake of this essential nourishment, the Sacrament of the Blood and Body of the one who gave himself for us and who is alive. He asked his Father to give unity to his disciples... right up until today: "I pray also for those who will believe in me: that all may be one..." In the diversity of this microcosm of humanity come from five continents to celebrate his resurrection here at Grandchamp, we are now profoundly united in him.

After the benediction, one more song: an *ostinato* from the Taizé song book—*Jubilate Deo*, introduced by the instruments. We can no longer keep still; first one sister then several begin to dance a *farandole* (an open line folk dance of southern France), and soon the whole assembly begins to dance in the open space before the altar. Rejoice!

The celebration continues with breakfast. Everyone is invited for a true *agape* feast. The sisters remain in white all day, as on their day of profession.

At dawn the Good News is announced by the angel to the women: "Go tell the disciples, Christ is risen and goes before you into Galilee!" In the evening we read the text which tells of the pilgrims of Emmaus who were joined by Christ himself in their grief. "Was it not necessary that the Messiah should suffer these things?" he asked. And they recognized him in the breaking of bread: "Didn't our hearts burn within us when he opened the Scriptures to us along the road?" (Luke 24:26, 32). Yes, he is risen, Christ our hope!

Community Worship and Personal Prayer

"My house shall be a house of prayer for all nations."

MARK 11:17; ISAIAH 56:7

A community of prayer, that which Christ asks the Church to be—and the Church exists wherever two or three are gathered together in his name—is a place where the glory of God is manifested in living power, where the whole plenitude of God's revelation is contemplated.

Those who pray are called by Christ to ascend the mountain of the Transfiguration.

A community of prayer is made up of witnesses to the Resurrection. Christ has visited them, nourished and forgiven them, and has given them the power to bring into the world of sin and disorder God's vision of the world, where Jesus reigns.

The apostles of God's love are those who live from the faithfulness of God, like branches attached to the vine.

The Spirit of Truth descends upon those in the shadows who have not yet received the light to bear witness to the Truth, to fill these shadows with the divine presence, revealing the glory of Christ. He carries out his royal mission in heaven, and in us. And his prayer in us becomes praise, adoration, the prayer of expectation of his coming in power . . .

MOTHER GENEVIÈVE, 1948

Personal prayer and common prayer are like our two lungs, and the Eucharist the heart of this body which we are forming in Christ. The liturgy is enriched, enlivened, and made authentic by our relationships, our work, the quality of our hospitality, our daily life, and everything we do outside the community. Our liturgy cannot therefore be static: it is a living thing!

As in every monastery, and contrary to in the spirit of the world, the center of Grandchamp is not the office of the prioress or the secretary, or the dining hall, but *L'Arche* chapel. In this place we experience intense moments of community. We gather there for prayer at least four times each day . . . beginning at the end of the day with the evening office, followed by compline, which ushers us into the night, then the morning and midday offices. Our liturgy is rooted in that of the early church and the Jewish tradition that came before it. Our liturgical life of common prayer is essential for the life and growth of the community, and always has been. Since 1936, the bell has gathered sisters and guests for prayer. Our life of faith and our spirituality are nourished by common prayer, culminating in the celebration of the Eucharist.

During the early years, the liturgy was rather simple, but still a place of living water for the sisters and guests. Each one could find unity and meaning in life through "being together before God." One sister was responsible for the services. Each day had its particular theme. She even chose the readings (at least at the beginning) and prepared the prayer of intercession, which had a place of honor alongside adoration. Spontaneous prayer had an important place in the liturgy, and the Scriptures were central to the praise, revealing the truly Protestant roots of the community. People from the village attended alongside the guests, and sometimes our neighbors' children, René and Simone (ages six and four), came all by themselves! Members of the *Veilleurs*, the earliest sisters soon adopted the little breviary of this Third Order–style group founded by Wilfred Monod.[21] Since that time, midday prayer has been focused on the Gospel reading of the day and on the Beatitudes.[22]

Practicing a more structured and more objective common prayer was an important stage in the development of the community. The Psalms, biblical canticles, and liturgical texts of other confessions also became "ours;" a path toward deeper communion with the Jewish people and other

---

21. Pastor in the Église Réformée de France, co-founder of the periodical *Le Christianisme Social*, and of the Protestant spirituality group, similar to a Catholic third-order, called *Les Veilleurs*.

22. The daily discipline of the *Veilleurs* included the midday recitation of the Beatitudes.

Christians. As soon as it came out in 1943, the sisters adopted the *Office Divin*[23] created by a group of Reformed pastors of French-speaking Switzerland for the enrichment of congregational worship, and later the *Office of Taizé*[24] which was an adaptation of the *Office Divin*. Again thanks to the brothers of Taizé, we began to sing psalms together using the psalmodies of composer Joseph Gélineau.[25] Before that, we had tried using Anglican psalmody, which does not work as well for the French language. More recently, we have introduced pieces (*ostinati*) from the Taizé songbook.

Following the visits of numerous sisters to the fraternity in Algeria where we experienced the Eucharist in our little places of prayer, very simply, on the floor, the desire grew to give more space in our chapels, including at Grandchamp, for kneeling more freely in prayer. Until then, everything was arranged in a very traditional way, with benches for the sisters at the front and visitors behind them. Emptying *L'Arche* chapel of numerous rows of benches radically changed our common prayer. The open space adds to a sense of the presence of God, but also, mysteriously, makes more evident the communion of saints in heaven and on earth.

When I arrived in 1958, Saturday evening and Sunday, candles were placed on the communion table alongside the cup and paten, but on Monday the table was cleared of its candles in order to avoid scandalizing anyone![26] Our experiences with other Christians have wonderfully enriched our eucharistic liturgy through the years.

The quality of our common prayer has also been enriched by visits of our sisters to our fraternities and fruitful visits to Catholic and Orthodox monasteries. Our community in Lebanon has contributed Eastern liturgical elements. Sister Sylvie, an art conservator, learned iconography. Over time, icons entered our chapels and our lives, new windows onto the kingdom of God. The *Icon of the Trinity* by Rublev, a great gift to the universal church, is among them. For many years, Sister Sylvie shared her knowledge with other sisters; today, Sister Olga continues to write icons and offers icon retreats with Marianne Drobot, a Russian iconographer. We are very grateful to Marianne and her husband, Father George Drobot, for their constant support, encouragement, teaching, and friendship. Retreatants and sisters alike can discover a way to experience, through icons, the image of God within themselves.

---

23. Église et Liturgie, *l'Office divin de l'Église Universelle*.
24. Communauté de Taizé, *Office de Taizé*, 1963.
25. Catholic liturgist, the composer of the earliest Taizé chant music.
26. Among Protestants, still very sensitive at that time to "catholicizing" practices.

Where song is concerned, Byzantine tones have come to us in part from our ties with Romania, and in part from our Orthodox and Melchite friendships in Lebanon. Upon her return from the Lebanon fraternity, our Sister Anne-Christine worked on a call to prayer inspired by these tones, and the presence of Father Boris Bobrinskoy[27] at Neuchâtel has helped initiate us to Orthodox chant, which is indispensable to the celebration of the Divine Liturgy.

To open up to receive all of this richness involves an inner journey for a community that is part of the churches of the Reformation, for our Rule states: "Let us pay close attention to the meaning of liturgical acts, and seek to discern in signs that are accessible to our senses an invisible reality that is of the kingdom of God. But let's be careful also, not to go overboard with multiple signs, but to keep them simple, the measure of their evangelical value."[28]

What are the norms of this evangelical simplicity? Keep moving, trust God, impose nothing, go slowly, understand ever more deeply that we do not all need to be the same, and respect the differences while searching for the best ways to support our common prayer—that is a summary of the way forward. Obviously, all of this could not happen without dialogue, sometimes even long discussions, to safeguard the peace of our common prayer, and to dare to develop further while retaining its simplicity.

Our liturgical life allows us to enter into a more appropriate attitude of faith, knowing ourselves to be in God's presence. For we have, first of all, to receive prayer, and not to create it ourselves, to invent or fabricate it, but to receive it as the Word of God that we must welcome in the silence, meditate upon, and put into practice before analyzing or studying it. "The one who prays is a theologian," said the Desert Fathers. In our liturgy, we experience that the reality to which we belong is greater than ourselves. "Lord, open my lips that my mouth may proclaim your praise." I am no longer alone with myself, given over to my own thoughts and desires. Everything in me opens itself to the presence of God the thrice Holy (Isa 6:3) who is a personal God, who is revealed in the history of salvation, in the history of the Community of Grandchamp, in my history.

We are together in the name of the Lord. By the invocation of the Holy Spirit, we enter into the prayer of praise, of adoration, like taking a breath of God's love—the true breath of the cosmos. Our prayer, as humble as it may be, is a participation in the adoration of the communion of saints in

---

27. Born in Paris in 1925, Father Boris Bobrinskoy was a Russian Orthodox Theologian who taught at St. Sergius Orthodox Theological Institute in Paris and was a member of Faith and Order.

28. Communauté de Taizé, *Rule of Taizé (1961)*, 18–19.

heaven and on earth, a participation in the intercession of Christ. Prayer is at the heart of humanity and of all creation, which "waits with eager longing for the revealing of the children of God" (Rom 8:19). The communion of saints strengthens us and connects us to all those who struggle for justice, peace, and the integrity of creation. This solidarity with them commits us to fervent intercession, putting into the Savior's hands all that we experience and carry in our hearts of the sufferings of the world.

Yes, each life of prayer is called to open itself to the whole world and to become ever more deeply rooted in Christ our only Lord and Savior, in communion, *koinonia*, with all those who have lived in his friendship and all the believers who follow him today.

Personal Prayer As a Source of Communion

"Come apart, seek his face, let yourself meet God in solitude and silence, disarmed and unified by his love," says the first call, which cannot be dissociated from the second: "enlarge the space of your tent..."[29]

Each day we have a time of silent adoration in spirit and in truth (John 4:24), and a time of meditation on the Word, and of *lectio divina* on our own. Once a month, each of us enjoys a full day of retreat... to come back again and again to the call, to the One who alone is necessary (Luke 10:42). As Jesus invited Peter, James, and John to go up with him onto the mountain of the transfiguration (Matt 17:1), this time is for us an invitation to follow Jesus in his intimacy with the Father, to listen to him and to enter into the process of transfiguration.

"First Love, then surrender," as Mother Geneviève would say. In Gethsemane Jesus experienced the intensity of that call to fully accomplish the loving will of his Father: "He took with him Peter, James, and John. And he began to be afraid and anguished. He said to them, 'My soul is sad unto death. Stay with me, watch and pray.' And going on a little further..." (Mark 14:33). It was only a plea: "Father, all things are possible for you. Take this cup from me." But his heart remained the heart of a son: "And yet, not my will but yours be done" (Mark 14:33-37).

"After having asked the Father three times, you arise. Your 'yes' now calls to action your whole being as a man who will be one with the will of

---

29. See chapter 1, "Taizé, Pomeyrol..."

the love of the Father, to the very end."[30] To this meditation on the Way of the Cross that I was asked to prepare for the Good Friday service in Rome in 1995,[31] I added this prayer for the church: "Father, open by your Holy Spirit our will to yours, that we may have the strength to watch and pray with Jesus in his struggle against evil. And that our communion in his sufferings may lead us to the power of his Resurrection."

"Watch and pray with Christ" to the point of shedding one's blood; "praying for others means giving the blood of one's own heart," says the *starets* Silouan.[32] It is to give ourselves with all of our strength so that Love might be incarnate in us, that the Love of God thrice Holy might continue the work of salvation in the world. Our vocation to prayer urges us to follow the Lamb of God everywhere he goes, to watch and pray with Jesus for our wounded world, so full of suffering and brokenness. Christ invites us to remain close to him, to become deeply vulnerable to the depths of human pain in order to carry their burdens, with him, into the heart of the Father. We are to be present in these places of brokenness,[33] to invoke the name of Jesus that the Spirit may raise up men and women of peace and reconciliation.

Christ invites us not to run away, but to stay wherever the Holy Spirit has placed us or sent us, to remain there even when the situation is difficult or even impossible. The Lord is close to the brokenhearted (Ps 34:18); a broken and contrite heart he will not despise (Ps 51:17). Mother Geneviève spoke of the life of prayer we desire to let live within us: "the life of prayer is impossible to live in the natural human heart. People pray, call, ask, implore. Only Christ has lived the life of prayer and only Christ in us can give us this extraordinary grace, the life of prayer."[34]

"To contemplate Jesus . . . is to stand before the bush which burns and is not consumed, it is to receive the light and ardor of divine love which sets the heart ablaze and transforms it."[35] It is to be thrown to the ground, values turned upside down—the death of the old self (Rom 6:6), of the ego turned in upon itself—to be raised again to the life of grace. It is to see Jesus

---

30. Vries, *Chemin de Croix*, [2].

31. In 1995 Pope John Paul II inaugurated a new "Way of the Cross" procession to take place every Good Friday in the Colosseum in Rome. Invited to participate in the preparations, Sister Minke wrote and submitted her *Chemin de Croix* (Way of the Cross).

32. Syméon Antonov (1866–1938), known as Silouan of Athos, was a Russian Orthodox monk.

33. The expression of Monsignor Claverie, O.P., assassinated in 1996 in Algeria.

34. Micheli, *Message*, 34.

35. Text inspired and edited by Sister Minke from Micheli, *Message*, 34.

only, to love him, he who draws so near that he touches us, so that all fear is taken away, even the fear of being unworthy. He raises us up again. He reassures us.

"Christ glorified is first Christ crucified. His suffering is at the center of the world. And this is the way in which all people belong to him. He loves them."[36] That is what the testimony of a community of prayer ought to be: the luminous Mount of Transfiguration brought into the midst of the dark night of humanity.

The Eucharist

People turn to God when they're in need,
plead for help, contentment, and for bread,
for rescue from their sickness, guilt, and death.
They all do so, both Christian and pagan.

People turn to God in God's own need,
and find God poor, degraded, without roof or bread,
see God devoured by sin, weakness, and death.
Christians stand with God to share God's pain.

God turns to all people in their need,
nourishes body and soul with God's own bread,
takes up the cross for Christians and pagans, both,
and in forgiving both, is slain.

DIETRICH BONHOEFFER[37]

Great is the mystery of faith! The memorial of his love, memorial that Christ gave us, the Eucharist, is made present by the Holy Spirit through each celebration. We receive it very concretely in the gift of his Body and Blood by way of the bread and wine: our communion becomes real in us, among us, and with the whole church. "Merciful peace, sacrifice of praise," sings the Orthodox Church. It is for us to receive his infinite mercy and to offer him our humble praise.

---

36. Micheli, *Message*, 31.

37. Bonhoeffer, "Christians and Pagans," in *Resistance et Soumission*, 361. Bonhoeffer et al., *A Testament to Freedom*, 549.

If the Eucharist is the ecumenical prayer par excellence, it is through my baptism that I first enter into the ecumenical vocation which is part of the covenant of love God has established with the whole creation (Gen 8:21–22), with his people Israel, and with the church. My very personal introduction into the tradition of my church, denomination, and country does not limit at all the universal perspective of the Christian faith. On the contrary, the first sacrament is called to grow and flourish under the loving will of God, Father of all humanity and of the entire cosmos.

Today I can recall with gratitude the road I have traveled: baptized two and a half months after my birth, I was confirmed at the age of nineteen, on Palm Sunday. The minimum age was set at eighteen in the Dutch Reformed Church; we had to know very well what we were doing! My father, the son of a Mennonite[38] father and Reformed mother, had not been baptized as an infant, and yet had taken catechism classes in the Reformed Church. He was baptized at the age of twenty-six before marrying my mother.

I rejoiced greatly in my first communion, a few days after my confirmation, on Good Friday, but I was disappointed—I didn't "feel" a thing! I had never before attended the Lord's Supper. On those Sundays, which were infrequent, the children had the day off! All was very solemn. Communion was served at long tables where we were seated in silence to listen to the words of institution. It was the day of the death of our Savior and we commemorated the extent to which Jesus had gone in giving his life. "For whenever you eat this bread and drink this cup you proclaim the death of the Lord until he comes again" (1 Cor 11:26).

Little by little I entered into this celebration. Love for Jesus, who had given us everything, even his flesh and blood, grew in me. "Here is what I have done for you. What are you doing for me?"[39] Seven years later, as a guest at Grandchamp, what an experience that first Lord's Supper was! The pastor was still in black, as in my home church. It was certainly solemn, but everything was lighter and we stood in a circle, like pilgrims—I was very touched. All this awakened me, without my realizing it at the time, to the mystery of his incarnation in the midst of our daily lives, rather than as a distant exception to normal life. And I was very struck by the words spoken by pastor and assembly before taking the bread and the cup: "Lord, I am not worthy to receive you, but only say the word, and I shall be healed," in receiving the consecrated bread, the body of Christ. Then, before sharing the cup of wine: "How shall I give back to the Lord for all of the good He has

---

38. One of the churches that came from the Reformation, in the Anabaptist tradition (adult believers' baptism only) and known for its pacifism.

39. Words of Count Zinzendorf, founder of the Moravian Church.

done me? I will lift up the cup of salvation invoking the name of the Lord (Ps 116:12–13). 'I call upon the Lord, who is worthy to be praised, so I shall be saved from my enemies'" (Ps 18:3). Those enemies are especially all of those inner thoughts which accuse us and fill us with guilt.

At Grandchamp, the Eucharist is celebrated every Thursday evening and every Sunday, and during retreats. Like me, the other sisters came with their habits of worship, often so different, even those of German-speaking Switzerland, or those who came from France, for each Reformed Church has its own traditions. When the German Lutheran sisters joined the community, especially those from the high church, they had to join in a liturgy which from their perspective seemed stripped down to the bare essentials. They no longer even dared to make the sign of the cross to avoid scandalizing others! Now people say our eucharistic liturgy is more Lutheran, while some find it too "Catholic." For me all of this is a sign of our openness.

A key question if ever there was one is this: what happens with the bread and the wine? What can we interpret in the mystery of a life, of a love? "The head must truly descend into the heart." With St. Thomas Aquinas, we need to adore the wonderful mystery. It is in this way that the understanding of the *sensus fidei* (the "sense of faith," or the intuition of faithful believers) grows, as well as eucharistic faith. Of course, the basic attitude must be not to cling to our own tradition, but to know ourselves to be en route toward the church of tomorrow and to keep in mind that our understanding will always remain partial. One thing is certain: beyond our various liturgical differences, our eucharistic faith is one. We are truly communing with the Body and Blood of Christ. At each Eucharist we consume fully, with boundless respect, the bread and wine, the Body and Blood of Christ.

What more can I say of eucharistic faith? Each sister gradually enters into the mystery by experiencing it, with theological instructions and especially thanks to the action of the Holy Spirit so tangibly at work.

For us the Eucharist is not the only moment of communion; we see each worship service as a whole. During Holy Week, our various eucharistic liturgies emphasize particular aspects of this unfathomable mystery. On Holy Thursday, for example, we highlight that the Institution of the Eucharist, which has become very solemn, began as a simple meal, taken by Jesus the Jew with his disciples, probably the Passover meal. So at the beginning of this liturgy we share a meal in *L'Arche* chapel, on low tables in groups of six or eight, with great simplicity and in silence. We listen to several texts, among them the story of the Exodus, which highlights the meaning we give to the coming of Jesus Christ: he liberates us from captivity. In preparation for the second part of this celebration, the tables are cleared of all food. During the offertory, the presider goes to the altar for the part of the liturgy that includes thanksgivings—the Eucharist. Then the sister deacons bring the Body and Blood of Christ to our tables. We receive communion there. This rich experience speaks to our whole being: soul, body, and spirit.

The Good Friday Eucharist accentuates another reality. On that day, we face the cross, which the arrangement of the chapel accentuates. Starting at the sixth hour, we pray there in silence, until the ninth hour. Then begins the Eucharist. After the readings followed by the long universal prayer, we stand together around the communion table. The liturgy is extremely solemn, recalling the incredible gift Christ gave us by his death: "Here is my body broken for you; here is my blood shed for all." On this day the gift becomes real; it is the immediate fruit of his death which flows from exclamation "It is finished" (John 19:30).

Through inter-confessional meetings, by visiting other churches, and staying in monastic communities, many Christians have realized that the Last Supper, now the Lord's Supper, which Christ left to his disciples, is first of all a meal of thanksgiving and gratitude for the vast love of the Father. In this context, the intercommunion now established between the various traditions of the Reformation is precious.[40] It is the fruit of our realization that through the action of the Holy Spirit, Christ himself invites us to this meal. The Eucharist does not belong to us! It is through Christ, with Christ, and in Christ that the Eucharist becomes the creator of communion, the sacrament of unity. That makes the impossibility of sharing communion at the table of the Lord with Catholics and the Orthodox all the more painful. On the eve of his passion, Christ prayed for our unity.

As we wait for this unity to become a reality, I want to remember a number of other exceptional events in the church which the Holy Spirit has sparked: a way of kindling our desire to attain to the visible unity of the Body of Christ. These events happened shortly after Vatican II, during a time when the wind of the Holy Spirit blew strongly. Dom Olivier Rousseau, a Catholic, was to give a conference at Neuchâtel and asked us if he could stay at Grandchamp. He was there for the Eucharist Thursday evening. At the moment of communion, we were all in a circle. Suddenly he found himself receiving communion. He was quite upset: "I don't know what happened. I could not do otherwise. I invite you to mass tomorrow to reciprocate." On another occasion, a Jesuit father en route to Rome for their general chapter participated in communion at Grandchamp. When he arrived in Rome, he confessed right away to his Father General: "There was such faith—it was not possible to do otherwise." Father Arrupe answered, "Go in peace, my son. That is the way it should be."

40. Concorde du Leuenberg (1973).

One day Dom Helder Camara was in Switzerland for the celebration of an Oratorio.[41] We had invited him to an ecumenical day for religious orders at Grandchamp. Many Catholic sisters were present, and a Eucharist was planned for them. Such unity was evident among us, such communion with the poor, that he invited us as well. It was an unforgettable celebration, anticipating the kingdom—a true epiphany. Before leaving, he wanted to visit our 99-year-old sister to ask her blessing. Sister Marthe gave her blessing in all simplicity.

As prioress of the community, I traveled frequently to visit our sisters in various places, or to participate in ecumenical gatherings. I still remember some of the prayer times together, especially the celebrations of the Eucharist. In Rome, in the chancel of St. Peter's, I was deeply moved by what was given me to contemplate: the universality of the church. I was invited by the Little Sisters of Jesus to attend the final profession of forty of their sisters. I was so touched by the diversity and universality of the Catholic Church: each sister made her final vow in her own language, and they came from everywhere. They were ready to go out to the four corners of the earth to live among the poor! This alone was enough to make the Eucharist we shared unforgettable. The place itself also impressed me and gave me a sense of connection with the apostles, the martyrs of the early centuries of Christianity whose blood nourished the spreading of the Gospel, and with all the pilgrims who had come there to pray—including Luther and Bonhoeffer!

Another memory is from my visit to Budapest during the communist regime with our Sister Lydia, who was Reformed and a member of our group, Servants of Unity. She took me with her to visit a Catholic community of sisters.[42] It was time for mass. A cupboard was opened—an altar and all that is needed for a celebration of the Eucharist—and the priest, still weak from his years in prison, offered us the Eucharist alongside the sisters. We left them refreshed in our faith and hope, filled with a love from on high.

When I was in Algeria, we were in the habit of meeting quietly with the monks of Tibhirine in their monastery, a haven of peace in a country that was becoming more and more dangerous. Theirs was the place of gathering for the whole little world of Christians from many different churches who remained in Algeria. The prayer times of the monks, especially at night, gave us strength. The monks were so simple, their chanting so weak but so full of the presence of God, and our communion together was beyond what can be expressed in words.

41. "La Symphonie des deux mondes," the Oratorio for which Dom Helder wrote the words, put to music by Pierre Kaelin. For a performance given in Switzerland Dom Helder spoke the words.

42. See Timar, *Journal 1957–1962*.

THE ADVENTURE OF OPEN COMMUNION

At the fraternity, the sisters tried to celebrate the Eucharist from time to time in their little chapel. When I visited them as prioress, they told me that for this communion service, Cardinal Duval would preside. The sisters asked the proprietor for a chair for the occasion—it was red! After the celebration I expressed my astonishment at his willingness to come. He answered, "My sister, I feel myself privileged to have come and to have celebrated with you and your sisters—are they not the only Christian presence among the forty thousand Muslims in this neighborhood?"

Then in Guatemala, a close friend of mine, Julia, who later came to Grandchamp for refuge for a few years, took me with her to visit Rigoberta Menchu.[43] One day we all went to a large gathering of catechists in the mountains. We were early and so were able to watch as the others arrived little by little; some had been walking for hours. How could we help thinking of the Gospel story of the multiplication of the loaves and fishes? We were seated on the ground sharing the Word, rejoicing in all the blessings of the Lord, in the communion we shared, through the body of Christ. What a joy it was to know ourselves engaged together in his service, and joined by true friendship. What an encouragement and hope! A few years later, many of these friends lost all of their belongings, some their lives, during the persecution. I remember them often during our Eucharists, especially when we use the low altar, as we did with Father Alfredinho of the Fraternity of the Suffering Servant (Brazil).[44]

Another highlight was celebrating the Eucharist with Father Oshida, O.P. of Japan. After the service our Sister Jacoba, who had spent the time of the occupation in Indonesia in a Japanese concentration camp, suddenly said, "Now I can finally forgive the Japanese," and all in a turmoil of emotions she embraced the priest, who was crying.

Our Orthodox friends are very happy to discover in the liturgy of Grandchamp some hymns with Byzantine tones. The separation we experience in the Eucharist on Sunday morning is all the more painful—to the point that they prefer not to attend this service at Grandchamp. There remains one other lasting seed of communion sown in the fertile soil of Grandchamp and experienced intensely there: a Divine Liturgy, celebrated within the framework of a retreat, which gathered Orthodox and Protestants together. On that occasion, before the Orthodox received the Body and Blood of Christ, the priest knelt before us and asked our forgiveness for not being able to invite us, too. We were moved to tears.

43. Rigoberta Menchu was a Guatemalan woman of the Maya people who was awarded the Nobel Peace prize in 1992. I saw her some years later at the Vancouver Assembly of the WCC in 1983.

44. Chapter 4, "Testimony of Sister Janny."

The Eucharist, Foundational Act of Nonviolence

In the Eucharist we celebrate together the victory over the forces of evil that do so much harm in the world, in the church, and in us by constantly raising countless walls between us. By his death on the cross and his complete willingness to do the will of the Father, Jesus Christ has given us and continues to give us a new capacity for communion with one another. He has shown us the way from death to life, from fear to confidence, from self-centeredness to openness, from self-justification to a humble return to the Father, from sterility to fruitfulness. The risen Christ leads the way.

Yes, the Eucharist is at the heart of our life. It is the prayer for unity *par excellence* which sums up all prayer. It is our sacrament along the way toward full unity, toward the second coming: "until he comes," in communion with all the faithful of every age and with all Christians spread across the earth.

The foundation of our vocation to prayer is Christ, risen from the dead. Rooted in him by baptism, our personal life and community life are restored and renewed in the celebration of the Eucharist and open us up toward the universal church. At each moment of the Eucharist, the love of the Father, which is seeking every human being, no matter how distant, pierces us and sensitizes us to the most hidden cry that rises up from the depths of human suffering, pushing us to intercession and to solidarity.

"Lamb of God, who takes away the sins of the world, have mercy on us; grant us your peace." In the risen Christ, I am joined in the depths of my being, to all of humanity, to the whole creation. In him I become a woman, a man, profoundly universal—catholic. Brother Roger wrote, "You know that Jesus the Christ came for all, not just for a few. Risen, he is united with every human being without exception. Such is the catholicity—universality—of heart, God has set within you."[45]

In the 1980s, Father Joseph Pyronnet introduced our community to an essential aspect of the Eucharist: its meaning as the foundational act of nonviolence. We learned that the Eucharist is not only the heart of our life, but also the source of our desire to live a Gospel nonviolence[46] daily, in our prayer and in our relationships. Here is a summary of this teaching: Jesus so perfectly carried out his nonviolent struggle against the forces of evil, against violence, against sin, that all of this evil turned against him, to kill him. At his baptism, Jesus took upon himself all of our collective, structural sin. Then he vigorously denounced the presence and toxicity of

---

45. Communauté de Taizé, *The Sources of Taizé*, 48.
46. For those unfamiliar with this phrase, see Taylor, *Love in Action*.

that sin within the most sacred institutions of his time: the Sabbath, the Tradition, the Law, the Temple. In so doing, he quickly attracted to himself all the hatred of the guardians and beneficiaries of those institutions and the established order.[47]

Jesus confronted the spiral of violence, a three-stage rocket, says Dom Helder Camara. In fact, Jesus focused onto himself all the forms of structural violence that are rooted in our personal and collective unconscious. First stage: the violence of the righteous reached its peak; Jesus was to die for the people (John 11:49-50). Second stage: the poor and the disciples, disappointed in their violent hopes (for the overthrow of Roman oppression) abandoned him, and one of them was even willing to turn him over to the authorities. Third stage: repression was allowed to be unleashed upon him, "there would be no tumult among the people" (Matt 26:5).

At that moment Jesus declared, "I lay down my life in order to take it up again. No one takes it from me, but I lay it down of my own accord" (John 10:17-18a). The process begun at his baptism led him to the final end. As John says, he showed them the full extent of his love (John 13:1). In an incredible act of love, he short-circuited the evil, violence, and sins of the world that came to rest very concretely upon him. He endured them, not only for us, but in our place and in our names.

He took bread and wine, which symbolize creation as well as the collaboration between God and humankind, "fruit of the earth, fruit of the vine, and the work of human hands."[48] Jesus identified himself with this creation now in revolt against God, to the point of becoming one flesh with it. He, who drew all of his life and strength from his communion with the Father, took on our nature, and also all that separates us from the Father. In this way he joins each one of us and all of us together, in our personal and collective darkness, conscious and unconscious, to himself. He thus consented to an apparent total failure, to total solitude. "This is my body . . . this is my blood" (Mark 14:22-24). Yes, Father, the Pharisees, the Sadducees, the Herodians with all of their rationalizations, this is my Body. The soldiers who tortured me, this is my Body. Pilate who schemed, this is my Body. Peter who denied me, this is my Body. Judas who betrayed me and the others who fled, this is my Body. The crowd that shouted, "Crucify him!" this is my Body. Yes, Father, all victims and all accomplices, they are my Body. In me they offer you my Blood, my life, my love, your love, capable of

---

47. Father Pyronnet has made a more complete presentation of this teaching in *Prier 15 jours avec Gandhi* [*Pray 15 Days with Gandhi*].

48. Compare with Liturgy of the Eucharist: Anglican, Roman Catholic.

transforming all of their violence, whether conscious or unconscious, into tenderness, your tenderness."

Just after the institution of the Eucharist, before his arrest, Jesus struggled at Gethsemane, with all the human distress he had taken on, in all of its worst forms; he collapsed, sweating blood. From the depths of this misery, of our misery, he cried out to the Father, "If it is possible, take this cup from me!" (Luke 22:42). But even in the depths of his disarray, his faith in the Father remained firm: "Yet, not my will, but yours be done" (Luke 22:48). Jesus has caused the tender mercies of the Father to pierce the darkest corners of our violence and separation from God. From now on, "nothing can separate us from the love of God revealed in Christ Jesus" (Rom 8:39). Like Jacob wrestling with God, Jesus did not let the Father go, but obtained from him a universal and eternal covenant that reaches into our deepest wounds.

The Eucharist is not only the celebration and offering of the death of Jesus, it is the offering of the Body and Blood of Jesus who died and was raised to life in the name and in the place of all humanity. The resurrection of Jesus is the response of the Father to the nonviolence of Jesus . . . The resurrection is the guarantee given by God that all acts inspired by this nonviolence are the road to healing and new life, the bearers of the invincible power of the living God. So the Eucharist is not only an important act of nonviolence, it is the fundamental act of nonviolence. It is part of a precise moment in history, but it expresses within history an eternal act of the love of God and is the foundation for the value and efficacy of all acts of nonviolence of the past, present, and future.[49]

Father Pyronnet explains well the link between participation in the Eucharist and our Christian engagement on the path opened by Jesus, the path of reconciliation and universal love, the path of unity among all human beings:

> I feel obliged to pose the question to all who participate in the Eucharist, "Do we have the right to participate in the sacrament of universal love if our minds are still made up to eliminate our personal and collective adversaries any way we can, to base our well-being on our bank accounts and our security on atomic bombs and the sale of weapons?"[50]

---

49. Excerpt of a lecture by Father Joseph Pyronnet for "Church and Peace," Leipzig, 1990, Grandchamp archives.

50. Excerpt of a lecture by Father Joseph Pyronnet for "Church and Peace," Leipzig, 1990, Grandchamp archives.

From the Desert to Communion

Christianity means community through Jesus Christ and in Jesus Christ . . . "He is our peace"[51] *Without Christ we should not know God . . . nor could we come to him. The way is blocked by our own ego. Christ opened up the way to God and to our brother/sister. Now Christians can live with one another in peace; they can love and serve one another; they can become one . . . Now we are in him. Where he is, there we are too, in the incarnation, on the cross, and in his resurrection. We belong to him because we are in him . . . we also belong to him in eternity with one another.*

DIETRICH BONHOEFFER [52]

"Love solitude but flee isolation!" This is a life-giving word for every woman and man touched by the call of Christ. It is indispensable to cultivate solitude with him in order to progress along the path of growth, maturity, and openness to others, reaching out ever more generously and freely to others. If this learning process is essential for couples, it is also essential in the various forms of consecrated life: religious orders, monastic communities—whether celibate or non-celibate—as well as for hermits.

"Love solitude!" This is a paradoxical proposition for those who, thanks to the call of Christ to follow him, have discovered brothers and sisters who are so happy to share this calling: "how good and pleasant it is when brothers (and sisters) live together in unity!" (Ps 133:1).

Solitude is the primary reality of our human existence, since we are created by God as unique beings. If I truly accept that this solitary, silent, desert time is essential to the fulfillment of my life, solitude sinks in over time: silence opens in me a space where the risen Christ lives, a place of hope in his glory. Solitude then becomes imbued with the presence of "the One who is closer to me than I am to myself."[53]

In this sense, the desert is a place of fundamental importance for each member of a religious order, as it was for Abraham and Sarah, or Moses

---

51. Eph 2:14.
52. Bonhoeffer, *Life Together*, 21, 23–24.
53. Augustine, *Confessions*, III, 6, 11.

and the Hebrew people. Jesus himself showed us the way. Having left Nazareth, he went to the Jordan to be baptized by John. There, becoming one with the human condition, he was confirmed: "This is my Son, the Beloved, with whom I am well pleased" (Matt 3:17). Then, driven into the desert, he let these words resonate within and endured the ordeal of temptation: his struggle with the devil and with himself. His will firmly rooted itself in the will of the Father. No, he did not grasp to himself this grace, this privilege of being the beloved Son, but remained until the end in perfect union with the loving will of the Father.

The desert, as an interior space, is the place of vocation, of the call to find again and again our first love, welcoming the "yes" of Christ to us, and his word, "Come, follow me." It is a place of unburdening, of purification, of dispossession, for there is only him, our one and only. Becoming poor, as he was, my inner ear opens to listen to his Word. My heart learns to love as he does, without exclusion, to be open to all those he sends to me, receiving this "whisper" with which he fills me and which is all my joy, learning to share it with them. In this place I become reacquainted with his face, and allow myself to be touched by his loving gaze which speaks to me of God and tells me again why I was created.

I must always guard against isolation, for I was created by God, who is revealed to us as communion. As a being of communion, God said, "It is not good that man should be alone" (Gen 2:18). This is the gift of Christian marriage, to which most are called: times of solitude must be rooted in mutual respect. Others are called to remain alone for the Lord, their one love. All together, we are on the road toward the kingdom of God. Our celibacy deepens our desire to see Christ face to face, to live only for his love, to reach for his coming and for his kingdom, from now on, "to prefer nothing to Christ."[54]

This celibacy, lived chastely, is a sign of the provisional nature of this world. All of the good I may experience in this world delights me, but the one essential is not there. The world and its idols cling to us and our hearts are constantly tempted. If we welcome chaste celibacy as a breaking up of the hard ground of our soul, our hearts can open ever wider to the presence of Christ in us, enabling us to walk with him toward the New Jerusalem, to live in this way the "not yet" of the promise. In loving Christ alone, we can freely reach out to others in his name, living out the compassion that we ourselves experience so fully in him.

We must sow seeds of communion with a simple, free, and generous love which desires nothing other than the healing and flourishing of the

---

54. Benedict, *Holy Rule*, chapter 72.

other in this same love of God and love of one another. This love watches over the other, that she may not close her heart in fear or remain isolated in her desolation (Matt 25:31–46). Following Christ, the first monks went physically into the desert to flee the spirit of worldliness, which had also affected the church. These giants of the faith found even fiercer demons there as well as confrontation themselves. Then the desert was brought into monastic communal life by planning for times of silence, especially the great silence of the night. Lately, some have started speaking of communal life itself, whether within the couple or the monastic community, as a desert, a place of temptation, especially that of taking refuge in isolation. But the monastery, the community, is a laboratory of communion, sowing the seeds of hospitality, openness, and ecumenical engagement through life together.

The challenge is clear: true freedom is not possible without times of solitude upon which our personal and communal lives are built. At Grand-champ we experience these times of solitude in the "desert time" of our retreats, and each night in the great silence. This experience is essential for our lives to be led by the Spirit, so that we are fit to let the Word of God resonate within our hearts, to let it take root and grow there. The quality of our interior silence determines our ability to live the Word received, for example, during *lectio divina*. It lets our inner ear open gradually through the Scriptures.

Once a month, each of us withdraws for a day into "the desert" in order to experience more intensely this reality of "solitude and communion." Similarly, before each important personal or communal event, we take a time of retreat, alone or together, to return to the freshness of our first love and to renew our commitment and our availability.

The liturgical year also offers us opportunities for community retreats: for example, at the beginning of Advent and at Lent. Between Ascension and Pentecost, the community takes a few days of retreat for a time in "the upper room." But there is no need to wait for an important liturgical time or a retreat to practice solitude, especially for those who live in the rhythm of the world. To experience a moment of "desert" is to enter that place of silence within, that space of solitude where Christ lives by the Spirit, where we are alone with him, where the Spirit speaks to us, where we grow with him in belonging to the Father, as beloved daughters and sons—the place where we are transformed to conform more and more to his image. It is important to be able to enter that solitude with Christ consciously, without getting stuck there however, for we are to flee isolation.

The dual reality of solitude and communion is called to become one in us. Living individually that inner unification leads us toward the fullness of *koinonia*[55] as a community. "The Prayer Cycle" that we received from Frau Vera[56] is valuable for making progress along this road: it creates, among other things, a solid link between the hours of the day and the key moments of Christ's life. Similarly, we have become aware that the liturgical year is not discontinuous with special celebrations such as Advent (the cycle of Christmas) or Easter (the Paschal cycle), which break into the ordinary rhythm of the liturgy. On the contrary, the three major periods of the liturgical year find their unity in Christ:

1. The time of creation and waiting on the coming of the Messiah among the people of the first covenant.

2. The coming of Jesus: his life, death, and resurrection, ascension, and the coming of the Spirit.

3. The sending of Christians into the world, confirmed by the Holy Spirit; they are Christ's body, his presence, the church on its way to fulfillment.

The liturgical year is found in the hours of each day. The cycle lets us live them in communion with Christ.

As a community, we first became keenly aware that Easter sunrise is at about six o'clock in the morning, and that Pentecost is around nine o'clock. Each time of day is thus marked by a moment in the story of the life of Christ. Permeated by this rhythm, our conscience opens gradually to him without any conscious effort on our part. This apprenticeship allows us to experience day after day, consciously and unconsciously, all the richness of the incarnation of the Lord, who entered into our human condition, all the gifts that he prepared in advance for us, he who is the Way. At the center of everything are Christ's death and resurrection. We continue to make discoveries. Sharing what we have received with our guests helps them understand more fully the meaning of each office and helps them to integrate these realities into their daily lives.

In nature, when the leaves fall in autumn, there are already buds appearing on the branches. At the end of one liturgical year, and the beginning of the next, there is a time when the alpha and the omega overlap: the feast of All Saints in November, with its readings from Revelation closely follows the feast of the birth of Mary in September.

The season of what has already been accomplished intertwines with the coming season. These examples show how different our time is from time on a clock, which counts the minutes one by one. Our time is more a

---

55. *Koinonia* Greek word meaning communion or fellowship.
56. Founder of the Community of Imshausen, see chapter 3, "The Mystery of Israel."

space, a rich season in which we proceed from beginning to new beginning, ever more firmly attached to Jesus Christ.

In this season the earth, exhausted by all the abuses, and humanity worn out by its non-acceptance of love, awaits "the revealing of the children of God" (Rom 8:19). In the middle of the afternoon, around three o'clock, those who toil begin to think of the end of their workday. Without knowing it, all participate in the work of birthing a new world, which some bring to the foot of the cross in intercession. The certainty that "it is finished" (John 19:30) grows steadily in the hearts of these sons and daughters of the Father. They carry the seed of the promise until it becomes a reality for all.

At Grandchamp, evening prayer is at 6:30. It is the time of gathering before God after a day of work: "How happy was I when they said, let us go up to the house of the Lord" (Ps 122:1). This is the hour of the Magnificat, the hour for remembering our vocation. To the daughter of Abraham it is announced that the Savior will be born to her (Luke 1:35): a new beginning, the seed of re-creation for all. Common prayer is followed by the evening meal, the joy of an *agape* feast, which once a month is also the time for our community evening.

The hour of compline leads us into the great silence of the night. We set our hearts and minds resolutely on intimacy with God in the solitude of the night, for communion among us is not possible through Christ unless we each freely embrace inner solitude. If we were unable to say "yes" to this solitude by being completely alone, for each of us is a unique human being, community life would be a disaster. This truth, taught by Christ, we will learn profoundly, in our time alone with him.

At the beginning of Compline, as at the beginning of a retreat, we take stock within ourselves: "Discipline yourselves, keep alert. Like a roaring lion your adversary the devil prowls around, looking for someone to devour. Resist him, steadfast in your faith" (1 Pet 5:8–9a). The time of silence that follows this reading is there for us to recall all that was good and beautiful in the day, then to take stock of our spiritual condition. Have I accumulated voices of doubt, false imaginings, tensions experienced during the day? Where do I need to open myself and allow Christ to come and visit me and give me rest at the end of the day? "Into your hands, Lord, I commend my spirit." I surrender to you. The time has come for the body to rest: "I will both lie down and sleep in peace; for you alone, O Lord, make me lie down in safety" (Ps 4:8).

But it could happen that a struggle begins, for the promise is put to the test. It is late, the time for waiting, for temptations, for doubts. The symbolic hours continue to succeed one another through the night. The hour of midnight is marked by the surprise of love in the birth of Christ, of the true

Light that shines in the darkness: "The Word became flesh and lived among us" (John 1:14).

Around three in the morning, comes the agony of Christ. Luther said, "The cross was made from the wood of the manger." During Lent we rise between two and three o'clock in the morning on Thursdays and Fridays, to contemplate together the passion of Christ: the Light was not welcomed (see John 1:5). He offered teachings, made disciples, and then experienced death on the cross in order to experience the full reality of the human condition, in order to love them to the end so that we can now place our limitations and failures into his "failure." And by his death, he has conquered death.

Six o'clock, the paschal hour: "Welcome with each dawn the presence of the Risen One. He opens us to God's today, to trust, and to freedom." Awakened to this flow of life, each of us meditates on the Word in her cell. Postulants and novices do so together in silence in the chapel.

Breaking the night's silence, we share in common prayer, then immerse ourselves again in *lectio divina*. We are on our way to a time of sharing; to the daytime hours; quite simply, to community life.

Around nine o'clock is the hour of Pentecost, the time of our "colloquy." The community gathers to begin the day together with this opening word spoken by the prioress: "Christ is in our midst." She reads a text from the Rule to guide us. Then there is a brief time of sharing, just the time to say "thank you" or "I'm sorry" or to give thanks for a gift or to make amends for a wrong done to another. In this way the communal body regains its unity by listening attentively to what is shared. In community life, the welcome and acceptance of those who are different from us is a reflection of the communion within the Trinity; community in Christ, by the Spirit, for the Father. In his icon of the Trinity, Rublev expressed this community with sensitivity and depth, as a dance of communion. The community is truly the fruit of Pentecost. Each of our sisters accepts her own responsibility to receive Pentecost as a gift by allowing herself to be guided by the Spirit.

Noon is the hour of mission. For us, it is to truly live out our communion in the spirit of the Beatitudes: "Shine like stars . . . among the people of this dark world" (Phil 2:15). During the Office we let a word from the Gospel of the day resonate within us, and we pray the Beatitudes.

At three o'clock we enter the last period of the cycle: all are invited to spend a moment in intercessory prayer at the foot of the life-giving cross. This is the hour of the martyrs, those whose blood is the seed of the church.[57] It is the time to prepare for a new day, which is welcomed and celebrated at Evening Prayer at 6:30 p.m.

---

57. Tertullian, *Apology of Tertullian*, chapter 50.

The Friday before Holy Week, at this hour of the day, we experience the Great Pardon, whether we are at Grandchamp, the Sonnenhof, or in a fraternity. This is a community time for which Lent has prepared us. This celebration of the Great Pardon, which is a communal reconciliation, includes all the humble gestures of reconciliation of daily life all year long, freeing us to fully experience Holy Week. Of course this does not exempt us from the duty of settling our differences with one another one on one, on a daily basis throughout the year,[58] and forgiving daily, starting over again and again. As the Gospels invite us, and our Rule recalls, "Forgive your brother, your sister, up to seventy times seven times" (Matt 18:22). Through these acts of forgiveness, we become in our turn seeds of communion.

In addition, at the beginning of the celebration of the Great Pardon, we read a text from John 20. Like the disciples, we often let ourselves be led into a natural movement of withdrawal and isolation for fear of others. In these situations we must let Christ break down our interior walls and receive his peace, which gives us joy. He then entrusts this peace to us and sends us out, as the Father sent him. In this way he teaches us that in order to be in communion, we must not keep the gift of his peace to ourselves. Christ also shows us his wounds, the proof that he suffered even death on a cross before saying, "If you forgive the sins of any, they are forgiven them; if you retain the sins of any, they are retained" (John 20:23). Here again he warns us: if community life is only possible in Christ who died and rose again, we cannot be content to live communion for our own comfort and happiness. Christ calls us to pass it on, and, like him, to hold nothing back.

To support our attempt to be open to the other, we can, when necessary, go to confession and be absolved of our sin by the chaplain of the community or other pastors who are friends of Grandchamp. Also, each of us has an opportunity to open up to a sister one on one (the prioress, novice mistress, or sometimes another sister designated by the prioress). This sister is simply a companion on the same road toward transparency and simplicity, someone who knows how to listen attentively, who does not impose her point of view, and does not judge. She doesn't have to be a model of virtue, but she offers this service as a witness of the Spirit.

On a personal level, our whole life is to be transformed in the light of the resurrection, including all of our failures and bad experiences. Whatever does not work in our relationships with others is not that important. It is enough to recognize and humbly accept this reality. Then everything in our personalities becomes like fertile topsoil. A newness of life, a new

---

58. "Be vigilant. If you are to admonish a Brother, let it be between yourself and him alone," Communauté de Taizé, *Rule of Taizé* (1961), 76.

beginning becomes possible when we can get outside of our selves and trust another. In seeking to simplify our lives and relationships, we become more accessible to our sisters and brothers. A real trust can grow which makes settling differences so much easier. In a community, differences in personality, thinking, culture, and life history build walls in our relationships; before we know it, we react according to some old script, some rigid set of ideas, which blocks communion with others.

Through all the small or major encounters of the day, we try to exercise concretely this attitude of authenticity with one another—a true asceticism. As soon as we notice that we are again playing a "role," we can humbly ask the Lord's forgiveness and return to authenticity. Sometimes we are tempted to withdraw because the others seem so much stronger than we are, and we fall back into fear. The simple reminder to ourselves of what we are before Christ, of his love for us, gives us new courage to reach out to others, to "flee isolation."

Honesty between sisters, openness to each other, is the fruit of our openness to God. It is subtle; completely different from a certain facility of expression which could be superficial or could crush others less gifted in their ability to express themselves, and completely different also, from telling all in an unrestrained, undiscerning attempt to appear transparent.

True transparency is seen in a profoundly welcoming attitude toward all. It is composed of listening, of wanting the other to be at ease and no longer afraid, of offering all the room that is necessary for her to be herself. It is a gift of grace given in the contemplation of the Risen Christ. Filled to overflowing by his endless mercy, we no longer need to make ourselves important, or defend ourselves, to justify ourselves, or make a place for ourselves. One of the deepest joys of community life is experiencing a foretaste of that kind of communion, that simplicity which will be perfect in the kingdom where God will be all in all (see 1 Cor 15:28).

Life in community at Grandchamp, as elsewhere, is a particular calling, and so a vocation to be discerned. On the road to this vocation, the fact of our belonging to several churches of the Reformation (which is a great richness in itself) can slow down our common progress if a sister imposes as absolute something that she learned and practiced in her church. Seeking to be welcoming and understanding of one another, in communion with one another, on the level of church unity, prepares us to be a leaven of unity among Christians on their way toward the church of tomorrow. In this sense, community is a laboratory for communion. We need a good sense of humor, for with all of our good intentions, we sometimes suddenly forget to take into account other sisters or sometimes the whole group.

The way of organizing the community has a big influence on the direction and quality of communal life. Here is an example from the 1970s: when the number of sisters living at Grandchamp reached about forty, we chose to get together in groups of six, changing the makeup of these groups every two or three years. This served to maintain closeness in our community relations, which become inevitably more distant with a large group. In expanding the connections between us, we risked falling into a sort of superficial "horizontalism" of endless chitchat. So the first result of this choice was a scattered life where, for many, silence and solitude were lost over time, along with the deeper meaning of their lives. It was necessary to develop and nurture a new way of being, to learn to take responsibility for the peace of others rather than seeking at all costs an emotional refuge for ourselves. This led us to put more emphasis on our solitude, on our alone times with God, our monastic roots.

Currently we meet in groups each week to share two or three meals, or a cup of tea, and review our lives together. Through simple sharing among sisters a Word from the Gospel reading, a passage from the Rule, or another text, through reviewing our lives together, or chats during a walk, we become more real. We discover little by little who we truly are. And thanks to the trust and positive attitude of the others, we can rejoice over our growth.

This example shows the understanding we have of our life together as a celebration of God's free gift of love: we sing of it in our common prayer and wish to live it out concretely in the joys and sorrows of a large family with a wide range of attitudes and ages. In addition to common prayer and meetings, our work is another place of sharing. We continue to do most of the work of the community ourselves, sometimes stretching the limits of our mental and physical strength—for example, when hospitality is especially busy (number of guests, number of directees or sessions to lead) and when a number of sisters get sick at the same time, while others are traveling, called outside the community, or when the garden is at an especially demanding point in the cycle of the seasons. Fortunately, the Lord sends his angels: a few youths or not-so-young people who come from the four corners of the earth to share our life of prayer and work for a time. Their presence is a gift well beyond the work they do. They are a part of our shared common life and enrich us and open us up a little more. We have also had the assistance of paid help from time to time, in order to maintain a wide welcome.

We must always remain vigilant, for a common life is dynamic in its constant seeking for unity within the community. Its growth is marked by a refusal to make efficiency the highest priority. Yes, more than anything else, it seems to us essential that we stay together in good times and in bad, until death parts us. To stay the course, taking each of our strengths into consideration, is literally to carry each other's burdens, and in this way to be signs of the kingdom of God in our society. At our profession,[59] when we promise to watch over our sisters in good times and in bad, we are in solidarity with them from now on. And I am also preparing myself to be dependent on them—literally on the younger sisters—when I am old or sick.

For several years, we have approached the reality of the difference between generations within the community in a new way, and we are discovering more and more how much the older sisters, far beyond the very real limitations put on them by age, are a gift to the community, yet another place where the fruitfulness of community is expressed. As for the young, it is for them to discover the way into the future!

Our faithfulness to one another can become the humble sign of God's faithfulness, and a true solidarity, which is the most fruitful witness. But we can only live in this way because of Christ and the Gospel, opening ourselves more and more to the newness of life that he gives us in all that we do.

Life in community is received continuously from Christ by the Spirit for the joy of the Father. It is a place of liberation, of maturation and of growth for each member, for the community gathers around Christ who lives among us and within us (Col 1:27). The Community of Grandchamp does not belong to us. It is not our task. It has no end in itself: it is neither a business to run nor a common ideal to work toward. Community is a place God has willed to dwell, in order to reveal God's glory there. A place where the love of God is loved, sung, celebrated, shared. We must therefore be watchful, never losing sight of the provisional nature of our community clutching at nothing—especially not the Rule, which we must live according to the spirit and not according to the letter!

Becoming a Parable of Community

The risen Christ, in the compassion and love he has for you, has chosen you to be a sign of brotherly love and a sign of newness of life within the church. By the gift of the Holy Spirit he opens you to joy, to forgiveness. He invites you to live with your sisters a parable of community in the spirit of Bethany according to the Gospel.

---

59. See promises made, chapter 1, "The Call of God . . . the Commitments."

Thus renouncing all thought of looking back, and joyful with infinite gratitude, never fear to precede the dawn to praise and bless and sing Christ your Lord.[60]

Adapted from *The Rule of Taizé*

At the beginning, community life among our first sisters was basic, but very real in all its simplicity. Each day, meditation on the same Gospel text and on the prayer of consecration: these were the things that brought them together.

"We give you thanks!" The joy of having been chosen together, and the response, "Here we are to do your will; our lives belong to you!" Then comes the realization that by depending only on our own strength, this life is hardly possible. "Lord, you know our weakness and our sins are not hidden from you. Forgive and purify us!" The more we know ourselves to be dependent on this forgiveness, on the limitless generosity of Christ, the more we can practice this gift of forgiveness toward our sisters: "Grant us the grace to remain in your love, to love one another in you."

"A life hanging on grace," said Mother Geneviève just before leaving us. The Holy Spirit is certainly the agent of this grace, the one who pours forth the life-source for an open communion. "Give us your Holy Spirit, that he may give us life, that your Word may light our way, that we may allow ourselves be led by you in all things . . . that we may remain in you that your name may be praised":[61] a grace of unity, of communion within us, among us, in the church and the world. All the inspiration is already there, like a stone thrown into the water whose ripples spread ever wider. Later, the first editions of the Rule of Taizé gave concrete suggestions and spoke more explicitly about the liturgical life of common prayer. The Rule approached vows in a new way, speaking rather of commitments,[62] and underlining at once the vocation to unity and openness to the world with the compassion of Christ. "Pray and work that He may reign;"[63] that Love may be loved, that love of the Father, which is communion, sharing, self-giving, gift, free grace, as revealed in the life of Christ.

---

60. Adapted by the sisters of Grandchamp from the final words of the *Rule of Taizé*, at once an exhortation and a calling, words which are recited at the time of profession. Communauté de Taizé, *Rule of Taizé* (1961), 77–78.

61. Mother Geneviève.

62. See the commitments, chapter 1, "The Call of God . . . the Commitments."

63. Br. Roger's first written expression of the Rule: Schutz, *Communauté de Cluny*, 4.

Common prayer and the celebration of liturgical feasts, especially Easter and the other major feasts of the Lord, cement our community together. Like the water of rivers, which carves the rocks as it passes, we are slowly formed by the great feast of Easter and the principal feasts of our Lord, as well as by the joy of a new profession, or by commemorating the origins of our community. We let all these celebrations resonate deeply within, in order to be renewed and revived together, awakened more and more to the newness of life we are called to bring to the world, and letting ourselves be more and more conformed to our calling to live a parable of community.

The two celebrations that are specific to us are tied to the history of our community and its two beginnings. Through the "yes" of Mother Geneviève and the first sisters, the Spirit was able to found a house of prayer in Grandchamp for all peoples whose cornerstone is Christ. This took place on November 9, 1952, the day of the feast of the Dedication, without anyone noticing this "coincidence" at the time, since our Reformed tradition is largely unaware of this feast. A few years ago, we had the joy of discovering it while staying at a Catholic community that we are close to. This feast day is a sign and a reinforcement of what God is doing with us: we are in his hands, individually and as a community. Since we are stones being built together,[64] we are to become ever more alive, authentic, and human: "In him the whole structure is joined together and grows into a holy temple in the Lord in whom you also are built together spiritually into a dwelling place for God . . ." (Eph 2:21–22). At once a house of prayer and of hospitality, a vine that grows, and a people; pilgrims on the road with the risen Christ, we seek to stand together before God for the world. The date of November 9, marked in the very flesh of the community, is to me a powerful reminder of the fruitful tension at the heart of our calling: to stand at once in the presence of God and in the presence of the world, for this date is a place of solidarity by its connection with the recent history of Europe. On this same date, in 1938, Europe experienced the Crystal Night[65] and then in 1989 the fall of the Berlin Wall.

The second celebration which is our own comes on December 7. It is then that we celebrate the birth of Mother Geneviève into heaven, as well as that of all our departed sisters. This openness to the communion of saints is, in a way, the second beginning of the community, the beginning of a fulfillment, a time of infinite gratitude for all that God has given us through our sisters, for this miracle, renewed daily, of the existence of our community thanks to the gifts of each and at times in spite of us! We also celebrate

---

64. 1 Pet 2:5.
65. Kristal Nacht: Nazi pogrom against all Jews.

birthdays and days of profession, as parts of God's good creation, in thanksgiving for our earthly existence.

We celebrate the handing on of the ministry of prioress on July 22, the feast day of Mary Magdalene. This woman, the female disciple par excellence, apostle to the apostles, is very important to our community. Deeply touched by Christ, his Word set her on her feet, and then sent her to bear witness to his resurrection. To the community and to each one of us, she speaks now, as she did then to the disciples. She was sent out to announce newness of life and to confirm each one in their relationship with the Father and with Christ. With her, we now bear witness to this newness of life by our whole life together.

The profession of a new sister is also a time of joy and strengthening for the community. Another living stone is added to the house of prayer, which we are called to incarnate in living this parable of community. The new sister is integrated into the communal body for always. Her "yes" freely given is confirmed by the Spirit, and it is a moment for each sister to remember her own profession and recommit to her promises. During the celebration of a profession, the prioress asks this question: "Sister, what are you asking for?" The answer: "The mercy of God and community with my sisters." The many symbolic gestures include prostration, and go well beyond the words spoken.

I've chosen two particularly significant moments that illustrate the vocation of the community. The first takes place after profession: the prioress girds the loins of the new sister with a sash, saying, with reference to the words the Lord addressed to Peter, "Up to now you have gone where you wanted to, but from now on you will go where He wants . . ." (see John 21:18). This act formally marks the crossing over, the adhesion of the sister to the vocation of communion which concerns at the same time each sister and the whole community. Each sister, very personally, for her life will henceforth be suspended on grace, commits her whole life before the Lord and asks his mercy. At the same time, she accepts that her life will be dependent on the vocation of the community as expressed by the prioress who receives her commitments, in her ministry of communion.

Another significant moment comes after the laying on of hands by the prioress, the presider, and a representative of monasticism, up until now a brother of Taizé, as well as by all the professed sisters and all consecrated persons who raise their hand to indicate their desire to participate. The new sister chants the Magnificat, which all sing together with her, and then she receives the kiss of peace from each professed sister. In turn she approaches the novices and postulants to give them the kiss of peace, saying, "My joy." And they reply, "Christ is risen," an exchange inspired by Saint Seraphim of

Sarov.[66] For the woman just fully received into the community, this gesture is the first "outward momentum" of the professed sister, to welcome others, to enlarge the space of her tent,[67] another way "to precede the dawn,"[68] where God will be all in all (see 1 Cor 15:28).

Each of these celebrations helps to strengthen the community so it will become a vibrant, healthy body whose head is Christ, rather than a fortress. By sharing the joy, a joy given by the Spirit, of each particular celebration as a community, each sister learns little by little what constitutes the communal body, in a subtle handing on of knowledge that cannot be controlled but that we can learn to receive.

All of the liturgical celebrations of the church year are important, but among them, the Transfiguration, the Visitation, and the feast at Bethany hold a very special place for us. The morning of the Transfiguration, we go on a little pilgrimage, as did the disciples, a walk together that we begin at night. We meditate on the biblical text "Be attentive to this as to a lamp shining in a dark place, until the day dawns and the morning star rises in your hearts" (2 Pet 1:19). We have the joy of being outdoors and seeing the sun rise. Sisters and guests climb the hill to the promontory, step by step, encouraged along the way by words from the Gospels.

This feast, like the luminous outpouring at Gethsemane, emphasizes the slow transformation of the shadows of our lives in the light of Christ; a light that heals and transforms. But on this same day in 1945, there was Hiroshima and the light which killed, with the destructive power of a light invented by humans, with its terrible consequences. Again, this dual dimension gives a particular weight to this day, to our prayer. To conclude our pilgrimage, we have a time of intercession on the hill, praying that the light of Life may swallow up the light of death.

For the Visitation, which we continue to celebrate on July 2, we rejoice together in all of the encounters led by the Spirit that we have experienced. All of the visitations that fill this book tell of the importance of this feast for the community. Every encounter sparked by the Holy Spirit requires our "yes," our availability to walk with others, including our own sisters, for fruitfulness is also a question of availability.

On July 29 we celebrate the feast of Bethany, as an expansion of our celebration of Saint Martha. Little by little, we came to realize that everything the Gospels tell us about Bethany—the healings, the encounters, the

---

66. Seraphim of Sarov (1754–1833) was a renowned monk and mystic of the Russian Orthodox Church who spread monastic teachings among the laity.

67. Isa 54:2.

68. Last phrase of *Rule of Taizé* (1961), 78.

teachings—have a deep resonance with the parable of community we are called to embody. We make our own the lines written by one of our sisters, and sung at the feast of Bethany: "You have chosen Bethany, O Christ our God, to manifest there the power of Life over death. Come, Lord, free us from the chains of death and pour over us the blessing of life like a perfumed oil. Lift us up that we may sing your glory, you who are the Resurrection and the Life."

Through Jesus' coming, Bethany, "house of tears," the symbol of the world's suffering and our own, has become a "house of praise," joy, and singing. A poor little village of no importance, Bethany was where Jesus liked to go to rest and enjoy its gracious hospitality. There he was freely and humbly loved, but also celebrated.

Bethany has become a sign of personal and collective resurrection. It is a house of communal fellowship, a cell of the church where each one has her own value: Martha who welcomes ("a woman named Martha welcomed him into her home")[69] as much as Mary who listens, contemplates, and worships ("Mary took a pound of costly perfume made of pure nard, anointed Jesus' feet, and wiped them with her hair"),[70] and Lazarus who reaches the end of life, still believing Jesus("now a certain man was ill, Lazarus of Bethany'))[71] Like Bethany, Grandchamp is called to become more and more a place where mutual service and encouragement are the order of the day. Jesus is our very first guest. "Behold, I stand at the door and knock"[72] He waits there like a poor man who does not want to impose. The "other" is, first of all, my sister. The Lord called each of us, without our having chosen each other, to live together fully the mystery of hospitality and communion. The "other" is also each woman or man or youth who knocks at our door, whom God is seeking to love through us and in whom we can meet the Lord. In this spirit, the spirit of Bethany, we are to offer hospitality in a spirit of retreat and of sharing. We are to do this even though our community's reason for being is less a defined service than a call to be, together, a place of prayer and of common life inspired and nourished by the Gospel. We confess and welcome the resurrection of Christ in the concreteness of our daily life as a reality that puts us in motion and transforms us as it did Martha, Mary, and their brother Lazarus.

Bethany prophesied the paschal mystery, the mystery which is at the heart of our communal life. Fear and rivalry can quickly weigh down our

---

69. Luke 10:38.
70. John 12:3.
71. John 11.
72. Rev 3:20 King James Version (KJV).

fraternal relations and push us toward isolation, as the disciples experienced in following Jesus: "They had argued about who was the greater" (Mark 9:3). It is then that we understand the words of the "confession of sins" in the Heidelberg catechism, which puzzled some of us for a long time, and even paralyzed or revolted some of us: "We are capable of no good, inclined only to evil."[73] This is not a moral reality, but the profound condition of our human will in rebellion, which we discover at the death of Jesus, as did the disciples, Mary Magdalene, and St. Paul.[74] It is the total failure of our good intentions! We cannot overcome this on our own. Jesus Christ took this evil, which is like a sickness, upon himself in his death on the cross, and even at Gethsemane. He wants to give to us the freedom he had during his passion: the freedom to obey the Father to the utmost, to give of our lives, to forgive our enemies, the freedom to let him work through us and become witnesses in our turn: "You are the light of the world" (Matt 5:14).

Those whom God sends to Grandchamp keep us very close to the suffering and the hope of today: women alone and abandoned, the young and the not so young, confused, wounded; but also people who seek to commit themselves, to deepen their faith. For them, we become a small sign of the kingdom that will come.

We are not here for ourselves alone, but to be a sign for others of *koinonia* (communion). One of us, the prioress, focuses especially on this ministry of communion so that we may be of one mind and of one heart (Acts 4:32) in the ministry God has entrusted to us and so that our unity of service may be fully realized.[75] Our commitment to accept authority puts the emphasis on the interdependence that exists between the community and the prioress. Father Enzo Bianchi, founder of the ecumenical Monastery of Bose, Italy, speaks of a "circular dynamic" between the community, the Rule, and the prior or prioress. Personally, I experienced as a second profession the moment when I became assistant to Mother Marie, with the responsibility for making decisions and presiding at the council. I was still young to be exercising such authority. Fortunately, rather than immediately casting a vision for the future, I had the good sense to listen first to what each of the sisters carried within her of the common vocation—how she saw it and lived it. Also, I immediately reread the chapter in the Rule on the prioress and the council, which is made up of all the professed sisters. At the

73. Heidelberg Catechism. Lord's Day 3, Q# 8.

74. Rom 7:19-20; Gal 5:7.

75. Fifth promise (commitment), see text in chapter 1. "Will you, so that we may be of one heart and of one mind in the ministry of communion which God entrusts to us, and so that our unity of service may be fully accomplished, adopt the decisions made by the community and expressed by the prior?"

beginning, I tended to value first what came from the community, then the Rule, and finally, what I sensed as prioress. I had a rather democratic view of my service at a time when the importance of the co-responsibility of each member was being discovered (during the 1960s).

Then I discovered, through experience, what Father Enzo considers "an important dimension of the communitarian dynamic,"[76] which is nothing less than the ecclesiology of communion emphasized by Vatican II. The sisters helped me on this journey through their trust in me and their kindness. A word had accompanied me since my time in Lebanon as a young professed sister: "Live communion and learn to be responsible for the peace of others." A few years later, some of the sisters developed a tendency to interpret the Rule with a more rigid monastic orientation, putting us in danger of missing the unexpected leading of God. Father Sophrony, spiritual son of Saint Silouan and founder of Saint John the Baptist Monastery in England, replied to my request for advice by saying, "My sister, the Rule is for the monk, and not the monk for the Rule."[77] Gradually, I came to understand that it is important for the one who leads to know where to take the next step on the road toward the kingdom, to let myself be better guided by the Rule, while still being attentive to each sister and constantly gathering us together through retreats, letters, visits, and especially the annual council. Father Enzo explains, "The Abbot is invited by the Rule itself to go beyond it, to discern what is more appropriate and in tune with the Gospel in a given situation with specific persons, to interpret the Rule for a particular community . . ."[78] According to the Rule, our prioress is a servant of communion among us, at the heart of the community. She speaks a word that gathers us and sets us on a path, that consoles and confirms, that encourages and leads us toward the one thing necessary: Christ and his Gospel. The "eye" of the community (Saint Basil), she constantly seeks, through the Holy Spirit, in prayer, and by listening to each sister, to discern the will of God for each one and for our common life, given the current realities of the community, the church, and the world. As Brother François of Taizé says, "true communion is only possible if it is inhabited by God, by Christ and if each sister takes responsibility for her life."

---

76. Bianchi, *Si tu savais le don de Dieu* [If you knew the gift of God], 256.

77. Allusion to Mark 2:27: "The Sabbath was made for man, not man for the Sabbath."

78. Bianchi, *Si tu savais le don de Dieu*, 256.

Reconciliation and Gospel Nonviolence

The commitment to ecumenism must be based upon the conversion of hearts and upon prayer, which will also lead to the necessary purification of past memories. With the grace of the Holy Spirit, the Lord's disciples, inspired by love, by the power of the truth, and by a sincere desire for mutual forgiveness and reconciliation, are called to re-examine together their painful past and the hurt which that past regrettably continues to provoke even today.[79]

JOHN PAUL II, UT UNUM SINT

Some of our collective wounds drag on from generation to generation, we must seek to penetrate these wounds with the forgiveness of God. It is not possible to be a church of peace and reconciliation without entering this way of proceeding which was Jesus' way, without accepting responsibility, and asking forgiveness for our collective and structural sins of the past and of the present.[80]

FATHER JOSEPH PYRONNET

"Lord, may Christians manifest the communion which is in you." This is our prayer of praise each morning during the time following Pentecost. It expresses our desire to be, together, a cell of communion within the universal church. It expresses the desire that among ourselves and within the church, we, sisters of Grandchamp, might live a monastic life of prayer and reconciliation, and live it ever more simply; that this life become an ever more transparent and inclusive reflection of the communion of love within the life of God, with the help of the Holy Spirit. For prayer becomes embodied

---

79. John Paul II, *Encyclical Letter Ut Unum Sint*, introduction.

80. Extract from "Asking Forgiveness of our Collective Sins," Lecture on "The Baptism of Jesus," Leipzig, 1990.

and is practiced in daily realities, in practical ways, in the flesh! It is there that we learn little by little, sometimes painfully, that our differences of temperament, culture, or even denomination can become a gift that enriches, complementary blessings instead of sources of conflict, of power struggles or resignation.

From the beginning, the community has emphasized unity, beginning with Christian unity. But very soon, and the adoption of the Rule in 1952 reflects this, reconciliation became a clear orientation of our life together. As a sign and a source, we are asked to begin afresh over and over again through mutual forgiveness, given and received.

Like the people of Europe and the world, all the sisters of our community carry memories of the painful experience of World War II. Sometimes, especially for the French, German, and Dutch sisters, it is extremely painful. But we were unaware that we also carried the roots of hatred and domination within each one of us. Nor were we any more aware that the "divider" (Satan) would work on us exactly there, in our personal and ecclesial woundedness. And that doesn't even include the wounds that were inflicted within our families of origin. It took us some time to recognize this and more time to begin to address it.

To illustrate the road to be traveled in this regard, I offer this example from my own experience. It had been eighteen years since the war had ended. Living for a time as a young professed sister at Grandchamp's fraternity in Jerusalem, I had the privilege of meeting a German doctor who was a missionary in Cairo. She shared with me the inexpressible suffering she experienced, with the entire German populace, at the time of the Allied bombings, especially of Berlin. As for me, I remembered my own experience in Holland, my joy at hearing the Allied bombers flying overhead at night toward Germany. They were a sign of hope, of relief. And soon there was an end to the war, an end to the unbearable, humiliating occupation of Holland. I thought, "It's all to the good." This thought, I now saw, took inappropriate joy in another's suffering. What followed this radical new awareness of my own sin was a profound conversion. A short time after this, I became novice mistress. As a Dutch woman, I welcomed several German sisters. We must live in our flesh the gift of reconciliation, the grace of forgiveness, the newness of life that Christ gives—as it is written in our promises at profession. And this continues even today. Our good will and our generosity are not enough. Each of us must get to work on ourselves so that as a community we can experience together this road to repentance, to reconciliation among ourselves, in Christ and for the world. That foundational experience in Jerusalem introduced me to the mystery of the life-giving cross, the only source of reconciliation and real love among the peoples, and the birth of a new humanity (Eph 2:14–19).

In the 1960s, the community experienced a very real solidarity with the world through our sisters living in fraternity. Our community felt deeply the wounds carried by the Arab peoples on the one hand (fraternities in Lebanon and Algeria), and Israel (fraternity in Tel Aviv) on the other. Each of us identified with the people among whom she lived. The great temptation was to take sides against one another. As a community we have experienced the impasse that is reached when, identifying ourselves with an oppressed people in despair over injustice, we can no longer see any way to liberation except through violence and accusation, through taking sides.

Julia, a close friend of the community, came from Guatemala and was a voice for the voiceless of Central America during our 1976 council. She confronted us with the impotence of our situation as pray-ers, and unmasked all the guilt we were carrying within ourselves for not being more active on their behalf, as well as the responsibility we bore for a complicit silence. But several of us asked the question this way: what is, therefore, the vocation of the monastic? And what meaning do we give to love for our enemies? Can one divide humanity into two categories, the good and the evil?

For years we had felt a call to solidarity with developing countries, and we had a great interest in liberation theology, new at that time. Before this council, we had already been introduced to nonviolence as a strategy for liberation through contacts with the Community of L'Arche de Lanza del Vasto by Mother Geneviève and several other sisters; through friendship with pastors Henri Roser[81] and Jean Lasserre,[82] both great peacemakers; through the presence of Joseph Pyronnet at Grandchamp; through prayer in our chapel during a demonstration at Bienne against the war in Viet Nam; and through a day of formation in nonviolence for several sisters in Neuchâtel in connection with MIR—the International Movement for Reconciliation.

This time the community was ready. Just before the end of the 1976 council, one sister saw a film with General de Bollardière[83] on a raft in the Pacific protesting nuclear tests, and asked herself, "Couldn't this be a path for us?" The next day, the table reading in the refectory was an article on Jean Goss.[84] It upset several sisters and helped us make up our minds; this

81. Roser, *Le Chrétien devant la guerre* [The Christian in the Face of War].

82. An ardent French pacifist pastor who knew Bonhoeffer. See Bonhoeffer, *Resistance et soumission*, 371–72.

83. Toulat, *Un combat pour l'homme: le général de Bollardière* [A Struggle for Humankind: General de Bollardière].

84. Mobilized in 1939, he participated in the Second World War. In June 1940, the night before his surrender to the German Army in Lille, he had an overwhelming

was the beginning of a new era and the beginning of our apprenticeship in Gospel nonviolence. On my way to Romania that fall, I met with Jean in Vienna, at the offices of the International Fellowship of Reconciliation (IFOR). A few months later, three of us attended a session given by Jean in German-speaking Switzerland. From our first session with Jean Goss, we were deeply touched by his sharing of experiences as a soldier and then as a German prisoner, especially because of the healing and reconciliation we were experiencing among ourselves at this time. We wondered if this new awareness we had experienced could have a broader impact than on the interpersonal level. Could it have an impact on the political and ecclesial level? This remains a vital question for us up to the present day. For our contemplative life of prayer does not separate us from humanity, but places us at its heart. The fate of oppressed peoples concerns us profoundly. Isn't the very meaning of the word *oecumene*, the entire inhabited earth?

For our 1978 council, the community chose Gospel nonviolence as the theme: "Live together today the peace and nonviolence of the kingdom," "The Christ of the beatitudes," "Lord, make me an instrument of your peace." To prepare, we read the works of several experienced pacifists, notably Thomas Merton[85] and John Howard Yoder.[86]

During the 1980s, active nonviolence took up much of our attention. Numerous activists came to Grandchamp, including the founder of l'ACAT,[87] Jean Goss and his wife, Hildegard Goss,[88] Jean Lasserre, General de Bollardière, Jean-Marie Müller,[89] Lanza del Vasto, and many others. We came to know the Mennonite Church as a peace church. Two of our sisters visited Elkhart, Indiana for a few months, while several American Mennonite women and Professor Yoder came to Grandchamp. Through them all, through our councils, and through the invitations that flowed from these contacts, we took part in the events that were shaking the church and the world. We became aware of the tremendous dangers that threatened our

---

experience of God's love for him and for the whole of humanity. It would be the beginning of a lifelong commitment. As a prisoner of war in German camps until 1945, he was sentenced to death but was saved by a German officer who was moved by his testimony.

85. Thomas Merton (1915–1968) was an American Catholic writer and mystic. A Trappist monk of the Abbey of Gethsemani, Kentucky and author of *Faith and Violence*.

86. John Howard Yoder (1927–1997) was a Mennonite theologian, professor and author of *The Politics of Jesus*.

87. ACAT (l'Action des chrétiens pour l'abolition de la torture), L'ONG Chrétienne Contre La Torture Et La Peine De Mort (Christian NGO against torture and the death penalty).

88. Goss-Mayr, *Oser le combat non-violent*.

89. Müller, *Témoins de la non-violence*.

world: "just wars," nuclear weapons, and the arms race. Two women especially impressed us during their stay because of their acts of mobilization in the face of the nuclear threat: Solange Fernex, a mother and member of the European Parliament, and Rosalie Bertell, a Catholic sister and scientist.[90]

At the same time, we were invited as a community, as a prayer support, to participate in the founding of Church and Peace, an association that includes traditional churches as well as peace churches (Mennonite, Quaker, etc.). Our discovery of nonviolence—to be lived out within our community also—nourished our monastic vocation, coloring it in concrete ways. For the Desert Fathers in particular, love of enemy is central and a proof of their love for Christ. That love consumed them, as it did Jesus. What does this mean for us today? There are personal enemies, but there are also, especially, those who commit injustice, who oppress the peoples, who abuse and enslave the poor: our collective enemies, which political and religious systems so obviously support.

Steps on the Road of Gospel Nonviolence

Jean Goss knew how to open the understanding of our hearts, and those hearts began to burn within us, as did the hearts of the disciples on the road to Emmaus. All that he said was very concrete and full of a great compassion, the compassion of the Father: no attempt at eloquent words, no spiritualism without substance. From then on, and until his death, Jean was like a brother to us, one who forgives and respects the other, and Hildegard, his wife, was like our sister.

God made this man, above all, a true contemplative, a great contemplative. In a sweeping vision, he was shown the world and humans as God saw them. Then he was given his mission right in the heat of battle on the front in World War II, on Easter day 1940, with this word from God: "Teach them to love one another as I love them; teach it to them quickly. I love them madly. I am their Father: I created them for myself, and I gave my life for them. But they do not know it, and that is why they kill each other instead of loving one another." He was afire with this love of God from then on. He was crazy with joy because of it, but he also was quick to learn that this love must be practiced, embodied in all the little details of daily life. In the prisoner of war camp, he asked his fellow prisoners of war to remind him with a little phrase: "Hey, Jean! Where is your love?"

Our common life is a life of relationships. It is up to us to make these relationships vital, simple, and transparent. In a life like ours, it is easy to

---

90. Fernex, *La vie pour la vie*; Bertell, *Planet Earth*.

go one's own way alone, while participating faithfully in all the community functions, easy to live our life of love of God while neglecting others a little. Well then, if I can say to myself, as a contemplative, "Hey, Minke! Where is your Love?" then I can begin to get back on track.

In sending us Jean, the Lord showed us some simple but challenging ways to live the depths of the Gospel in the spirit of the Beatitudes. Christ wants to share his love for others through each of us. We cannot simply let go of a relationship if it isn't working, or work against the other or talk about them with others. On the contrary, we must try again and continue the dialogue without giving up. On this road, the teaching of Jean Goss, developed with his wife, Hildegard, remains a treasure: not as a recipe, but as a beacon on the path of good relationships in a community.

> Step 1: Discover the truth about the other, the good that is in her, and tell her.

> Step 2: Discover in yourself the wrong the other is doing, that you see in the other, and tell her about it, asking her to let you know each time she sees it in you, and to help you to stop doing it.

> Step 3: If we see that we or the other are so caught by this wrongdoing, that we cannot free ourselves and that we are hurting others, then we must fast and pray, receive the Eucharist, and bring to it the inner struggle we are facing.

> Step 4: In the face of lies or injustice, speak the truth with respect and love, while making the injustice obvious. Never be complicit even by remaining silent, and refuse to participate in lies or injustice (for example, by accepting a privilege). Be willing to pay the price for telling the truth, revealing an injustice or refusing to participate in it.

The connection established from the first meeting with Jean and then Hildegard Goss is a good example of reciprocity; we prayed faithfully for them as they traveled all over the world giving seminars and retreats. We were happy to read their logbook and welcome them at Grandchamp. All of this expanded our horizons.

In retracing the steps God took to lead us through to our vocation of reconciliation. I marvel at the way our encounters over the years have led us to turn to a contemplative activism of nonviolence. For example, in 1980, we invited the Orthodox Father Jean Breck. He spoke to us about fasting within his tradition. Shortly afterward, a doctor, Françoise de Toledo, while staying with us for a time, taught us an aspect of nonviolence that is complementary to the practice of fasting: growth in respect for our bodies as instruments of praise of God in harmony with the whole creation.

On the road of Gospel nonviolence, Joseph Pyronnet and Grandchamp became traveling companions. Around Christmas 1987, Father Pyronnet came to give a retreat on the theme of inner healing. The following year he began giving sessions on the spirituality of nonviolence. He emphasized more and more the connection between inner healing and active nonviolence, and started a retreat called "My Christian pilgrimage in light of the Word of God." Each retreatant starts a journey of reconciliation with herself. The last session opens with questions designed to guide her return to daily life and to stay the course. Here are a few of these final questions: "Do the most difficult times in my life, times I failed to react well, have meaning for me now? Do I accept them as part of myself? Do I accept myself as marked and shaped by my *whole* life history? Do I recognize my life story as a sacred history? Have I had the experience of recognizing that in such and such a circumstance, I react according to my past, which prevents me from living in the present? In what way could this experience be the starting point for healing? Is my forgiveness of the best possible quality?"

I helped Father Pyronnet with that first retreat of this type at Grandchamp in 1987. Deeply struck by this process, we decided to use it in the "communion cell group."[91] Since then, this process has become an important step of personal spiritual growth for many sisters and has become part of the formation of novices.

That year, Father Pyronnet needed an assistant to replace me and called on Simone Pacot.[92] Both of them were open to the action of the Spirit and had met at the Community of L'Arche de Lanza del Vasto. She became a close friend of Grandchamp and our sister in Christ. We welcomed her, encouraged her from the beginning of the sessions she created in faithfulness to her calling and her charisms. So began the adventure of the Bethasda sessions of "Evangelization of the Interior Life," which continues to this day.

The Bethasda cycle includes three sessions over a year's time: teachings, sharing groups, individual direction, and "steps." Simone Pacot passed along her knowledge and methods to the whole team of sisters who assisted her through the years, and has remained very close to them. Several sisters now accompany individuals during the Bethasda cycle, and continue to receive training. In view of the success of this approach, which takes into account, without confusing them, both psychological and spiritual issues, the sessions have spread to other francophone areas in France, Belgium, and

---

91. "La cellule de communion"—A small team of sisters which advises the prioress.
92. Pacot, *L'Évangélisation des profondeurs*; *Reviens à la vie!*; *Ose la vie nouvelle!*

Quebec. But as Simone Pacot writes, "Grandchamp remains for the whole team our foundation and our bulwark of prayer."

The journey proposed to retreatants during this cycle leads to an experience of the paternal (God gives us the guidelines for a fruitful life) as well as the maternal (mercy, welcome, tenderness) love of God. It is focused on reorienting each life in its entirety, body, mind, and soul, according to God's will. Each one is invited to open herself to the grace of Christ, the light of the Spirit, and then to a rereading of her history, the ways her identity has been formed, her inner freedom. Each discovers the impact of past wounds and her reactions to them on her present life. The goal is to bring to light the way she refuses to accept the limits of the human condition, unhealthy relationships she has formed (enmeshment, influences, role confusion, co-dependence, envy, rivalry, emotional overdependence), to recognize and deal with hidden emotions, experience the mourning associated with each loss, whatever its nature, and finally to leave the paths that lead to death in order to take the paths that lead to life. Each of these steps will chart the course.[93]

The Bethasda cycle takes each retreatant on a journey toward unity of the self by way of a teaching on the incarnation. What a joy it is to see how these sessions renew each person, including members of religious orders, along with their whole community as a result.

So many other encounters and examples of daily interactions within the community could be mentioned. But the example of our little pilgrimage at dawn on the sixth of August (feast of the Transfiguration/commemoration of Hiroshima) is a sign of the ever deepening relationship that unites our life as intercessors, our responsibility in the world, and the path of Gospel nonviolence: a way of proclaiming our faith in the transformation of the world in its darkest places, where evil takes on the very traits of infernal light.

---

93. For more on the Bethasda Sessions, see www.bethasda.org.

CHAPTER 3

Together in Solidarity with a World in Travail

So many walls have gone up through the years, and especially from century to century in Europe. I want to reflect on some experiences I had between 2002 and 2006, which were attempts to go over those walls, to be a pilgrim of peace; to work for that peace; attempts to heal memories without "doing" anything, but simply by "reaching out," in an ecumenical spirit. From among these travels I have chosen to present three: Eastern Europe, Auschwitz, and the Holy Land, where one encounters the mystery of Israel.

Again and again, we must dare to let the light of Christ penetrate the wounded places in our deepest selves, our subconscious, and then bear witness so that through simple sharing, without our knowing how, the Spirit is at work: new perceptions and understandings of the world and of ourselves open a path toward reconciliation. The Spirit is at work everywhere, in different forms, inviting us to experience each encounter as a true visitation.

On the Road to Eastern Europe

The Community of Grandchamp is a microcosm of the universal church, especially in what it carries, through each sister, of the twentieth-century European experience. Our communal life began at the beginning of World War II and the first professions were made in the middle of the Cold War. In 1954, we established a retreat house in German-speaking Switzerland, a first step toward Eastern Europe. Our welcome of German sisters into the community dates from 1961, the year the Berlin Wall was completed! Germany was cut in two and Europe, and the world, divided into two major blocs. Several of our sisters felt keenly their separation from their home country and from a part of their family. This reality wounded their hearts and through them, the heart of our community. Since then, so many of our interior walls have gradually fallen and have given us, by the grace of reconciliation, the strength to reach out to others.

In 1965 we opened a fraternity near Frankfurt; Sister Marie-Madeleine, the first sister to go to the Sonnenhof, was put in charge. The following year, Ilse Friedeberg, a member of our Servants of Unity[1] and a translator for the World Council of Churches (WCC), created Philoxenia,[2] a group that facilitates meetings between Orthodox Christians, coming from the East to find work, and Western Christians, including us. Through this association several of our sisters have forged bonds of friendship with brothers and sisters of the different churches living on "the other side" through meetings, pilgrimages, and so on. Two years later, after a Serbian Orthodox sister had stayed with us for several months, Sister Sylvie spent time at Manassia with a Catholic sister, invited by the abbot of that renowned monastery.

In 1972 Protestant deaconesses living in East Germany asked us to give retreats for them at Eisenach and Gernrode. For twenty years now, we have been sending one or another of our German sisters there, often accompanied by a Dutch sister. Many relationships continue to form with Catholic communities in the area as well.

In 1976 Sister Myriam participated in a meeting in Laski, Poland, which gathered delegates from the Catholic and Protestant churches of Germany, which were separated by the Berlin Wall. They were all welcomed by the Franciscan sisters of the area. Father Christopher Lowe[3] of the Anglican community of Mirfield discreetly planned these meetings during the years when Europe was divided by the Iron Curtain. Our presence there strengthened our relations with the Christians of Poland and, through personal contacts, opened us to the Judeo-Christian dialogue going on there. Today the meetings at Laski are called Christopherus, and have expanded to include Orthodox participants.

Our openness to Orthodox spirituality is as old as the community. The first relationships with Orthodoxy were established in the 1930s between professors Leon Zander, Paul Evdokimov, and Mother Geneviève. Theirs

---

1. See Grandchamp website: www.grandchamp.org. Servants of Unity, faithful to the church of their Baptism, these women pray for the visible unity of Christians and of the world, "So that God may be all in all" (1 Cor 15:28). "A vocation of contemplative prayer within ordinary life in the world."

2. Circle of friends who are Orthodox, Catholic and Protestant which facilitates the meeting of Western and Eastern Christians, their sharing and mutual support.

3. Christopher Lowe was an Ecumenist, an indefatigable "passeur" (one who passes ideas across barriers, as a smuggler passes goods across borders), in spite of the political difficulties of the Eastern bloc. See Brother Johannes, "Christophorus," 17.

became a profound friendship that continued to grow. Other Russian immigrant theologians living in Paris, including Father Boris Bobrinskoy, were also close to the community.

In 1968 Father Boris, future dean of the Institut Saint-Serge[4] in Paris, brought Timotei, a young Romanian theologian, to Grandchamp to serve as deacon for the Divine Liturgy celebrated in *L'Arche* chapel. Both of them were visiting scholars at the Faculty of Theology of Neuchâtel. Around 1972 Father Timotei, by then a priest, returned to Switzerland for another year of studies at Fribourg. He visited Grandchamp and found everything he needed there to celebrate the Divine Liturgy, including vestments and icons, which were gifts from the Patriarchate of Romania by way of their priests who stayed with us. (Among these was Father Plămădeală, who became Bishop of Sibiu.) Father Timotei brought with him two deacons who were students at the Catholic Faculty of Fribourg. One of them, Brother Franz Müller, now a Dominican, has become a true brother to Grandchamp, treasured for his wise counsel.

During the 1960s, more and more Romanian priests visited Grandchamp. Their presence meant an Orthodox celebration for the Orthodox of our region and for our community as well. But we couldn't be naïve, with the political situation being what it was. On one occasion *L'Arche* chapel was full of people in uniform taking photos!

Little by little, Romanian parishes formed in Geneva-Chambésy, in Fribourg, and in a Lausanne basement of a Reformed Church, to our great joy. Romanian celebrations at Grandchamp became more rare, to our regret! For alongside all that we have received from Anglican and Catholic communities, Orthodox spirituality has opened us to cosmic and resurrectional dimensions, especially through Paul Evdokimov, Olivier Clement, and their writings, and through Father Boris Bobrinskoy and Father Ion Bria, who worked at the WCC in Geneva. When we were in Lebanon (1957–63), we developed friendships with young Orthodox who were experiencing renewal. Several monasteries were the fruit of this renewal—monasteries that were always ready to welcome us. Teaching on the Fathers by Father Corbon, a Melchite priest, enriched this experience.

In 1973 our Sister Irmtraud and Marie-Dominique, a sister of the Poor Clares, visited Agapia and Varatec, two of the large monasteries of Moldova, at the invitation of the WCC representative of the Romanian Orthodox Church. Four years later, Sister Sylvie, an iconographer, and I, then prioress of the community, were invited to visit by the Patriarchate. In our hearts, we sang the Orthodox praises, antiphons (choruses), and hymns we learned in

---

4. Orthodox theology faculty founded by Russian immigrants to Paris.

the small choir of sisters which was formed, in the late 1960s, to accompany Father Bobrinskoy in the celebration of the Divine Liturgy at Grandchamp. We were received at the Patriarchate by the Patriarch Justinian and his vicar Anthony Plămădeală, well known by our community. We visited Bucharest, then under the communist dictatorship of Nicolae Ceaușescu. I have vivid memories of our stay at the monastery of Agapia. We were greeted by Mother Eustochia, an extraordinary woman of God, full of faith and openness. Later she came to visit us several times thanks to ecumenical sessions for women in religious orders.[5]

The first Congress of Orthodox Women was being held at that time, at Agapia, a blessing that allowed us to participate in a Divine Liturgy led by Monsignor Hazim, who came there from a Lebanon in flames. We were forever marked by that service. The celebration was at once a long supplication with *Kyrie eleisons* in many languages, and a hope against all hope: Lebanon was at war and many Orthodox countries were weighed down by the communist regime. Monsignor Hazim,[6] later Patriarch of the Antiochian Orthodox Church, remains close to our hearts, especially because of his kindness to our sisters during the time they lived in fraternity in Lebanon.

In 1978 I was able to make a second trip, without an invitation this time, through the Balkans. There were three of us, including a former WCC employee who had just retired from her job in the reception office in Vienna. She had built strong relationships with Reformed and Lutheran Christians in these countries as well as with Orthodox Christians. At Sihastria Monastery we had the joy of receiving a word from the abbot, Father Cleopas, a true *starets*.

When I recall these pilgrimages in Eastern Europe before the fall of the Berlin Wall, I also think of our meetings with the Orthodox of our region, with the monastery of Saint John the Baptist at Maldon, England, a community founded by Father Sophrony, a disciple of the *starets* Silouan. We were very touched to receive at the time of its publication, the French translation of his book, *Le starets Silouane*.[7] This spiritual bond has continued. Soon after the death of Father Sophrony in 1993, the Saint Silouan Association was formed with members from the Catholic, Orthodox, and Protestant churches of the area. We are members as well, and have hosted several of their retreats at Grandchamp. On these occasions the Orthodox Divine Liturgy is once again celebrated in *L'Arche* chapel, to our great joy.

---

5. E.I.I.R. (Inter-confessional International Meetings of Religious).
6. Died December 5, 2012.
7. Sophrony, *The Monk of Mount Athos*.

Three years ago we rejoiced in Metropolitan Joseph's visit to Neuchâtel, at the request of some Orthodox Christians in the area who wished to form a parish to be led by young Romanian Orthodox theologian, Alexandru Tudor. This parish was born, linked to the Romanian Patriarchate, but with a real pan-orthodox openness that makes it possible to avoid the pitfalls of nationalism. In fact, because of its tiny but diverse Orthodox population, the canton of Neuchâtel up until then had not seen the formation of any Orthodox parish at all. During his visit, Monsignor Joseph[8] asked us to pray for this would-be parish. To support its birth, at first without a place to meet, and to come alongside its young priest as he entered the priesthood, several Orthodox Christians, with a few of our sisters, began to meet together regularly to pray the "Jesus Prayer," in a style close to that used at Maldon. All of this is a source of joy and hope for the Orthodox of the area and also for us. We accompany them with our prayers, our friendship, and our caring presence. What a joy it was to attend the ordination of Father Alexandru Tudor as a deacon and then as a priest, and for one of us to take part in their liturgies on major feast days.

Three Pilgrims in the Spirit of the Beatitudes

All of this gave me a longing to return to Romania, where I had encountered the heart of Orthodox monasticism. For years I had wanted to do an ecumenical pilgrimage through Europe to Romania. One of our friends, Elisabeth, offered to take me in her car, opening my way to a new journey eastward in July 2006.

We set out like pilgrims: Elisabeth, long-time pastor of the Reformed Church of Gelterkinden, near Basel, and a close friend of Grandchamp by way of her ministry, and me. At Cluj-Napoca, capital of Transylvania, a third "pilgrim" joined us: Thomas, a Hungarian pastor who spoke Romanian well.

Since 1972 Elisabeth and her congregation had lived in solidarity and close contact with Reformed Christians in Transylvania, like many Reformed parishes in Switzerland and the Netherlands. These ties were established in the sixteenth century, when the Reformation affected a large part of Hungary. Student exchanges among the Reformed continued through the centuries.

The three of us had such different experience of relations with other Christian traditions, in particular the Orthodox tradition. So here we were, on our way in the spirit of the Beatitudes as our Rule requires of us, poor,

---

8. Metropolitan of the Romanian Orthodox Church of Western Europe, headquartered in Paris.

simple, living in the present moment, open to what the Holy Spirit had prepared for us in the encounters to come.

To those we met along the way I spoke of an ecumenical pilgrimage, and learned with astonishment that the word "ecumenical" did not have good press, and even troubled some who offered us hospitality. So it was better to speak simply of pilgrimage. It was certainly our desire to encounter others who were different from us, but who were also motivated by the same deep thirst for God.

We arrived in Budapest which stretches along the banks of the Danube, then crossed the plain that extends to the Carpathian Mountains. The villages still had their bell towers, just as in Switzerland. Here the churches were Reformed or Catholic, whereas in Transylvania, though the architecture is almost the same, they are Orthodox, Greek Catholic (some Slavic and Romanian Churches have had relations with Rome since the seventeenth century), or Reformed. Under the dictatorship, all Greek Catholic churches were forcibly integrated into the Orthodox Church, exacerbating the painful situation in which minority ecclesial groups found themselves. After the fall of the Berlin Wall, some of the churches were returned to Catholic communion, some were not. But beyond the buildings, the challenge is the same everywhere—the recognition on both sides of the suffering that has taken place, and the ridiculing of religious beliefs. In some places, the wounds are still fresh; in others they are infected by lies, oppression, and power. How painful is this road we must walk in love and truth. What could we say to the wounded hearts we met, whether Reformed, Greek Catholic or Orthodox? Yes, in Christ the first step is to remember, to welcome the truth of each church's painful history in this region. We tried to respond in the spirit of the Beatitudes. We suffered with some of them and rejoiced with others, meeting those who were open to, or eagerly seeking, dialogue.

We reached Cluj-Napoca, the largest city in Transylvania, in the morning. After passing the border (so easy now), we saw many Romanian flags flying next to European Union flags. It was a delight for me to go to Thomas' house this time. In 1978 we had been able to visit, but were required to stay at a hotel, as all relations were subject to strict government surveillance. This time, Thomas' house was our home base while in his city, which gave us great joy. We visited Cluj-Napoca and the surrounding area, especially major Protestant sites, including the Faculty of Theology. I also got to know the Reformed Church a little better: its courage and its exhaustion, for the times continue to be difficult.

The first stop on our pilgrimage was the Greek Catholic hermitage of Sainte-Croix, close to the Moldavian border, founded by Mother Éliane of the Carmel Saint-Elijah in Saint-Rémy near Dijon, France. Shortly after the fall of the Wall, in 1994, Mother Éliane, filled with evangelical vigor and faith, was able to fulfill the intuition of Mother Élisabeth, their founder, to work for unity among Christians in Romania, by sharing in the same prayer as the Orthodox, as is done at Saint-Elijah. The hermitage is the fruit of relationships built over the years, some through the inter-confessional meetings for religious,[9] with the Orthodox and the Greek Catholics of Romania.

For several years I had been invited by Mother Éliane to visit; she renewed the invitation when we met at the celebration of Monsignor Emilianos' ninetieth birthday, which was held "at her home," the Monastery of Saint Elijah,[10] in the department of Côte d'Or.[11] Never lacking in creativity or perseverance, Mother Éliane had succeeded in gathering for the occasion a collection of tributes[12] to the ecumenical and spiritual work of Monsignor Emilianos. A few years earlier, she had done the same for the Orthodox theologian Elisabeth Behr-Sigel.[13]

At the hermitage of Sainte-Croix, the life of prayer is led by two sisters who live in a central building, close to a small wooden church surrounded by hermitages. They are served by a priest. Recently, a deaconess stayed there for a month, sharing in their prayer. Our visit made it possible for my fellow pilgrims, Elisabeth and Thomas, to become a little more familiar with the liturgical life of the Eastern churches, for the liturgy is celebrated in the Byzantine rite and in the language of the country, as it is at the Carmel Saint-Elijah. There also, a small group has formed around the sisters for meetings, visits with Orthodox, Latin Catholics, Greek Catholics, and Protestants of the area, and for dialogue with Jewish communities there.

This little foundation already has a wide influence. Greek Catholics come from afar to this place of peace and silence that encourages prayer, hospitality, and openness in a region still so wounded by the Orthodox/Greek Catholic division. The choice of date for their annual assembly is a hopeful sign: the day of the Transfiguration, the sixth of August and the day the church was consecrated.

We pilgrims took to the road again, headed for Iași, Romania, where the Metropolitan Daniel, whom we had met at Bossey, lived. Unfortunately he was not there. But there we celebrated the great feast of the apostles

---

9. E.I.I.R., supported by Don Hernando and Monsignor Emilianos.

10. Monastery of Saint Elijah, a Carmelite monastery of Byzantine rite, founded in 1974 by four Carmelites.

11. Cote d'Or is one of 101 departments of France. It is in Burgundy, near the city of Dijon.

12. Carmel of St. Rémy/Stânceni, *Qu'ils soient Un!* See a tribute by S. Minke on p. 371.

13. Carmel of St. Rémy/Stânceni, *Toi, suis-moi*.

Peter and Paul, and were impressed by the fast the Orthodox are invited to observe in preparation for Pentecost. We shared the joy of the celebration with Father Justin and his parish at the psychiatric hospital in Socola, in a structure which had been built to house the first seminary for Moldavian priests. Father Justin is another of those former visiting scholars at the Faculty of Theology in Neuchâtel. During the 1990s, he came regularly to Grandchamp to celebrate the Orthodox liturgy, and even got us to celebrate the Easter night vigil with him—an unforgettable experience for the whole community who participated in song and prayer.

We were very warmly welcomed in his parish and by a group of spiritual friends of his who support him in his ministry, forming a support unit for the parish. Father Justin introduced us at vespers, a service that lasted forever due to the great number of people who wanted to make their confession before the Sacred Liturgy. I was filled with joy by this celebration. Elisabeth and Thomas, who were strangers to this world, had their first experience of the fervor of the Orthodox people, for the first time from the inside so to speak. I sensed this time of quiet prayer of the people as a balm of consolation, an experience so different from so many hurtful confrontations they carried as a member and pastor of the Reformed Church. During communion, which lasted a long time, we received all of the kind attention Father Justin could give us between the comings and goings of the sick in hospital gowns, members of the nursing staff, and others. Yes, it all filled me with joy.

Thanks to Christine, one of the members of the parish support group, we were able to visit with the contemplative sisters of Sion who had just established a prayer presence in one of the large houses of the Congregation. Before the war, half of the population of Iași was Jewish. The massacres were terrible. It is difficult today for the sisters to find a way to minister here.

In the evening we got together with Father Justin, who was exhausted from the day's activities. We enjoyed a meal together with his parish support group. But I had a painful experience that evening: a turn in the conversation led to some negative remarks about the beginnings of the Reformation which lacked understanding, and it hurt. It was difficult for me to regain the spirit of the Beatitudes that night, and even to maintain a friendly attitude in our encounters. Yes, encounters of this type are perilous in this region that has experienced so many years of oppression and lies, where disagreement often meant death! We need to fast and pray again and again to receive in the depths of our beings and of our churches the healing power of an encounter in Christ as was experienced by the apostles Peter and Paul.

The next day, after a pleasant breakfast with Father Justin and his parish support group, we left them, full of gratitude for their gracious hospitality.

As pilgrims, we continued our journey, heading for Agapia. There we were warmly welcomed by Mother Olimpiada, who arranged for us to stay in a new house, "Eustochia house," named for a deceased member of the community. As we drove through the forest to Sihastria, I remembered my first time there, when I came on foot accompanied by a sister of the monastery. This time Sister Cecilia, whom I had met at the meeting of the E.I.I.R. (Interdenominational International Meetings of Religious) in Basel in 1989, came with us. We started at Sihla, a small monastery of monks which her father, Cleopas joined twenty-five years ago while her mother lived at Agapia. Father Visarion, who knew him well, invited us to his little hermitage where, at ninety-six, he spends his time praying. Next to his hermitage a path goes up through the rocks toward the cave of Saint Theodora, where this hermit lived a totally solitary life, as did many others, persecuted by the Turks who ruled Moldavia at the time. It was a moving experience to be in this holy place.

At Sihastria, after visiting the tomb of Father Cleopas, we came back down to earth. Vespers were beginning. Several of the monks participated in the office in their cells or seated on their balconies, thanks to a loudspeaker. Elisabeth and Thomas were deeply moved by Father Visarion, the hermit, and by the prayerful attitude of those who attended church services, often on their knees, according to Romanian Orthodox tradition. They were impressed but also wondered if this was too emotional. The road toward other Christians different from ourselves really does take time.

We returned to the monastery of Agapia just before a storm broke. The pilgrims prepared to sleep under the stars, as planned, but in the end we were invited into the monastery, which is made up of numerous small houses, and into the church itself.

The next stop was Voronet and its church, famous for the beauty of its interior and exterior paintings. A small monastery has been erected next to it to re-establish monastic life in the area and to return this jewel, "The Sistine Chapel of the East," to its primary vocation: prayer. The restoration of this church is ongoing. What a joy it was to share the table of Mother Irina and the two sisters who were guides, Elena and Gabriela. What a gift to end our pilgrimage with a visit to Monsignor Timotei, now Bishop of Arad. We found him to be a man of openness, a man of relationships, with an ecumenical concern in a diocese where the population is very mixed. The Orthodox Church of this region has relied for a long time on the Orthodox Church of Serbia on the other side of the southern border.

Mgr. Timotei and two assistants welcomed us; one a priest trained in Chambésy near Geneva, the other a deacon who studied for four years in Lugano. On the way to the women's monastery we had a big surprise; we found ourselves standing before a newly constructed Reformed Church. The pastor came out to greet us and showed us photos of the latest Week of Prayer for Christian Unity where even the rabbi was present.

We left Eastern Europe carrying with us the joys and sorrows of all those we had met and those we could not meet because of the wounded memories of the people and the churches. Stronger than ever was our desire to pray for the unity of the church with Christians of other traditions, many of whom are prisoners of the past who, like us, are in search of the true Light, God's Love. We left it all in the hands of the Risen One who lived the spirit of the Beatitudes to the fullest.

"Memory for Peace" at Auschwitz

There was another experience that marked me for life. I had the great privilege of participating, with Magda Hollander-Lafon,[14] in the "Memory for Peace"[15] (Mémoire pour la Paix) trip organized by Father Émile Shoufani,[16] a priest in Nazareth, and Jean Mouttapa.[17] Out of discretion, Father Emile did not speak of pilgrimage. How could Auschwitz, site of "the desolating sacrilege"[18] of the Jewish people and of all of humanity, be a place of pilgrimage as are Jerusalem for example, or Mecca? But yes, it is a place of memory, of "Memory for Peace." There were five hundred participants: three hundred from Tel Aviv, and two hundred from Paris. They included Jews, Arabs—some Muslim, some Christian—and a few others, like me, some Christians, others not.

During the days of preparation in Paris, I met several of the people involved, including Muslim and Jewish girl scouts and boy scouts. At Auschwitz some of these relationships deepened, without many words needing to be spoken. I felt a need for silence there, to maintain an interior space. What I saw there left a profound imprint on me. Everything spoke to me, struck me: the buildings or what was left of them, the vast expanse of the grounds that we walked across for two days. In the center was the railroad track installed to "welcome" as "efficiently" as possible 400,000 Jews from

---

14. Nouvelles de Grandchamp 2008. Hollander-Lafon, *Quatre petits bouts de pain*.

15. Shoufani, "Memory for Peace," 73.

16. Father Emile Shoufani is an Israeli Arab Christian, educator and activist for peace, archimandrite of the Melkite Greek Catholic Church. He won UNESCO Prize for Peace Education (2003).

17. Jean Mouttapa organized the French participants in the "Memory for Peace." See Mouttapa, *Un Arabe face à Auschwitz*.

18. Or "abomination that desolates." Dan 12:11; Mark 13:14; Matt 24:15.

Hungary, including Magda. We saw the remains of row upon row of barracks, miles of barbed wire, and the "sorting" area, where we held the closing ceremony of the event. And above all, there were the faces, the testimonies of the deportees.

This ground on which we walked, Anne Frank, Etty Hillesum, Edith Stein, and Alma Rosé had crossed just once as they walked to the gas chambers. Magda's testimony helps memorialize so many others who remained anonymous:

> My life stopped at age 14, in the middle of adolescence, amid conflict with my parents. At Auschwitz I left my mother and my sister without a backward glance, without a gesture, and when I became aware of their absence, a Polish *kapo*[19] told me, in an indifferent tone, "Look at that chimney with the flames leaping up. They are already inside." My life stopped for a second time.[20]

We were told that not a single blade of grass could grow on this ground, a mixture of ashes, blood, and tears, crushed by boots, fouled by dogs; this ground trod by thousands of humiliated, wounded, sorely tried feet. No bird remained there, in this place of desolation invented and developed by human minds, where the air was un-breathable, thick with the smoke of the crematoriums.

What a strange contrast now, with this explosion of nature, the smell of fresh-cut grass, birdsong, flowers. I picked a few growing in what had been Magda's barrack. I brought them back to Grandchamp, where I placed them in L'Arche chapel at the feet of Christ, a crucifix made by a Brazilian artist friend of the community, a Christ whose body is no longer anything but an immense cry of pain—pain the artist knew from his days of torture during the dictatorship.

Nothing remained of Magda's barrack but the brick outline—I can still see her husband walking there, absorbed in thought. And Magda had not returned to this place since the end of the war. She told story after story: "and there at the end of the path is the door we passed through on our way to work. My job was to carry the ashes to the pond."

That evening at the hotel a young Muslim with an important post at the Grande Mosque in Paris—as I learned later—gave me a crucifix carved from olive wood. "Is this yours? I found it when we were with Magda in her barrack." The next day at Orly airport he worried again: "Have you found the person it belongs to?" What to do? In the end I brought it home to

---

19. Concentration camp inmate appointed by the SS to be in charge of a work gang.

20. Hollander-Lafon, *Quatre petits bouts de pain*.

Grandchamp and set it in my prayer corner. A few weeks later a woman, "Juliette," wrote to me. Magda had told her of the crucifix, which belonged to her.

For each of us who participated in the "Memorial for Peace" at Auschwitz, there was a before and an after. We were no longer the same. Auschwitz inspires you or sends you into despair, if it does not cause you to just run away. After Auschwitz, how can we believe? How can we hope? How can we love? Chagall opened a path for me with his White Crucifixion. This Jewish believer, in the pandemonium of anguish, desolation, and horror of his people in 1938, painted a Jeshua abandoned by his own, who surrendered himself completely to God in his "yes" right through to the very end. Chagall placed lights at his feet, a reflection of the light that comes from elsewhere, as a certitude. When all seems lost forever, light springs forth from darkness, a seed of life, of love, of hope against all hope, like a spring of goodness, of humanity.

As the closing declaration read at Birkenau expresses it,

> We, Jews and non-Jews, beyond our various origins, beyond the beliefs or non-beliefs, or philosophical options of each person.
> . . .
>
> Together, we affirm that every man and every woman, for as long as he and she lives on this earth, from childhood to old age, bears in himself and herself a sacred spark which is worthy of the highest respect . . .
>
> Together, we commit ourselves to be bearers of the memory of the Shoah and to do the task we have in common which, based on the teachings of that memory, will allow us to explore together the horizon of peace.[21]

Pilgrimage for Peace in the Holy Land

All the suffering and all the hopes borne by the peoples of the world are intensely concentrated in the life experiences of those who live in Jerusalem. Through our personal intercession and communal prayers at Grandchamp, through the prayers of so many believers all over the world, how often we have invoked peace upon this city—holy ground for the three monotheistic religions—and on the entire Near and Middle East! When the situation there seems to be deteriorating (such as the blitzkrieg in Lebanon in 2006),

---

21. http://www.notredamedesion.org/en/dialogue_docs.php?a=3b&id=168.

the highlights of my pilgrimage there in the spring of 2002, the Pilgrimage for Peace in the Holy Land, come to mind and take on even greater significance.

Five of us went. Five instead of the thirty who had planned to go, due to increasing tensions between Israel and the occupied territories (the second *Intifada*). The Church of the Nativity was occupied by Palestinian fighters, resulting in a siege of Bethlehem by the Israeli army.

A little earlier the Latin Patriarch Monsignor Sabbah[22] had addressed the Christians of the world, asking them not to stop coming to Jerusalem, reminding them that in former days they had received much from this ancient church as well as from the holy places which it has tended throughout the centuries. He spoke of the necessity of maintaining solidarity among Christians today—especially since those of the Holy Land depend on pilgrims for their living—and of recognizing in this way the vital importance of this ancestral and indigenous Christian presence in the region. Touched by the Patriarch's call, Hildegard Goss[23] had the idea of making a pilgrimage. She was able to gather pilgrims of peace from a diversity of Christian confessions and European countries. We were neither an official delegation nor an activist group: Paul Lansu, of Pax Christi International (Brussels); Hildegard Goss (Vienna); and peace activists Clemens Ronnefeldt (Germany) and Christian Renoux (France)—all from the International Fellowship of Reconciliation (IFOR/MIR)—and me. In Vienna, as a send-off, we celebrated the Eucharist in an attitude of repentance and intercession with some of those who had decided not to go, but accompanied us with their prayers.

Our group, though modest in number, was thus supported by many others. Some of these gathered at Imshausen to fast and pray during our pilgrimage. Others participated in the prayer chain. The numerous emails we received also encouraged us throughout our pilgrimage, and we in turn became messengers to those we encountered.

We had left the safety of our homes without knowing what we would find, having heard the call of God, like Abraham, the father of all three monotheistic religions. We were sure, as he was, of the blessing of God on our pilgrimage which was also a journey of self-discovery, and sure of a deeper understanding of our vocation as artisans of peace and reconciliation. The first condition was to be poor in spirit, to shed all that encumbers, especially our ready-made presuppositions. As pilgrims, we would rediscover

---

22. Born in 1933 in Nazareth, Michel Sabbah was the Archbishop and Latin Patriarch of Jerusalem from 1987 to 2008.

23. Austrian nonviolent activist and Christian theologian.

our basic condition as Christians: nothing more than travelers, nomads, strangers on the way toward the kingdom, in the spirit of the Beatitudes. We were going to Jerusalem, the city of peace for Jews and for Christians; for Muslims, the Holy City. Jesus wept for her and died outside the city, outside the camp. In all of our encounters, in all that we would experience and hear, we were joining Christ in his humiliation (Heb 13:13–14). The story of the disciples' encounter with Christ in the locked room, reported in the Gospel of John (John 20:19–31), was read the eve of our departure and gave us strength: we heard it as a renewed call to allow ourselves to be led by the Spirit in order to be freed to forgive sin, to free others from their sin, their inabilities, their anger, and hatred.

In Jerusalem we stayed at the Austrian residence in the Old City, hosted by Father Wilhelm Bruners.[24] The first day we went to the Mount of Olives, where Jesus wept over Jerusalem: "My house shall be called a house of prayer for all peoples" (Isa 56:7). We spent the afternoon at the Church of the Holy Sepulcher, which the Orthodox call the *Anastasis*. The empty tomb opens onto a space stimulating openness in us! Through his love, which endured to the end, on the cross Christ destroyed in his own flesh the wall of separation; all the walls of separation. We all sensed these truths of the faith in the City where exclusion rules, in every sense of the word.

The next day we met with our friends Dalia and Yehezkel Landau, who were working for reconciliation and dialogue. Their "Open House" in Ramla is a former Arab home where Dalia, a Jew of Bulgarian origin, grew up. They run a daycare facility for Arab children who have less access to daycare than Jewish children in the same area. The house also offers a space for gatherings of older children and adolescents (mixed groups of Israeli Jews and Arabs). In the same spirit, events such as summer camps, trips outside the country, as well as follow-up sessions are organized. This place of healing really impressed us as a concrete sign of the desire for peace that motivates many people. But work for peace in these circumstances becomes a superhuman undertaking, as it is located in Neve Shalom, a village where Jews, Arab Christians, and Arab Muslims live together. Another highlight was a visit to Yad Vashem,[25] where we were very moved by the memorial reading of the names of children lost to the Holocaust.

While still in Jerusalem, we met an amazing Sufi Muslim named Nafez Assaily,[26] from Hebron. During earlier, more "calm" periods, he invested

24. German Catholic priest, author, poet and hymn writer who, during eighteen years in Jerusalem, worked with Jewish poets still writing in German.

25. Yad Vashem, Israel's official memorial to the Jewish victims of the Holocaust, established in 1953.

26. It was a talk given by Mubarak Awad, a Christian Arab, which convinced Assaily

himself in the education of children. He used a mobile library, "Library on Wheels for Nonviolence and Peace," to spread a message of peace and respect for human dignity inspired by the Qur'an, by his role model, Gandhi, and by the Qur'an, the Torah, and the New Testament read with a Muslim sensibility. One of his projects was to help the Palestinian activists of Jerusalem find slogans which were more concrete, less general, and closer to their daily realities: for example, "Jerusalem, open city," "The holy places should be accessible to all three religions," or "Share the water equitably."

What a blessing it was to be staying just steps away from such symbolic holy places: the Wailing Wall for Jews, the Church of the Holy Sepulcher for Christians, the Temple Mount, and El Aqsa mosque for Muslims. In this old city where many Palestinian Christians live, we met with Patriarch Michel Sabbah. He was happy we had come but very tired because of all the difficulties in Bethlehem due to the occupation of the Church of the Nativity. Other important encounters included the Justice and Peace committee and the director of Caritas (at Notre Dame) who was very involved with the transport of medical supplies and food to the city of Ramallah and other towns which were occupied or isolated by the hostilities. We also met with Lutheran friends including Marylène, who courageously works to raise awareness among the young Israeli soldiers at the checkpoints using leaflets and personal contacts. She also helps Palestinian women exhausted by the waiting, the long walks, and the red tape.

We also had the great privilege of meeting Israeli peace groups: "Women in Black," "Machsom (Checkpoint) Watch," "Peace Now," and "Rabbis for Human Rights." Each of these groups resists nonviolently, attempting to speak the truth as much as they can. They seek to establish contact with Palestinians and collaborate with them. They are small in number and their work is immense, but their popularity is growing among Israelis, in spite of the difficulties.[27]

Our pilgrimage was supposed to have continued into Palestine. Unfortunately, because of the situation, we could not meet the nonviolent groups in Bethlehem. But each day we spoke with them on the telephone, even one day from the Ecumenical Center at Tantur, from where we could see Bethlehem. They were all grateful that we had come, in spite of everything. They shared with us their feeling of being imprisoned, of their fears, and of the violence all around them. There were several cranes in the fields among the olive trees. I realized much later that this was the beginning of the construction of the wall.

---

of the efficacy of nonviolence as a strategy for peace and justice.

27. In 2016, the time of this translation, each of these groups was still active.

Words by the thirteenth-century Sufi mystic and poet Rumi, taken from one of the twenty-six pages of supportive emails, accompanied us: "Beyond our ideas of right-doing and wrong-doing, there is a field. I'll meet you there." It is so natural for humans to take sides. And that is why the situation is deteriorating more and more. God alone can raise up persons who are truly open to both sides. They are there, certainly few in number, but a leaven of the kingdom, sowing peace.

I stayed on for four weeks with our sisters at St. Elizabeth/St. John in the Desert, not far from Hadassah, Ein Karem. My visit with André Chouraqui[28] and Rabbi David Rosen,[29] and our contact with the Abbot of Dormitio,[30] were moments of great encouragement. Bethlehem finally reopened the day after my departure. Sister Maatje immediately joined our friends engaged in nonviolence, to the great joy of Noah Salameh, a Muslim, and Zougby Zougby, a Christian, both leaders of centers for peace, reconciliation, and mutual aid initiatives. She also visited the Little Sisters of Jesus at Beit Jala, and other friends as well; visits which were difficult for her, as she saw with her own eyes the damage done by Israeli forces in the city, the centers, the family homes, often without reason. She heard stories of thefts, threats, and violence toward simple folk. It was heartbreaking to hear news of Jenin, Ramallah, Bethlehem, and elsewhere, for we love the Palestinian and Jewish peoples.

Suicide bombings result in great anxiety among Israelis and confirmed many of them in their gut-level convictions that the Palestinians would like nothing better than their disappearance, and that the whole world is against them. This constant fear in turn helps justify many acts of violence. Yesterday's victims are always at risk of becoming in their turn the executioners, and the spiral of violence continues to escalate. For many Palestinians, the attitude is the same. All the wounds they suffered unjustly in 1948 and since 1967 were reopened: "They are trying to push us off what remains of our land . . ." "We are shocked by the corruption of most of our leaders, but at least they are defending us—who would do it otherwise?"

And finally, the ideology of "Greater Israel" is a major obstacle to an authentic peace process. Based on the Bible, this ideology, dear to fundamentalist Christians, numerous in the United States, is unjust and dangerous.

---

28. André Chouraqui (1917–2007) was a French Sephardic Jew born in Algeria who was part of the resistance in France during WWII, worked for interfaith understanding while based in Jerusalem where he became Mayor, and wrote many award winning books and articles on these topics.

29. Former Chief Rabbi of Ireland, a leader in inter-religious dialog.

30. Dormitio Abbey, Mt. Zion, Jerusalem.

Four years have passed since our pilgrimage. The construction of the wall between Israel and Palestine has become a reality, but the question remains: What is the solution? After listening to different perspectives, we have come to the conclusion that only the creation of two independent states would guarantee dignity, justice, and peace for all. That probably will not happen without the help of an international mediator.

It is urgent that at the heart of the two peoples, more and more men and women of peace, able to rise above this desperate situation, meet and pray together, drawing hope from their respective faiths. The night before my departure, for example, a peace demonstration in Tel Aviv brought together between sixty thousand and one hundred thousand participants. The leaders of this sort of action need to feel the support of others in order to persevere when the tide turns against them.

One question haunts me: Are we ready, as members of religious communities, to open ourselves today to the suffering of each side without judging either one? I believe it is our responsibility to encourage peacemakers by our inclusive prayers and an open, non-partisan attitude: "What comes out of the mouth proceeds from the heart" (Matt 15:18). In this way, with them, we become artisans of peace and reconciliation.

I experienced another sign of hope during this trip when I took part in the first prayer gathering held in the garden at St. Anne's Church in the Old City. It was profoundly moving to hear, in addition to French and English, prayers in Hebrew and in Arabic by members of the two peoples, either by birth or by ministry, and from all three of the monotheistic religions—all of this in the presence of the leaders of the churches, including the Latin Patriarch. What a powerful experience! Three weeks later, on the Vigil of Pentecost, a second prayer gathering took place at Dormitio Abbey on Mount Zion, more specifically Christian this time, crying out to the Spirit of peace. Jews and Muslims also participated. The church was packed. Yes, we must pray, pray, gather in prayer, crying out to the one God, thrice Holy,[31] to open pathways and to support today's peacemakers in concrete ways.

In Jerusalem the sufferings of the human family, painfully giving birth to a new world, are experienced intensely. What a call to dedicate ourselves to loving the whole world inclusively, with a love that knows how to go through the narrow gate[32] of forgiveness and compassion for the other! What an impact this could have on the entire world!

---

31. Allusion to the Trisagion (thrice holy or Holy, Holy, Holy), a hymn of the Divine Liturgy of Orthodox Christianity.

32. Allusion to Matt 7:13.

The Mystery of Israel

"It was not the Jews who crucified you, Lord Jesus, but us!"

From a seventeenth-century Dutch poem learned in childhood

"Great is the mystery of the faith,"[33] and like an echo, "Great is the mystery of Israel." Like Moses before the burning bush, we must contemplate this mystery of God's presence with fear and trembling. Yes, we must approach the mystery of Israel, beloved people of God, in the Holy Spirit, just as we do the mystery of the church, the Body of Christ.

"Now the chief priests and the whole council were looking for testimony against Jesus to put him to death; but they found none . . . All of them condemned him as deserving death" (Mark 14:55, 64). In 1995, during Good Friday's Way of the Cross in the Colosseum, these words came to me in response:

> Your heart is heavy with suffering at this tragic moment when the gulf is widening between you and your People, the beloved People of your Father. "Yes, I am the Messiah, the Son of God," and the gulf is still widening . . . but you never repudiated your people. "Father, forgive, them, for they know not what they do." But we, your Church, we have been repudiating them for 2000 years.[34]

If, from the beginning, we Christians had been able to live in communion with the people of Israel in spite of our differences and separations, in spite of all the aggression against the newborn church, we would have realized that exclusion is not the only way to deal with those who believe differently from us. This might have taught us how to avoid the other schisms that fill our history. But the fullness of time[35] had not yet come . . .

It is up to us today to find this path of communion within diversity which always begins with repentance. Our community discovered this gradually, for the Holy Spirit was working on us from all sides. Our prayer of the psalms, liturgical feasts, teachings, and meetings challenged us. God's instruments also included Sister Jacoba, our fraternity near Jerusalem, and

---

33. The phrase from the mass in French, used by Sister Minke, "Il est grand le Mystère de la foi," is "Let us proclaim the mystery of faith" in the Catholic mass in English.
34. Vries, *Chemin de Croix*.
35. Allusion to Gal 4:4.

others, such as our Armenian friend who put his whole heart and all his energy into a service for "the forgiveness of Israel," inviting us all to a true repentance by recognizing our wrong doings.

The Spirit worked on us first through the Divine Office: during the revision of the Office of Taizé, the translation of the psalms was modified. The word "fear" was changed to "adore."[36] That astonished me. As a child I had learned "the fear of the Lord is the beginning of wisdom" (Ps 111:10). So I sent a sister to the nearest rabbi, in the town of La Chaux-de-Fonds. He taught us the deep meaning of "fear," which evidently had nothing to do with being afraid, but was not adoration either. "Reverential fear is a relationship of respect; it is to know oneself a creature, but also beloved by the creator." At the time of this meeting, one of our sisters had discovered her own Jewish roots! The many teachings we received through the years, notably by Rabbi Rouche, who later moved to Jerusalem, enlightened us greatly concerning the Jewish roots of our Christian faith. And this way of seeing our faith deepened through other friendships, notably with Colette Kessler and Armand Abécassis. These meetings and teachings, which took place and continue at Grandchamp, introduced us to ancient and modern readings of the Bible by Jews, helping us to grasp the vitality of today's Judaism. Others accompanied us along this way as well, among them the Prayer Union of Charmes[37] which is very open to the mystery of Israel, and Father Pierre of the Monastery of the Epiphany in Eygalières.

Once we had understood the profound meaning of the feast of the "Presentation of Jesus at the Temple on February 2," we renamed it the "Encounter of Jesus with his People," as it is called in the Eastern Church. With the help of Pastor Jacques Serr of the Union of Prayer of Charmes, we developed our understanding of this great mystery even further.

Yes, the Spirit has often spoken to us through the liturgy. We began to use the menorah, lighting it on Friday evenings to celebrate the beginning of the Sabbath with the Jews. In this way we wanted to show our loving closeness with the Jewish tradition. We began this practice without considering the risk of mimicry that accompanies it. Now we place the menorah under the icon of the Trinity on Saturday evening to celebrate the beginning of the Lord's Day. Our Orthodox friends feel right at home with the seven-branched candlestick which is always lit on their altar during the Divine Liturgy, signifying that Jesus Christ is the Messiah of God. In synagogues the menorah is not lit, since the Jewish people are still waiting for the Messiah.

---

36. I.e., Ps 34:9 "Adorez le Seigneur . . . ," Communauté de Taizé, *La louange des jours*, 558.

37. *Union de Prière de Charmes*, founded in 1946 by Louis Dallière in Charmes-sur-Rhône, France.

This reminds us that our relationship with Judaism is unique—that it will never be the same as our relationship with Islam, even though believers of all three religions are the children of Abraham. This reality is a source of reciprocal suffering for Jews and Christians that an infinite respect for one another cannot erase, for Jesus did not come to abolish the law, but to fulfill it. And the Hebrew Scriptures, the first testament, are an integral part of our faith. The way we have appropriated the psalms, concluding them with the glorification of the Trinity, is another telling example of the unique relationship between Jews and Christians. What belongs to them also belongs to us, in part.

Concerns over incorporating elements of the Jewish tradition into our liturgies by simply imitating them can hold us back at times. What is called for is an inspired discernment which is far from all ideological intolerance. We must find the right path in order to enter ever more clearly into an understanding of all the ways in which the Jewish people and their traditions enrich our understanding of God's present moment,[38] integrating them according to our faith without taking them over. Fortunately, since *Nostra aetate*[39] of Vatican II, Catholics no longer see the church as superseding the People of Israel.

At Grandchamp we have the incredible privilege of greater freedom when it comes to liturgical renewal. Always careful to avoid injuring another church, another people, or another religion, we try to update our liturgy according to our experience. For example, we have adapted the intercessory prayers of Good Friday from the Catholic liturgy. At Grandchamp we no longer pray "that the Jews may again find the light"; instead, we pray for the beloved People of God, the chosen people who endured the Holocaust, for their safety and for justice. With equal vigor we also pray for the Palestinian people. In other ways as well, the Good Friday prayer is becoming ever more inclusive at Grandchamp.

When our life includes the gift of Jewish friends visiting Grandchamp, what a joy it is to begin the Sabbath, thanks to them, with the blessing at the beginning the meal, lighting the two candles, then breaking the bread and drinking from the same cup. The link with the eucharistic meal becomes so striking.

I am amazed to observe that the first communities with whom we have forged the closest ties, after Taizé and Pomeyrol—Bec-Hellouin, Imshausen,

---

38. Allusion to Brother Roger's first published book, Schutz, *Vivre L'Aujourd'hui de Dieu* [*This Day Belongs to God* or "God's Today"] in which he uses a phrase from C.S. Lewis's *Screwtape Letters* referring to the present moment of time, wherein God can act.

39. Paul IV, *Declaration on the Relation of the Church to non-Christian Religions*, par. 4.

Eygalières, and Bose—had this same concern to signify in their liturgies the continuity between the first and second covenants. Through our contacts with these communities, our liturgy has been enriched with Hebrew responses and melodies. Their help has been so important for us in deepening our understanding of the mystery of Israel.

At the beginning of Lent in 2000, Pope John Paul II, successor of Peter, led his church on a journey of repentance through a liturgy of "forgiveness of debts." In March of that year, he went to Jerusalem and placed his prayer of "confession of sins" into one of the many niches in the Wailing Wall, where many Jewish people have also traditionally prayed and left prayers. Likewise, the Ecumenical Charter signed at Strasbourg in 2001 included a passage that makes explicit the desire to combat anti-Semitism and anti-Judaism in all their forms in the church and in society. It is up to the churches to stick to this charter. These gestures reveal how far we have to go until each one has begun a process of the purification of memories. On another front, our relations with Israel today have become more complex because of the political situation and because of a certain religious fanaticism. I believe that for us as Christians this is the moment to renew our vigilance, to guard against identifying others with the wrong they do, and excluding them, whether they be Israeli or Palestinian.

"So when you are offering your gift at the altar, if you remember that your brother or sister has something against you, leave your gift there before the altar and go; first be reconciled to your brother or sister, and then come and offer your gift." (Matt 5:23–24) If he agrees to be reconciled with you, "you have regained that one" (Matt 18:15). If not, keep your heart open.

The second key attitude we must have is found in John 20:23: "If you forgive the sins of any, they are forgiven them; if you retain the sins of any, they are retained." This concerns every Christian, especially every monastic man and woman. As Christians we must accept this formidable responsibility of forgiving those who do us wrong. The greatest witness to the truth of the Gospel is to be found in the humble welcome extended to the other who also carries the divine spark within, who is infinitely loved by God, and for whom Jesus Christ suffered and died.

As a community always in need of God's help, we seek to situate ourselves on this road of hope. In 1963, after my stay in the Arab lands of the Maghreb in the Near East, upset after my visit to a Palestinian camp in Jerusalem, it was very difficult for me to return to our Sister Jacoba "on the other side," in Jewish territory. But suddenly, seeing a number tattooed on a man's arm, I reconnected with the suffering of this people who were denied everything, even the right to exist.

The presence of Sister Jacoba in Israel from 1957 to 1990 was of fundamental importance for our community. She showed us the daily reality in Israel, first in Tel Aviv, then in Jerusalem. Our sister was a pioneer, truly called by God to live in the Holy Land—she who, through her own personal story, was so close to the Jewish people. She was forced to cross Germany on November 9, 1938, during *Kristallnacht*, when synagogues were looted and burned. It was through her that André Chouraqui became a good friend of the community. Also thanks to her, we were able to establish a fraternity at Saint Elizabeth, on the grounds of the monastery of Saint John in the Desert on the outer edge of greater Jerusalem.

Our Ties with the Community of Imshausen

Among the places where attention to the mystery of Israel is great, I must mention Imshausen.[40] Our ties began with the relationship between Mother Geneviève and Frau Vera (1906–1991), the founder of the Community of Imshausen and the sister of Adam von Trott.[41] Those ties were reconfirmed when I met her in November 1963. At the time of our meeting, I was still filled with thoughts of my trip to Lebanon and the months with Sister Jacoba in Israel. I had a dawning awareness that, as a Dutch woman, I was not beyond reproach, but that my hatred was no better than that of the Germans.

We had both come to the Sonnenhof for a meeting with Karl Barth. The participants were about to leave when Sister Vera called to me. There was immediately an amazing rapport between us. We talked of nothing but Israel. She had been there the year before and had met with Martin Buber[42] and others.

Our meeting was a true visitation, like that of Elizabeth greeting Mary, an encounter full of God's presence. Her whole attitude, her trust and respect for me in the duties I was undertaking at the age of thirty-five, as novice mistress and leader of the community, helped me so much, for I felt very shy about taking on those responsibilities, which seemed so far beyond me at that age. Today I am convinced that our encounter was one of the fruits of her meetings with Mother Geneviève, a gift of God. Fortunately, though I did not have many conversations with Mother Geneviève, I had

---

40. Community situated in Bebra in the state of Hesse, Germany, near the border between East and West Germany.

41. A German diplomat who was part of the failed assassination attempt on Hitler in 1944, for which he was arrested and then executed.

42. 1878–1965. An Austrian-born Israeli Jewish philosopher best known for his philosophy of dialogue.

truly encountered her in that I had profoundly sensed what motivated her and what life together as women in community, following Christ, could be. I treasured her first words to me, "Christ alone!" Her last words, "I have confidence" still echo in my heart today.

In Frau Vera I discovered that same clarity of vocation: "It is about nothing but Christ, and his compassion for the world." She would say, "We must live from the living Lord who heals the world," and often recalled this word from the Gospel: "You will see me; because I live, you also will live" (John 14:19b). She lived for this calling, to become the Bread of Life for the world.

Frau Vera was a true spiritual mother to me, as Mother Geneviève had been for her, but always within the freedom of personal responsibility. Others have been a great help in opening me to an understanding of the universality of our vocation, but Frau Vera played an irreplaceable role, just as quiet time alone with God is also irreplaceable.

From the early 1950s, Mother Geneviève and Frau Vera shared everything that was important in great depth. They enlarged this sharing to include both communities of women. In 1954 for example, Frau Vera, Brother Hans, and a dozen members of their community came to stay with us for the Ascension retreat given by Brother François of Taizé. Sister Vera is the *Wegbereiterin* (forerunner) of the community, meaning that she is the one who opened and prepared the way. Her love for humanity made a great impression on me. She often said to me, "Each human being has the innate capability for doing the worst," and "I know what compassion is because I am myself an impossible person."

Imshausen, a German Protestant community of brothers and sisters with its roots in World War II, and born just afterward, has a very unique history. We are very close to them because of these personal ties as well as their founding principles. In 1938 Frau Vera von Trott moved into the Untermühle, a house on the outskirts of Imshausen, on the estate where her mother had lived. There she served as a parish assistant for girls and the children of the region until the Nazi regime prohibited her work. During the war she gave shelter there to children sent to the countryside because of the bombings in the cities, to soldiers on leave like Hans Eisenberg, a theologian from the Russian front (later he would become Brother Hans), and to deserters who were trying to escape capture and imprisonment by the Americans. Immediately after the war the house became an orphanage.

To mark their jubilee of 50 years of living in community, working together to heal the wounds of the war, the brothers and sisters hosted a "debt forgiveness" celebration. "In the vulnerability of their old age the community radiates strength and gentleness—what a joy! The fruit of their humility today carries the seeds of the future," remarked one of our sisters. She was very moved, as many of us were, by all that this community has made possible for us on the road to healing after the ravages of the war; not to mention all that we have received through "the Cycle"[43] of prayer sent to us by Frau Vera. This is a method for remembering the great moments of Christ's life through the hours of the day, thus integrating the different aspects of daily life into a great liturgy of peace and unity.

The deep ties between our communities began with the visits between Mother Geneviève and Sister Vera: theirs was an intense spiritual bond existing between two very different people. Through the years Frau Vera, Brother Hans, and the sisters and brothers of Imshausen have been a source of renewal for many of us. I always felt supported by their prayers and their love. What I found there was a space, a large space, and a creative way of thinking, for wrestling with the questions of the moment important in the history of humanity, alongside a constant seeking for ways to live our vocation in God's and the world's present moment.

Visits between our two communities have never ceased. I rejoiced greatly in the recent visit by our novices to Imshausen, a visit made on the way to and then again on the way back from a commemorative visit to Buchenwald concentration camp. The following impressions were written by the group of novices after their 2006 pilgrimage:

> In these places [Imshausen, Herrenhaus] so dear to the von Trott family, it is impossible not to think of Adam von Trott, Dietrich Bonhoeffer, the Kreisau group,[44] and their willingness to work together to open a way for peace and liberty in their own country, an enterprise that cost them their lives. There one is face to face with their experiences of the war, the Holocaust, and resistance to an ideology that imprisons and kills, and one gains a better understanding of the poem "Who am I" by Bonhoeffer.[45] The suffering and absurdity of the concentration camp are beyond all reason.
>
> On the return from Buchenwald we had a discussion with the Community of Imshausen that sent us back once again to that burning question: complicity or responsible freedom? And along this painful road, are we to repent or to forgive? Brother Peter went with us in the rain to the cross erected in honor of

---

43. See chapter 2, "From the Desert to Communion."

44. A group of German dissidents centered on the estate of Helmuth James Graf von Moltke at Kreisau, Silesia (now Krzyżowa, Poland).

45. "Who Am I?" A poem from Bonhoeffer, *Letters and Papers from Prison.*

Adam von Trott and his companions. The requirement to "lay down one's life for one's friends"[46] and certain passages in our Rule now took on their full meaning.

To grasp the suffering of the victims, but also to sense that of the executioners, and empathize with both, and from this common ground to turn toward reconciliation through unceasing prayer for yesterday, today and tomorrow: this is what God asks of us in order to free us, reconcile us, and lead us toward life that is stronger than death. The Community of Imshausen is a constant reminder of this. At the foot of the cross, on this wind-beaten plateau, there is a sense of the presence of the God who suffers with each of us and causes us all, victim and executioner together, to pass from death unto life. Bread and wine set upon the altar: in the Eucharist celebrated that Sunday was recorded the past and the present of the Community of Imshausen, our experience at Buchenwald, and the love of Jesus on the cross. For a moment all became one: the history of the country, and beyond that, of our humanity, our entire humanity.

In this testimony of our novice sisters are outlined the profound concerns that tie our two communities together: finding our way along some of the darkest paths of this world, and traveling along them again and again in order to let the Light shine in that darkness.

The Winds of Renewal

We have already mentioned several of the people who have allowed themselves to be led by the Spirit, among them Mother Geneviève and the Abbé Paul Couturier. Is it not being open to the Spirit, and the charism of the person, that allows the Spirit to give fresh life to the church through new monastic or missionary communities? The Spirit often works in hidden ways, but also works from time to time in a dynamic way, awakening Christians in great numbers and causing them to become witnesses. The power of the Spirit seeks again and again to express itself in all the churches—in Rome, Constantinople, Canterbury, Geneva, and elsewhere. The Spirit works for the renewal of the church, often without our realizing it, through networks of men and women who have set out for the kingdom, leaving signs of communion today along the way.

Before his death, the Abbé Paul Couturier had known pastors touched by the awakening that occurred in the 1930s in the Ardèche, a region of

---

46. John 13:15.

France with a large Protestant population. Pastor Louis Dallière, working with other pastors, supported the charismatic movement while discouraging further divisions within the Reformed Church. Mother Geneviève greatly respected this man of God. So upon my arrival at Grandchamp in 1958, I went to his retreat center at Charmes-sur-Rhône in France for the Pentecost retreat. The theme was "The Holy Spirit, Reconciler," a message inspired by the Word of God and the teachings of the Fathers of the church. This gave me a solid foundation for all that I was called to experience afterwards.

Several of our sisters were then and are still today members of the Union of Prayer of Charmes, a fruit of this renewal movement. A number of the pastors who were part of it have been invited to lead Grandchamp's annual Pentecost retreats. All of them have been open both to the significance of Israel for the church and to ecumenism. That is why I went to Pastor Dallière looking for answers about Mary, Mother of the Lord. Back then, I was worried by the exaggerated proportions popular devotion to Mary sometimes took on among Catholics, which risked, I feared, overshadowing the importance of Christ. I wondered, "How far can we go in our open attitude with regard to the unity of the church?" Pastor Dallière knew how to calm my worries. He helped me to put into perspective certain forms of piety, to leave them on the sidelines, in order to make central the Mystery borne by Mary, daughter of Israel, who was steeped in the tradition of her people and mother of the Lord. The Reformers themselves, Luther, Calvin, Zwingli, had great respect and endless gratitude for Mary, the one who bore our Savior—Mary, image of the church. She who goes before us on the way and calls us to become in our turn the servants of the Lord holds an essential place in the Scriptures. Several years later, Vatican II and then the Groupe des Dombes produced important documents on Mary.[47] So, in 1995, when Pope John Paul II asked me to write a "Way of the Cross" for the Colosseum, I could say, with Mother Geneviève, "She hears the voice of Jesus: 'Mother, here is your son.' And tenderness fills her heart, the ineffable consolation of a love which reveals to her a different kind of maternity."[48]

The Catholic charismatic renewal began in the United States at Pittsburgh in 1967, coming out of a Protestant milieu, and then won over students and teachers at the University of Notre Dame before spreading to Europe and the world. The Union of Prayer of Charmes as well as several council fathers (Vatican II), considered the emergence of the Renewal as an answer to their prayers, a confirmation that a new Pentecost had begun with

---

47. Second Vatican Council, *Dogmatic Constitution on the Church*, chapter 8. Groupe des Dombes, *Mary in the Plan of God*.

48. Geneviève Micheli.

Vatican II. At the same time, the Union of Prayer of Charmes sent us invitations to international charismatic meetings in England, then in Belgium.

In the community, as in the church, the charismatic experience was greeted by some with enthusiasm, by others with fear. Years earlier, I had had a life-changing experience in the context of an awakening in Holland. With a group of sisters, I went to visit a small community of Poor Clares, friends of ours, where Father Caffarel[49] gave a talk on the outpouring of the Spirit. It was an important experience for everyone except me. I returned with a bad migraine due to an upset stomach. At first I was disappointed in the experience, which in reality helped me very much. As prioress I was very careful not to disturb the proper balance of the community.

The Union of Prayer persevered in its invitations: I went with another sister to the first large charismatic gathering in France, at Viviers.[50] There were five hundred participants, half Catholic, half Protestant, many of them priests or pastors. Since we were a little late, we heard them singing in tongues from a distance . . . it was like the sound of many waters (see Rev 14:2–3). Entering the large assembly room of the Seminary, I was astounded to sense the power of the Spirit at work; all of these people participating in a prayer of praise! I received no specific gifts at the Viviers meeting either, but something within me let go, opened, and I saw what the Spirit can do. It was real! I received fresh momentum for accomplishing the heavy task which was mine: courage and strength, and especially the vision of a church united! I also received a renewed wisdom, happy for what the sisters could receive in this movement, without discounting those to whom it did not speak. All of this took place in 1973 among Christians of several churches who were not in the habit of meeting together.

The diversity of reactions to the charismatic renewal in the community did not present an obstacle to hosting the first large charismatic meeting in French-speaking Switzerland at Grandchamp. People who had been touched by the renewal began to visit Grandchamp, among them Father Philibert Zobel, prior of Bec-Hellouin, and Father Jean-Baptiste Gourion,[51] a brother of that priory, who was later sent to Israel with Sister Ignace to found a monastery at Abu Ghosh. Both were a great support to our sisters

---

49. Henri Caffarel (1903–1996) was a French Catholic priest, the founder in 1938 of Teams of our Lady, formed to encourage and support Christian married spirituality as a way of holiness. He was an early leader in the French Catholic charismatic renewal, through his prayer gatherings and teachings.

50. See *Viviers 1973*.

51. First prior of Abu Ghosh, he was subsequently its Abbot, then became the auxiliary bishop of the Latin Patriarch Monsignor Sabbah, particularly responsible for the Catholic community of Hebrew expression. Deceased in 2005.

in Jerusalem, and their communities continue to be supportive. Others who visited us included Cardinal Suenens[52] and many other pastors and priests of the renewal.

The charismatic experience was a source of renewal for our common vocation, but the Spirit did not allow us to attach ourselves to it, or to turn inward to what we had been given through that experience. We integrated into our daily lives what we had received in the renewal, especially the understanding that the Spirit is present and at work everywhere. In particular, it opened the way toward evangelical nonviolence and "Evangelization of the Interior Life."[53] Like the disciples at Pentecost, we had been witnesses to extraordinary manifestations of the Spirit in the church. As the disciples had let themselves be led by the Spirit to hear their call in the world, we took care to allow the Spirit to act in our daily lives and hospitality: "If we live by the Spirit, let us also be guided by the Spirit" (Gal 5:25). And that is the sum total of our responsibility.

From Visitations to Visitations

In monastic life, the work of the Spirit generally does not make a lot of noise. Instead of the "many waters" of the Apocalypse, there is the manifestation of a still, small voice, as Elijah experienced it (1 Kgs 19:12). Since all monastic or missionary life is by definition inspired by the Spirit, it is "normal" that our respective community stories include many visitations. It is up to each of us to remember and commemorate them, with gratitude.

First, I would like to mention the encounter between Mother Geneviève and Mother Marie-Élisabeth de Wavrechin, the founder of the Benedictines of Sainte-Françoise-Romaine. That year, 1938, Geneviève Micheli was just one of the leaders of the silent retreats at Grandchamp. But already the Spirit was making use of their friendship in the Lord. On February 14, 1939, the future Mother Geneviève brought Sister Marguerite to their monastery, where Marguerite received a vision and call to community life during the vespers service.[54] The conversation with Mother de Wavrechin that followed confirmed it: sharing a common life could begin at Grandchamp. This exchange bore much fruit!

---

52. Belgian leader in the Catholic charismatic renewal. Suenens, *Une Nouvelle Pentecôte*.

53. Simone Pacot and the Bethasda sessions. See chapter 2, "Reconciliation and Gospel Nonviolence."

54. See chapter 1, "The Great Field (*Grand Champ*) of the World."

Later, in 1956, strengthened by their profound friendship and their shared vision for unity, these two women planned an ecumenical retreat on "Women in the Life of the Church." For sisters who were leaders in their Catholic, Protestant, Anglican, and Orthodox[55] communities to meet together for a retreat was an extraordinary event in the church. It would not be until 1967 that another such gathering would take place, this time thanks to Mother Claire of the Congregation of Sisters of Saint-André. Since 1966 these sisters had lived in the village of Taizé, helping the brothers with hospitality. We came to know them through this collaboration, especially Mother Claire and Mother Tarcisius, the novice mistress, and then through other sisters of the community. A woman filled with the spirit of unity, Mother Claire initiated two inter-confessional meetings of men and women monastics, pastors, and priests, in their mother house at Ramegnies-Chin, Belgium. She organized them together with Brother Roger of Taizé, Father Nicolas, prior of Chevtogne, and Mother Marie of Grandchamp. All of them were on the road toward a church in full communion, yet were unable to share together in the Eucharist. But monastery doors were opening; mutual hospitality was beginning. As John Paul II emphasized thirty years later at the Synod on consecrated life, in the document *Vita consecrata*,[56] "I entrust to the monasteries of contemplative life the spiritual ecumenism of prayer, conversion of heart, and charity." We are called to put these words into practice in the 21st century.

The Spirit prepared other visitations as well. In 1970 Father Hernando Garcia,[57] director of the Ecumenical Center in Madrid, arrived at our door with Bishop Emilianos Timiadis, a delegate to the World Council of Churches, representing the Ecumenical Patriarch. He asked us to host the first of the Inter-confessional International Meetings of Religious (E.I.I.R.). Today monks also participate in these meetings, originally organized for women. This first meeting was well beyond our means, but we said "yes" and asked our neighbors to help us with the hospitality. This gathering was life changing, as was the meeting at Bossey the following year. Several participants caught the ecumenical bug. Among them was the Secretary of the International Union of Major Superiors, who later asked me to participate at a round table on ecumenical prayer during their international meeting in Rome in 1973. I took part in a panel with Mother Marie of Bethlehem and Sister Mariangela, a Franciscan Missionary of Mary. I remember that

---

55. Mother Eudoxie of Bussy-en-Other.

56. John Paul II, "Vita consecrata, no. 101." http://www.vatican.va/roman_curia/congregations/ccscrlife/documents/hf_jp-ii_exh_25031996_vita-consecrata_en.html.

57. Julián Garcia Hernando, founder of Misioneras de la Unidad and author of *Pluralismo religioso en España*. Later he became a bishop.

the preparation for this round table was difficult, because I was already accustomed to ecumenical meetings where there was prayer. What could I say on prayer that would be new? Fortunately, the charismatic meeting at Viviers had given me a whole new perspective: I had seen the church united in its praise and adoration of the Glory of God. I had experienced in the depths of my being the scandal of the division of our separated Eucharists. And I talked about the Eucharist as the ecumenical prayer par excellence. One beautiful fruit of this visitation was my first audience with the Holy Father. Others would follow.

Another initiative began in 1971. The Swedish Pastor Bengt Thur Molander, in charge of the department of *Diakonia* at the WCC, organized a meeting at Bossey for the leaders of deaconesses and missionary sisters with the leaders of contemplative communities who were already linked by prayer and friendship (Mother Marie-Therese, Carmelite in Mazille, Sister Elisabeth of Pomeyrol, Mother Marie of the Monastic Family of Bethlehem, and me, prioress of Grandchamp). Deaconesses and monastics deeply understand one another, since we are all contemplatives. The meeting was such a success that the participants wanted to form a small ecumenical group so that the spirit of this meeting could bear fruit in the churches. That is how Kaire was born. While recognizing that men and women monastics have a common vocation, we women have perhaps the special ability to experience an especially fruitful visitation.

The very existence of Kaire demonstrates this, including the name chosen: *kaire*, Greek for "rejoice," is the first word of the angel's greeting to Mary. This name, proposed by Mother Marie, a sister of Bethlehem, was adopted immediately. Mother Claire of the Congregation of the Sisters of Saint-André became our secretary, a role she passed to Grandchamp for a brief time in the 1980s. Thus our ties with that community continued to grow through Kaire, becoming for both of us a true visitation. One of the first meetings of Kaire took us to Corrymeela, the nonviolence center in Northern Ireland. There we met with women touched by the charismatic renewal, both Catholics and Protestants, compelled by the Spirit to act together to resist violence, and to share their passion for reconciliation against all odds.

The prehistory of Grandchamp attests to other important visitations that are still signs for us today. Among them is Mother Geneviève's encounter with Sister Antoinette Butte at Saint-Germain-en-Laye, where the Community of Pomeyrol began. These words from Sister Antoinette reveal the challenge of our meetings at that time: "The unity of the church is not something to do, but to recognize. We must recognize it." How true this still is today, and what a calling! We also are indebted to the Community of

Pomeyrol for introducing our first sisters to the realities of communal life before they experienced it themselves. And there have been so many other visitations through the years; what a gift.

Our ties with Pomeyrol made possible another important encounter, this time with the community of sisters of the Monastery of the Epiphany at Eygalières, who live in the same area (Provence). One day, Sister Renée, while on a visit to Pomeyrol, drove one of the sisters who was convalescing to that small new monastic community that was still finding its identity. Arriving there, the sister was disturbed to find that she was being put into the care of Catholic sisters. How would that be possible? Such a thing occurring in spite of the troubled history of several centuries of the Protestants of this region! Sister Renée met the founder of the community, Sister Simone, for the first time. Their Catholic community incorporated elements of the Syrian and Byzantine Orthodox liturgies into their monastic life and prayer after Vatican II. The sisters were encouraged in this direction by, among others, Father Corbon whom we knew well through our fraternity in Lebanon. Some years later, they were also challenged by the Jewish tradition, "the root that supports"[58] us, and without which progress toward unity cannot move forward. Several elements of our own liturgy are inspired by theirs. Their way of life, with an emphasis on solitude, helped us to revisit the basics of our own calling to silence and solitude. They also practice an open hospitality, allowing guests to share meals in silence with the community. A profound fellowship was created between our two communities, with a very fruitful reciprocity: Sister Renée spent several months there, then Sister Albertine, who did iconography with Sister Claire, and many others, made visits to Eygalières. Several sisters of Eygalières also made visits of various durations to Grandchamp. This exchange continues today.

Our first encounter with Sister Magdeleine, foundress of the Little Sisters of Jesus, also left a deep impression. Sister Marie-Catherine of the Little Sisters of Jesus remembers this encounter very well. It was at El Abiod in Algeria:

> Between these two women I sensed more than respect and friendship, but a sort of complicity and deep understanding. In her usual way, Little Sister Magdeleine went straight to the point and asked me this: "When we start fraternities in Switzerland, where would be a good place for a workers' fraternity?" I immediately replied, "At Bienne!" Little Sister Magdeleine looked surprised, then turned to Mother Geneviève, who smiled and said to her, "You win!" And in my presence she asked Mother

---

58. Rom 11:18.

Geneviève to watch over their first steps at Bienne, near Grandchamp—and "when we are there," she said, "come to visit as a mother would," in her place, since she would be traveling the world.

The fraternity of Little Sisters began at Bienne on Christmas of 1953, and our sisters started a fraternity in Algeria the following year. That same year several Little Sisters from Hong Kong, Algeria, and the Congo came for an extended stay at Grandchamp. These in-person visits are as necessary as our prayers for one another. Just as the visit of Mary to Elizabeth that inspired the Magnificat encouraged them and gave them the strength to follow God's will, these visitations between communities make tangible the work of the Spirit in our communities, increase our desire for unity, and bring us a step closer to that unity.

One other visitation was very important for me: the arrival of a young man at Grandchamp toward the end of 1967. His name was Enzo Bianchi. He was preparing to found the Community of Bose and had come to see how Grandchamp did things. I was just beginning my new responsibilities and was working alongside Mother Marie. He returned a year later, in November 1968, asking if we could send a sister to Bose to live for a time among the women who had joined the founding brothers of the community. I gave myself a night to reflect and pray, and in the morning, without hesitating, I sent one of our novices who spoke Italian. The communion between us, which began then, has continued to deepen. Today one of their sisters comes from time to time to teach our novices on various themes related to coenobitic monasticism in the early church. Another of their sisters wrote several icons for our chapel. One of the first brothers of Bose, educated at the Faculty of Theology in Neuchâtel and called to live in Israel with two other brothers, continues to be an important support for the sisters in our fraternity there. Father Enzo himself likes to come to Grandchamp to give lectures and retreats. His visits are another example of the great joy of fruitful visitations.

Even though we know that our lives are led by the Spirit, we are sometimes tempted to take this presence for granted. Fortunately, the Spirit watches over us and wakes us up! As an illustration, in 1983 two young monks from Bec-Hellouin asked to make a retreat at Grandchamp for the Week of Prayer for Christian Unity. At the time, this Week of Prayer did not have the same importance for us that it does now. After all, we had ecumenical gatherings all year long. Thanks to these two brothers, the full meaning of the Week of Prayer again became clear to us. At the end of their retreat the two brothers, one of whom was originally from Belfast, received the call, each independently, to live their ecumenical vocations in Northern Ireland. Their Father Abbot, the impressive Dom Paul Grammont, immediately gave his approval. The challenges have been many as they have traveled this road. In 1987 the two brothers were recalled to Bec and in 1998, this time accompanied by three other monks, they were again sent to Northern Ireland. In 2004, during the Week of Prayer, their monastery at Sainte Croix (Rostrevor), near the border between Northern Ireland and the Republic of Ireland, was dedicated. What a celebration! How moving it was to participate in an act of repentance and to hear the testimony of a Methodist pastor who lost his brother and sister-in-law in an IRA attack, and that of a Catholic father whose son was killed by loyalist paramilitaries—gripping testimonies of the way of forgiveness. Their monastery is truly a place of reconciliation and of ecumenical encounter.

Pilgrimages, visitations: why these journeys, these encounters and others, as well as all those we have personally? What meaning do they have for our common life? To hold fast to prayer inspired by monasticism and at the same time cultivate the ground in order to prepare the way toward peace and reconciliation—this is the challenge of our lives set apart, of the witness we are called to bear as communities. I was confirmed in this inner attitude while still the mistress of novices, by Sister Vera and Brother Hans of Imshausen, who never hesitated to reach out to Grandchamp and Taizé. Sister Vera herself had come to understand her vocation in this way, in part through her encounter with Mother Geneviève. Over time I grasped ever more clearly that in all things we must adopt a spirit of pilgrimage and of visitation. Those paths open us to the fruitfulness of the Spirit.

CHAPTER 4

Testimonies of "Otherness" within the One Love

In Places of Brokenness

THE ECUMENICAL VOCATION OF the Community of Grandchamp, its call to reconciliation, becomes concrete in its ties to the world: the connection of prayer but also the connections embodied in daily life. Through the presence of sisters in Algeria and a fraternity in Israel (Sainte-Élisabeth), the community goes to places of brokenness, places where the children of Abraham often struggle to recognize and respect others with confidence. In the Netherlands, their presence is more a sharing of their grounding in God and relating to those on the margins of the church through creative Bible study.[1]

Sainte-Élisabeth Fraternity,[2] near Jerusalem

Testimony of Sister Maatje, who has spent twenty years in this fraternity

Our presence *in* Israel is a presence in the Holy Land, a land which is larger than just the state of Israel. Being present *to* Israel is being present to the Jewish people, of whom there are many more than the Jews living here. Our presence in the State of Israel is a presence to all its citizens, including the 18 percent who are Arabs. To be present to Jerusalem, a holy city for the

---

1. Texts collected by Marie-Laure (see introduction).
2. Closed in 2014.

three Abrahamic religions, is to be present to the Jewish world that lives its Jewishness openly; to the Muslim world, to which the great majority of those living in East Jerusalem belong; to the universal church, present here in all of its forms, including the local churches, both Hebrew-speaking and Arab-speaking.

All of these worlds are split by divisions. Living here in this way one is always rejoicing with one group and mourning with another. It is multicolored! But the basic color of the fraternity is that of prayer for unity, peace, and reconciliation. Being present here also means living near the source, the roots of our faith in Judaism, always trying to understand it better.

Our vocation of reconciliation implies being in contact with the two peoples who live in the Holy Land and refusing to take sides. The strong emphasis we place on intercession is nourished by our relationships with people from both sides who work for peace and reconciliation, encounter, and dialogue, as well as by our contacts in multiple churches.

We try to be a simple presence of friendship. We visit Palestinian groups working for nonviolence and for the resolution of conflicts in Bethlehem. We have contacts with the Rabbis for Human Rights, the women of Checkpoint Watch, the ecumenical Fraternity of Theological Research (Jewish–Christian dialogue), and others. We participate in worship services in synagogues, especially on Jewish feast days, and we have contacts in the neighboring village.

Since 1973 we have lived in a building whose chapel dates from the time of the crusades, and other parts of the house from the fifteenth century. The house is on the grounds of the Franciscan monastery of Saint John of the Desert, on the West side of Jerusalem. According to tradition, John the Baptist lived here until he was thirty and began his mission: calling people to conversion and baptism in the Jordan.

At the Franciscan monastery is the cave and the spring where John is said to have lived. Our chapel, according to tradition, contains the empty tomb of his mother, Saint Elisabeth, dug for her by John the Baptist himself. Our residence belongs to the Franciscans and so our presence here is in itself an ecumenical sign! We offer simple hospitality in silence, thanks to two hermitages placed at our disposal. Everyone is welcome: Christians, Jews, Muslims. All are welcome to participate in our daily liturgy. This diversity is a joy to us.

Presence in Algeria

*Testimony of Sister Renée,[3]
in Algeria since 1955*

As I remember our beginnings, I am so grateful for the welcome we received when our fraternity moved into a slum on the outskirts of Algiers in 1955. The revolution for the independence of the Algerian people had just begun. We were not prepared, knowing neither the colonial context, the language, the culture, nor the religion, Islam. In spite of this, the people welcomed us as friends, as sisters, and took care of us—we who were strangers! Several months later we learned that without our knowledge they had organized guard duty around our shed each night so that no one would bother us. They were masters of openness and generosity.

Now, only two of us remain, elderly sisters living a humble presence in the midst of a young population. Our friends accept us in our fragility and are happy in their awareness of our presence and happiness in their midst.

The church is made up of Christians of diverse confessions, small, but persevering in prayer and service to the people. We try to live together as reconciled persons. Algeria is an Islamic country. All of our friends are Muslims. God is present in their lives, but they too must deal with their own diversity and elements of reductionist fundamentalism. So they share in our prayer for reconciliation with all their hearts!

For now it is given to us to live in Algeria, a few Christian brothers and sisters with some Muslim friends—all together, seekers of God. Having formed small fellowship groups, we get to know each other in depth, learn to respect our differences, and trust one another. We support each other in moving toward God. We pray for peace.

These groups are small oases in the desert of violence, indifference, and negation of the other. They help us to restore our vitality and recover the impetus we need to keep moving forward. Others, pilgrims like us, come to quench their thirst for truth and fellowship. These groups are small drops of hope, seeds which need protection so that they may grow. They are an active prayer that all people may recognize one another as brothers and sisters, even in their differences, and that peace may come to this land.

Each year our visit to Grandchamp is a precious opportunity for sharing our experiences in depth with all the sisters. The same is true for visits by one or another of our Algerian friends. Our ties are constantly maintained through the year by various written or audio exchanges with our sisters

---

3. Died 2014.

about meetings, retreats, and efforts to find ways to live Gospel nonviolence, as well as everything essential for our community life.

Though we are always connected by prayer, this coming and going keeps us in fellowship, sharing each other's lives openly and transparently. Year after year we have reconfirmed this need at the annual council: though living very different realities, we remain united.

Testimony of Sister Anne-Geneviève, in Algeria since 1958

I live my presence in Algeria as a Presence of Christ among "the least of these,"[4] in continuity with the vision of the first sisters when they decided, in the 1950s, to send two or three sister to live in fraternity in various places.

This is a long-term presence, of the community since 1954, and for me personally since 1958—nearly fifty years. I have experienced deep friendships here through joys, challenges and sorrows, deaths and births, even a simple shared cup of coffee. These friendships endure, even though I am no longer in the slum or in the "assimilated" quarter. Since the "black decade" of the 1990s, I have been living within the enclosure of the Protestant parish in the city.

I remember very well my first encounter with the Algerian people. Upon arrival I discovered that these very poor people around me were Muslims—in other words, of a faith different from my own. Their faith was lived very simply. It filled their lives. I felt fully at home there, for prayer is the heart of our vocation: "Praying among other pray-ers," as the Trappist monks of Tibhirine used to say. From the beginning I experienced the mutual respect of each season, from Ramadan to Lent, and all the others, experiencing the presence of God, communion, and rejuvenation in each of our daily exchanges, and that continues.

This immersion in the Muslim world happens in specific groups with Muslim friends, Sufis and others, who desire to learn about the faith of the other and to pray together. The Ribat es Salam (Link of Peace) begun at the monastery of Tibhirine continues to meet. There are also encounters with women friends—less formal but not less profound. In these I sense the expansion and enrichment of my horizons through experiencing the faith of the other.

My presence in Algeria is also a presence in a diverse but united church where we welcome one another and share a fellowship that speaks of the unity desired by God, both in our prayer and in the worship service. This

---

4. Matt 25:40.

church, with its enthusiastic awakening to the Christian faith (especially evangelical) by young Muslims, touches me deeply, as many of them wish to join the Protestant Church, often in order to have legal standing . There is a lot of work to be done in a spirit of communion, for these evangelical Christians tend to be fiercely independent of all "institutions."

In all that I experience, I feel strongly connected to the community, even if the form has changed, for after many years in fraternity I now live alone. But there is the daily connection with Grandchamp through the prayer of our liturgy. Our vocation to unity is expressed there, as much in the church as in our relationships with Muslim friends. This reality is important. Our presence in Algeria, Sister Renée's and mine, is a good eyewitness source of information for the community, about this Muslim world, which is becoming ever more important everywhere. In all of this, the community supports us, welcomes us, and shares the experiences we have here.

Presence in the Netherlands

Testimony of Sister Christianne, who arrived in Woudsend in 1986

It was in the middle of the 1980s, after a visit of Maria de Groot to Grandchamp, that I joined in the spiritual adventure of Flearstift, a small "school" of biblical interpretation in a women's context, a space of welcome and encounter in all of our diversity and poverty. At that time our community was opening itself to feminism and the work being accomplished at Woudsend, as well as the spirit in which it was done, was very inspiring.

When I consider my experiences of immersion during my presence at Flearstift, the first thing that comes to mind is certainly immersion in the biblical texts featuring women. This is done in order to experience, in the confrontation of the texts with our own lives, the message of these texts for women today: women who are searching, inside or outside the church.

I also became immersed in the stream of liberation theology, of which feminism is an important part. This happened naturally through the movement Vrouw en Geloof (Women and Faith) in base communities and in some parishes.

Then there is the immersion in this mass of individuals who are disappointed in ecclesial institutions but are passionately drawn to Jesus and his message. They are on their way out of the church, if they have not already left it. Today they make up what one could call a "church outside the walls."

All who take part in this interpretive reading of texts done in a variety of voices and hearts are given the opportunity to experience a form of contemplative reading. By creating a space of silence and freedom, this liberating reading allows new insights to emerge, including sometimes unexpected interpretations. It also allows for a shared empathic experience. In its way, it answers Nicodemus's question: "How can one be born from above?" (see John 3:1–7).

Since our work is fundamentally about understanding the message of the Bible as women, this kind of study is always directly engaged with the questions of our society which can be translated, in the context of Flearstift, through a series of questions: How can we express the good news in the language of today's men and women? In an always changing world, how can we remain followers of Christ? How can we make sure that our founding texts retain a Gospel freshness and a liberating, thirst-quenching power? How can we live daily life with a God who is constantly evolving in his never-ending search for his creatures? And how do we live joyfully with questions without always seeking to cling to certain answers? Yes, the question is, how do we cultivate joy and hope?

Finally, in the footsteps of Abraham and Sarah, how do we keep moving toward our deepest desire? Sharing with the community my experiences in the Netherlands has been a learning experience for all of us. Hitching the little boat of Flearstift to the great *Arche* (Ark) of Grandchamp has required a great respect for persons, shared stories, and a certain flexibility and creativity, if not spiritual boldness. It has called for freedom as well: that freedom given by the Spirit.

In this link between the North Sea and the banks of Lake Neuchâtel, slowly, timidly, a story has been woven. The spirituality of Grandchamp, a spirituality of openness and reconciliation, has found its place in the daily experience of Flearstift and in the life of its small groups. And since life is about sharing, this enrichment did not happen only in one direction. From the coast of the North Sea to the banks of Lake Neuchâtel, waves never cease their coming and going, enabling a dialogue on diversity. Thanks to this dialogue, we all feel caught up in a movement that leads us ever onward. A spiritual adventure has taken shape, with one foot in the church, one foot in the world, and both feet in the Scriptures!

The Daughters of Abraham

At Grandchamp, *L'Arche* chapel is a place of peace. Men and women passing through from all over the world never cease telling us so. This space has subtle traces of the friendship in God which unites all the children of Abraham. Best of all is their presence at the services. In this section a few of these women offer their testimonies.

When a stone is thrown into the water the ripples spread farther and farther, getting larger as they go. It is the same with all spiritual families. From the very beginning of our community, men and women felt at home with our spirituality while still feeling called to work in the world. Martha Westphal, the convener of our Servants of Unity, writes in this section on their origins and current activities. Barbara Kwast introduces us below to the spirit of the Third Order of Unity, another group associated with Grandchamp.

Testimony of a Jewish Woman

An excerpt from the testimony of Dina, an Israeli woman living near our Fraternity of Sainte-Élisabeth

"A good way to know God: talk to his friends, for this will be to your great advantage," writes Teresa of Avila. How much greater an advantage there would be in not only talking with them but in praying, working, sharing meals, crying, laughing, and being silent with friends of God, a whole community of them, every day for nearly two years! Such has been the blessing I received when I was welcomed by the sisters of Grandchamp as one of their volunteers in 2002 and allowed to share in their life.

As a Jewish woman from Israel, I did not know what to expect in a contemplative monastery. It is marvelous to realize that ever since my arrival I have felt safe and secure, very welcome, and—strangely enough—at home. Not a single sister tried to convert me! I had to revise my ideas about Christians. To my great surprise, I found at Grandchamp a great respect for Judaism, affection for Israel: on Saturday nights a menorah in the chapel, sisters who speak and read Hebrew . . .

The sisters planned my schedule so that I could have a day of rest on the Sabbath. They anticipated my needs with regard to Jewish feast days. Sabbath candles and flowers were placed on my doorstep that day, matzos for the week of Passover, two "tablets" of stone with the Ten Commandments, and branches of four "species," and a sukkah branch for the Feast of Tabernacles (Sukkoth); they drove me to the synagogue for Yom Kippur services and for the Passover Seder. The "miracle of the oil" happened when a sister bent the community's nutrition rules to make pancakes with oil for dessert at Hanukkah.

What makes me want to return to Grandchamp whenever I can? One reason is the sense of time and space, which is so different from that of the world. Monastic life has its own rhythm. The bell calls us to prayer and to meals. Time is marked by the liturgy. A night and a day, time of silence and of solitude, and then a time of communion.

Each volunteer is accompanied on her spiritual journey by a designated sister. Mine allowed me to open myself up and to become a pilgrim on the way. It was hard work for the two of us. She has become a friend for life. What a blessing! Becoming aware of the events which have marked my life means that nothing is as it was before . . . nor is my opinion of Christians.

Testimony of a Muslim Woman

Lalia, from Algeria, a friend of the community for more than 50 years

My meeting with the sisters of Grandchamp remains a miracle of God, the One who guides us all. In this slum on the outskirts of Algiers, we never thought we would find sisters like these, so full of goodness and love for neighbor. Our meeting was immediately positive and later meetings with sisters who came after the first ones has only made our circle of friendship and sharing grow larger.

After six years of friendship with the sisters in Algiers, I made my first trip to Grandchamp. And there I found what I had been looking for since forever. God had guided me well. Grandchamp, a vast welcoming space where one encounters so many differences and at the same time so many similarities: warmth, conversation, joy, happiness, and especially their sincere faith, worn so serenely on the trusting faces of the sisters.

They welcomed me with sisterly affection and with such joy that it has stayed with me and will forever. I have found there so much wisdom and love, so many enriching exchanges and comfort. The younger sisters, so alive, seem like quiet but active and efficient bees. The greatest gift was, and still is, the great wooden chapel, like a sea going vessel which seemed to be taking us toward infinity. The beautiful and comforting prayers have entered my heart. They have carried me through many trials and long illnesses. God is present everywhere and envelops us in his gentle light. Grandchamp, a place of peace, comfort, faith, joy, and happiness, is a place where we can meet the other without fear but always with hope for taking steps toward one another. My encounter with the sisters in the slums of Algiers, where for the love of God they gave themselves with confidence and abandon, in joy and serenity, is the greatest gift God has given me. Thank you, and in the love of God we remain united, always in hope and faith that God will keep us on the true path that leads toward him, toward his will, and toward the light.

From the bottom of my heart, I am grateful to those who are my sisters. I remain close to them in sisterly love. I am happy to have been with them as we prayed for Brother Roger of Taizé. May he rest in peace in the glory of God.

"Praises to God, Compassionate and Merciful—Lord of Judgment. It is you whom we adore and it is you whom we ask for help. Direct us in the straight way, in the way of those whom you have approved and keep us from the way of those whom you have disapproved for their sins." Amen.[5]

The Spiritual Family of Grandchamp

Servants of Unity

Martha Westphal, convener

At Grandchamp, there are lots of trees: fruit trees, flowering trees, trees hundreds of years old, European and exotic trees, ash, lime, ginkgo, apple, pear, cherry trees . . . this variety rather reflects that of the community and other groups that have come into being from it. All are nourished by one and the same earth, and draw from the same source.

So it is for the Servants of Unity, born out of the intuition and hope of two people: Mother Geneviève of Grandchamp and Brother Roger of Taizé. At the end of the 1950s, Brother Roger was hearing about the difficulties experienced by Czech monks, nuns, and religious people in living out their vocation in a country where the Church had been reduced to silence. It became clear to him that the only way for them to survive was to live out their vocation discreetly, on their own.

At the same time, Brother Roger wondered if it was suitable in Western countries to offer the possibility of making life vows to men who did not have a call to community life. These brothers would live out their vocation, on their own, in their working life right there where they lived. He wrote a text for this purpose called "Servants of Unity."[6]

---

5. Qu'ran, *Sūrat Al-Fātiḥah* (opening prayer).
6. 1959. Gradually he gave up this project: leading a new community as well as trying to form a new group for lay brothers seemed too difficult to him at the time.

As for Mother Geneviève, she saw single women coming to the Community of Grandchamp who evidently had a vocation to contemplative prayer but not to community life. These were often widows or divorced people as well as unmarried women. So, Br. Roger's text was adopted as a basis—we call it the "Basic Text"—and as a Rule of Life for these women. Here are some sentences from the beginning of this text:

> In view of visibly uniting Christians separated by century-long divisions, we need to support men (women) to live out their vocation in their own church and life situation, in a society where people have become deaf to the Gospel, partly because of the inconsistency of our Christian divisions: nothing spectacular, but people whom Christ himself has inspired to live out the call to the visible unity of Christians in the one church of Jesus Christ, in the here and now. Only by living a hidden life with Christ in God can one persevere day after day, for the call to unity lived out to the full involves a struggle both within and without.

It was Rosette Genton and the first group of women who were responsible for exploring how to discern and to express this vocation, helped by Mother Geneviève and Roman Catholic women who belonged to religious congregations or secular institutes. Thus the ecumenical dimension was there from the start. The vocation of the Servant of Unity, today, can be described as one way of living out a life dedicated to the Lord without any outer sign that distinguishes that person from those amongst whom she lives. So, it is a contemplative life right in the world, marked by a solitude that is wholly turned to the kingdom of God. This solitude is accepted for the sake of the unity of believers that will only be fully realized when God is all in all and when it is at the service of all. This unity of believers also implies unity of all humanity in a creation that is reconciled, as well as the inner unity that is so necessary for people to accept others in their differences.

This vocation is lived out in a spirit of attentiveness to the Word of God, to the people around us. It is lived out in solitude and with receptive discernment for the signs of God's presence in the world and for his call to us to work with him in his plan for the whole of creation. We live our Baptism commitment through the three traditional, monastic promises of chastity in celibacy, poverty and obedience, whether they be vows taken publicly or in the heart. In our day this can seem a mad, unbearable demand, but we receive it as a gift offered to us, and we embark upon it with Christ and in his prayer: "That they may all be one . . . so that the world may believe that you have sent me" (John 17:21).

So we always seek this communion with Christ and the Father through the Holy Spirit, by listening to the Word, by prayer, and sharing in Holy Communion, for that is where the real source of our consecrated life lies. There are also visits, meetings, and exchanges with other Servants, as well as the annual week together and occasional weekends and meetings with a minister, priest, or religious from outside. We are scattered in many countries, but we have a minimum of structure to link us with one another: there are the times together, the circular letters, visits, and telephone calls.

An elected "Collegiate Group" is responsible for the running of the whole. These people see that decisions taken in the various meetings are carried through and they are attentive to what the other Servants say. The "Recueillante," or contact person, is elected by the whole group and is charged with the Collegiate group to keep the unity of this body which we form as Servants of Unity. She keeps in touch with Grandchamp and in particular with the prioress, especially when a new member wishes to make her commitment. The Community of Grandchamp is our church reference point together with our chaplains, both Protestant and Catholic. The Servants of Unity are thus born out of this terrain that is common to Grandchamp and Taizé, and are rooted in a similar spirituality of joy, simplicity, and mercy.

Why did we start by mentioning the apple trees of Grandchamp? In a text called "The Parable of the Apple Tree,"[7] Daniel Bourguet has a conversation with an apple tree! After noting that the apple tree never feeds on its own apples, as these are for others to enjoy, he asks again: "Dear apple tree, tell me just one more thing . . . what is your food?" – "On this point I will not tell you everything," replied the tree. "Just know that my food is given to me in secret. I draw it with roots you cannot see and my roots have to remain hidden; with those I draw my nourishment in the shadows of the earth, all the time. Without this food, I would not produce any apples. Know too that my fruit comes from what I draw with my roots and that is the reason no doubt that the fruit looks nothing like me. In fact the fruit doesn't come from me at all. That's enough explanation just remember that it is the same with you human beings. What you need in order to love is drawn from God in the secret place of your prayer. I shall not tell you any more: apply yourself to prayer and you will be covered in fruit!" To this, we as Servants of Unity can say, "Amen."[8]

---

7. Bourguet, *Dieu au cœur de nos vies,* 22–27.
8. www.grandchamp.org. Servants of Unity, English translation.

The Third Order of Unity

An excerpt from the testimony of Barbara Kwast

The Third Order of Unity has just celebrated its 50th anniversary. It is made up of men and women who promise to live according to the spirituality of Grandchamp, drawing on the Rule for their orientation toward life.

After twenty years of life in a different culture, I came to Grandchamp for the first time in 1985. In Ethiopia, my work as a midwife was both blessed and anxiety producing because of the poverty of the women, the social injustice in which they live, their high mortality rate, and the terrible famine. My personal fountain of life, that of which the prophet Isaiah speaks, the "spring whose waters never fail,"[9] was by that time a mere trickle!

Here at Grandchamp there is a fountain from which water flows abundantly: and Jesus said, "Let anyone who is thirsty come to me and . . . drink" (John 7:37–39). He was referring to the Spirit that would fill those who would believe in him. The warm welcome by my designated sister for that visit, as for all the others, the feeling of being welcome in this monastic community with an ecumenical vocation, the silence, their spirituality, their liturgy (*Louange des Jours*), all of this was a balm to my soul. I could be myself; I had found a place where I could be renewed.

For a long time I had been feeling a desire for a life and service more profoundly rooted in Christ, and the need for fellowship with a community that felt itself called to truly be a "large field," a *grand champ*. My wanderings had taken me to diverse cultures and religions in Africa, Asia, and Latin America, and had led me to work among Christians—Protestants, Catholics, Orthodox—as well as Jews, Buddhists, and Muslims.

In 1986, providentially, the work schedule at the World Health Organization in Geneva made it possible for me to spend several days at Grandchamp, usually on personal "accompanied" retreats, but also for feasts such as Christmas and Easter. I prayed the *Louange des Jours*, but without consciously living the Rule. It was not until 1998, in the Netherlands, that I met the Third Order of Unity and discovered its connection with Grandchamp. It was then that the Rule came to life for me. With each cautious step I felt a desire growing within me to join the Third Order of Unity.

The Rule of Grandchamp and Taizé starts with "Pray and work that God may reign." Paul says, "The kingdom of God is justice and peace, and joy in the Holy Spirit" (Rom 14:17). Welcomed into the Third Order, in connection with Grandchamp, living and working profoundly rooted in prayer;

---

9. Isa 58:11.

all of this fills me with wonder and gratitude. I also find there the hope of ongoing spiritual growth.

During the last twenty years, my work has been prayed over by the sisters and later by the Third Order in the Netherlands as well. Each visit to Grandchamp or to the Sonnenhof has become for me a homecoming where I find love and joy. And finding women from Africa in the community today, as well as the extension of the Third Order into Benin, warms my heart.

Learning to live by the Rule has opened me to new horizons and has made me aware that the Rule can, and is intended to be, liberating. Rooted in the Word and the love of God, it is a tangible support, an encouragement, maybe even a challenge. My priorities are ecumenism lived daily and the Eucharist, and I hope always to hold firmly to both.

I realize that prayer of the *Louange des Jours* and reading the daily Biblical texts with Grandchamp deepens our communion and emphasizes the importance of contemplation alongside action. Finding peace and inner unity in the love of Christ in the silence of contemplative prayer is a pure grace of God. "Become filled with the spirit of the Beatitudes: joy, mercy, simplicity."[10] These have given a new dimension to my life. Surrounded by so many experiencing poverty, loss, and misery, I have often prayed for the blessings of the Beatitudes to fill their lives, but neglected to receive them for myself. Inner joy was especially difficult for me, as if it were blocked. My way of living in solidarity with those in the developing world experiencing great injustice, especially when it came to women—injustice that I believed I should take upon myself and carry with them—made me joyless. But the mercy of God comes to carry my burdens! I can leave them at the foot of the cross, walking through the desert toward Easter, because God has said, "Behold, I am doing a new thing; now it springs forth, do you not perceive it?" (Isa 43:19). Yes, I receive as a gift this new connection through the Rule which reinforces my fellowship with the community of sisters of Grandchamp so that I may remain faithful to my promise.

At the Heart of the World

Solidarity with the world also involves each sister in her own otherness. Sister Anne-Emmanuelle tells of her experiences in Porto Alegre during the Ninth Assembly of the World Council of Churches in Brazil.—a powerful experience of the church, while Sister Janny speaks of the Fraternity of the Suffering Servant, in which several sisters participate as prayer partners.

---

10. The third rule of spiritual direction from the *Rule of Taizé (1961)*, 8.

A Look at Porto Alegre

Sister Anne-Emmanuelle, present at the 2006 Assembly

For us, the World Council of Churches is, at the level of the universal church, the "parable of community" that we seek to live out together at Grandchamp as a small cell of that church.

The Assembly was a colorful and vibrant celebration, full of the life of God. That is my most important impression of Porto Alegre: that life is stronger than anything else. At the same time, it was a place where the cries of suffering could be heard and were transformed because they were gathered into this fountain of life that springs from the sharing of faith.

I will remember Porto Alegre for the rich blessing of encounters with many others who were also there seeking God. How beautiful it was! And how it gives one hope to realize that everywhere, the struggle is the same to make the world a more humane place where all can live and thrive. Suffering has no borders, but neither does the power of life!

Another essential and welcome step was taken by this assembly toward creating a process for arriving at consensus decisions. It establishes a better method for listening, for dialogue, and for seeking agreement together. There are no longer winners and losers, but a desire to strive together for the common good, attentive to the Holy Spirit. This brings us closer, in a concrete way, to bearing witness as a visibly united church and supports our desire to be the one Body of Christ, his church. "We do not see consensus as a technique to help us make decisions, but rather as a process of spiritual discernment."[11] This new approach allowed a way forward together with the Orthodox churches, which were feeling less and less heard or understood in their aspirations, their differences, and the riches of their distinct heritage.

Yes, at Porto Alegre I was like a fish in water! I was profoundly aware of our own vocation to prayer for unity and reconciliation. It is a vocation which opens us to the world, far and near, even in the process of living in community and offering hospitality to others. I was amazed to see so many familiar faces and so many who knew of Grandchamp. I was so thankful for all of the blessings I have received here, the knowledge I've gained of the history of so many countries through our guests, volunteers, and ecumenical and religious contacts.

At Porto Alegre I experienced the mystery of God present and at work transforming lives in the heart of humanity. It was so amazing and so encouraging to experience the vitality of the church in its universality as the

---

11. Rev. Dr. Samuel Kobia, of the Methodist Church in Kenya, was general secretary of the World Council of Churches from 2004 to 2009.

life of the Body of Christ. He has a face! There I was glad to be a Christian and I was renewed in my desire to continue seeking life breathed by the Spirit who is at work transforming those who consent, who open themselves continually to his action, on a daily basis. Some do so in simple, often hidden ways made up of small, ordinary things; others do so in the struggle for life. At Porto Alegre I experienced a church open to the great challenges of today's world, engaged, desiring to bring the abundant life promised by God for all people and for creation. As Dr. Kobia said, "I invite you to see the spiritual basis of the ecumenical movement as the 'celebration of life'; the ecumenical movement as a movement for life, open to the signs of the transformative grace of God."[12]

Each liturgy gives us the opportunity to continue the experience of Porto Alegre wherever we are—the experience of a great communion of the whole church everywhere in the world!

In the Fraternity of the Suffering Servant[13]

Sister Janny, one of the Grandchamp sisters who participates as a prayer partner

"I know that my redeemer lives!" (Job 19:1). Job's words have been a source of strength in the life of Father Alfredinho.[14] He lived them and shared his trust and faith with those who suffer the most. He showed the people that they are pearls of great price: how else can God be welcomed, except into a needy heart? My somewhat coincidental encounter with Father Alfredinho was planned by the Spirit. Right away he accepted me as a consecrated prayer partner in the Fraternity of the Suffering Servant, which was born in Brazil among people who are poor, marginalized, oppressed, and exploited. These people formed groups for sharing, acting, and praying together. Now the Fraternity has spread to Canada, the United States, Madagascar, France, Italy, Spain, Belgium, and Switzerland. "If you are not poor, then what are you?" Father Alfredinho asked us during the retreat he gave at Grandchamp in 1994 after our meeting. Suffering can become a road toward this poverty and toward joy, communion, and fraternity.

Part of our vocation as a community is follow the Suffering Servant, as does Father Alfredinho, becoming servants through our suffering and

---

12. Kobia, "Celebrating Life."
13. Mesters, *La mission du people qui souffre*.
14. Fredy Kunz, priest and brother of the *Fils de la Charité* (Sons of Charity), born February 9, 1920, died August 12, 2000.

inner poverty. We are to become a place of communion and compassion. Forgiveness and reconciliation are also part of our call.

In 1996, after discernment, Nara, a Brazilian woman who lives in a slum, and I committed ourselves to express together our profound unity and our quest for unity in the church from within the Fraternity. This commitment was made together at Grandchamp and the relationship between Nara and the community continues to grow and become a life force. Since then, a few other sisters have heard a similar call, in total harmony with their personal reality.

Like the Hebrews exiled in Babylon, exploited and crushed, those who suffer, whether rich or poor, have too often lost confidence in themselves, lost hope, lost their identity, and even lost the very meaning of their lives. God speaks to them, as in the past, through the songs of the prophet Isaiah:

> There are among you men and women who are oppressed but who do not oppress others, men and women who suffer violence but do not react violently, men and women who receive little love, but around them they are building a world of love. Rise. You are the seed of the future, the seed of God's world.[15]

In the footsteps of the Suffering Servant, each member of the fraternity makes the words of the prophet Isaiah her own. Among the orientations our community shares with the Fraternity of the Suffering Servant are these: living in a spirit of nonviolence, non-vengeance, and daily forgiveness; attentiveness to the most disadvantaged among us, to the suffering; being alert to the dangerous mechanisms of consumerism and taking care to share our everyday resources with those in need; actively seeking God, praying that those who suffer will find the way to the Suffering Servant who is Life; seeking ways to unite separated Christians; and inviting those who are marginalized to join together in fraternities in order to go through their sufferings together and with Jesus, the Suffering Servant, and to be witnesses to his resurrection.

---

15. Statement of the francophone group of the Fraternity of the Suffering Servant, 2003, taking up themes from Isaiah 53. "Il y a parmi vous des hommes et des femmes qui sont opprimés mais qui n'oppriment pas, des gens qui subissent la violence, mais qui ne la rendent pas, des gens qui reçoivent peu d'amour, mais qui construisent autour d'eux un monde d'amour. Levez-vous. Vous êtes semence de l'avenir, semence du monde de Dieu."

Conclusion

Toward the Fruits of Grace

"Find inner peace and around you multitudes will be saved."

SAINT SERAPHIM DE SAROV [1]

REMEMBERING THE EXPERIENCES CONNECTED with events large and small, in the near or distant past, and then putting them in perspective as I have done in this book—experiences of life, community, the church—makes no sense except as they are allowed to add life and hope to our present world; events of the past can become like corpses over which we lament. That's a temptation. It is also tempting to evoke with nostalgia all the promising sparks of life we have seen come to nothing, among those especially the great hopes raised by the ecumenical momentum of the postwar years. Each time we give in to this nostalgia, each time we slip toward discouragement, our memories, whether accompanied by tears or by laughter, trap us in a sterile kind of nostalgia that yields no fruit for the present moment.

The challenge is elsewhere. All of us, beginning with the earliest sisters, have a duty to remember, not in order to lament, but in order to give the community a second wind, to give momentum to the newness of life in us and around us, to stimulate what is not yet but will come in the future, to be involved in solutions to current challenges and assume as Christians,

---

1. (1759–1833) Russian Orthodox monk and *starets*. Saying quoted in Ware, *The Inner Kingdom*, 133.

especially as members of religious communities, our rightful share of responsibility.

The instability of the Near and Middle East, the endless conflicts, the ongoing impoverishment of many peoples, including here at home, the feeling of helplessness that comes with globalization, echoed by the media—these are just some of the realities we must face.

In all of this upheaval, are we ready to hear the first question addressed lovingly to Adam one evening: "Adam, where are you?" Has each of us become clearly aware that God himself raised up the community in which we live, the church to which we belong, so that God might act, might manifest his Love in the world?

The words of God to Moses are also addressed to us: "I have observed the misery of my people ... I have heard their cry ... I know their sufferings, and I have come down to deliver them ..." (Exod 3:7–8). Are we ready to enter into loving synergy with our Creator, to take the peace of others as our responsibility both through prayer in solidarity with them and through concrete acts that are signs for our world?

One day while I was prioress, Father Gibbard said to me, "You have to be a rock." I answered, "I agree, but a rock that weeps." And the text from the Gospels that he showed me then was: "When he saw the crowds, he had compassion for them, because they were harassed and helpless, like sheep without a shepherd" (Matt 9:36). That's a description of the church, the role of the church: to be full of compassion and mercy.

"I came not to judge the world, but to save it" (John 12:47b). As Christians, especially as those who pray, let us gaze upon the face of the transfigured Christ and allow to resonate within us the words he said to his disciples before going up on the mountain to pray: "The Son of Man must undergo great suffering, and be rejected by the elders, chief priests, and scribes, and be killed, and on the third day be raised up" (Luke 9:22). Gradually, his face of glory grew gaunt, becoming the face of the man of sorrows at Gethsemane and on the cross. We hear his cries, his groans: "Father, if you are willing, remove this cup from me" (Luke 22:42).

At the same time, we must always remember that we are not "the good guys." Evil is not someone else, someone who is different from us, some other people, some other culture, some other religion, some other confession, an agnostic or an atheist. Evil is not the world either. No, evil is in us. And there is our field of combat, the place where the commitment of our baptism needs to be put into practice and renewed each Easter vigil, when we renounce evil, "Satan and all his works," the fertile soil of our own potentially murderous identities. In response to each fear that grips us, sometimes more profoundly than we wish, it is up to us to return to our primary identity as the sons and daughters of God.

Remembering is first of all an inner attitude. Remembering is important for being thankful of course, but also for recognizing our personal, communal, or collective weakness. As I wrote this book, I rejoiced, but I also revisited times of trial through which I and the community have had to pass. We don't have to be superhuman. Our life as monastics invites us to face our faults and to pick ourselves up in Christ each time we fall, for it is in our failures that we most clearly experience the power of grace.

Remembering helps us to understand ourselves. In conflicts with others, even the most ordinary ones, we must learn to remember what connects us, enter once more into the conviction that the other person is a gift, that she or he belongs to God.

To work toward the healing of memories, those of peoples and of the churches, is urgently important in our time. Even if we had nothing to do with the wounds our collective histories bear, we are invited to enter into an attitude of repentance where we can become humble agents of healing within the human family. In the same way, when we are wounded we must not hold onto what hurt us, but approach the other in an attitude of blessing that surpasses all fear: "Bless and do not curse them" (Rom 12:14b).

So with Isaac of Nineveh we willingly say, "Those who know their own sins are greater than those who raise the dead." This entire journey of reconciliation that we experience ever more deeply, first in ourselves, then among us, can become incarnate. It can gradually enter into our churches and our world, the true seeds of communion carried to Christ through us and through our community. And so our interior walls fall by the power of Christ who has broken down the dividing wall of hostility (Eph 2:14).

The Creation

"To the Lord [is] the earth and its fullness, the world and all its people . . ."

(See Ps 24:1-2)

The duty to safeguard and, more broadly, to care for the creation which has been entrusted to us is our particular responsibility. Without being preoccupied with political economic issues, we need to support, with discernment, proposals and actions that are positive steps in this direction, wherever they come from. Are we ready, with Samuel, to say, "Here I am" (1 Sam 3:4)?

"Here I am" to accept my responsibility of being a human being in the ecosystem of my own body, of our food, our gardens, our dwellings, homes, monasteries, towns, or villages, and to fully exercise this responsibility that God has given me in relation to his creation, and consequently give up some of my personal or communal actions in order to assume this responsibility.

When taking a walk alongside a pond, I contemplate creation, praising God for so much beauty. Suddenly my eye is caught by some fish, floating belly up . . . What is the right attitude to take? To meditate on the mystery of suffering and of our fallen nature? Remove the dead fish from the pond so they will not disturb my meditation? Look the other way in order to see the beauty of creation elsewhere? Look in some other direction that does not offend me? Or to take action, not just for the sake of doing something, but by necessity in order to accept our humble human condition as sons and daughters of God? In material terms, does this not invite us to involve ourselves as good citizens? "Father, protect them . . . I am not asking you to take them out of the world, but I ask you to protect them from the evil one" (John 17:11, 15).

Watch Over the World

The incredible boldness of the inter-religious World Day of Prayer for Peace held at Assisi, initiated by Pope John Paul II, touched me profoundly: seeing the representatives of so many religions from all over the world, so different from one another in their clothing and beliefs, and yet gathered on the same platform, with the Jewish representative near the Christians, was a moving sight. The pope had the strength to make his idea a reality: the urgency of meeting one another around a common desire for peace for the whole inhabited earth, for all the world. To me it was the first fruits of *Pacem in terris*,[2] a peace experienced not individually, later on in heaven, but together, here and now—peace on earth. In turn, a representative of each religion prayed according to their tradition. And the Holy Father was among the delegates of the various confessions, one Christian among the Christians, while a woman had been chosen to lead the prayer of intercession in the name of that little "community," the church.

I was touched by this vision of the church, at this moment so obviously, so simply one. Truly, the prayer for unity Christ prayed on the eve

---

2. John XXIII, *Encyclical Letter Pacem in Terris*, on establishing universal peace in truth, justice, charity, and liberty issued April 11, 1963.

of his passion remains an urgent call for all disciples of Christ. That is why, once we understand it, we must not let ourselves be trapped by routine or the spirit of worldliness, or vacillate between "What's the use?" and "What a nice meeting." The vital issue that the ecumenical spirit, straining toward church unity, represents must be kept at the heart of our endeavors. We must remember that this unity is not an end in itself, but a requirement to be lived out "so that the world may believe" (John 17:21). Getting past our confessional identities remains an impossible task for many. Even we, whose lives have been set apart, are we ready to answer, as Jesus did, or rather with Jesus, "Father . . . not my will but yours be done" (Luke 22:42)?

Once again, we must follow the path of repentance. Whatever church we belong to, "if we say we have no sin, we deceive ourselves" (1 John 1:8). Theologians have done a lot of work on reconciliation of the churches, notably in France through the Groupe des Dombes (documents on Mary and on the conversion of the churches)[3] and through the WCC Commission on Faith and Order in *Baptism, Eucharist and Ministry*.[4] Within Europe, the Charta Oecumenica,[5] submitted and signed at Strasbourg, which most of the churches of Europe adopted, is another major ecumenical initiative. However, all of this theological work is having trouble being received in the local churches. The meeting at Sibiu in 2007, the third meeting of the two groups that signed the Charta Oecumenica (Conference of European Churches or CEC and the Council of European Bishops' Conferences or CCEE), was intended to give impetus to the engagement of various European churches (reconciliation of peoples and cultures, commitment to dialogue and collaboration).[6]

Knowing this Charter, reflecting on it and promoting it, is a concrete ecumenical commitment for today. With five loaves of bread and two fish, Jesus fed a crowd through his disciples (Matt 14:17-19). Let us not be afraid to share with others the distinctive treasures God has entrusted to each of our churches, and let us trust that they will be multiplied to feed all. May we be fortified by what we most treasure in our traditions so that we may reach out toward others with open hands. "For he is our peace; in his flesh he has made both groups into one and has broken down the dividing wall, that is, the hostility between us" (Eph 2:14-15).

3. Groupe des Dombes, *Mary in the Plan of God*.

4. In addition, more recently: World Council of Churches, *The Church*.

5. Agreement for cooperation signed by the Conference of European Churches (CEC) and the Council of European Bishops' Conferences (CCEE), Text in five languages: English, French, Russian, Czech, German. www.ceceurope.org/ and www.ccee.ch/.

6. "Fourth Stage: Sibiu, 4-9 September 2007." www.eea3.org.

Praying together, and not just for one another, is another key step on the road to unity. Even in old age, we can continue to pray in solidarity with one another, bringing to God the realities that each of the churches is going through. All of us can be strengthened by the witness of other churches.[7] In addition, under the auspices of the WCC, Christians of various churches are planning an ecumenical martyrology. We can intercede every day with this cloud of witnesses, the community of saints in heaven and on earth. In these ways the sap can circulate in and among the branches of Christ's vine (John 15:5).

Let us accomplish all of this "Not by might, nor by power, but by my spirit, says the Lord of hosts" (Zech 4:6). It is God who sends us, far and near, in our churches, to other churches, and out into the world.

---

7. A suggestion for ecumenical prayer can be found in the Ecumenical Calendar proposed by the Community of Bose, Italy, which gathers together the feast days of different Christian confessions and of the Jewish tradition.

APPENDIX

Several Communities Introduce Themselves—2007

1864/1948—Abbaye du Bec (France)

A community of Benedictine monks of the Notre Dame du Bec Abbey (France). Founder: Father Emmanuel André (Mesnil-Saint-Loup, 1864); Father Abbot: Dom Paul-Emmanuel Clénet. By establishing his community in Bec in 1948, Abbott Paul-Marie Grammont gave new life to the Abbey of Saint Anselm and renewed the connections Bec had maintained with the Church of England in the Middle Ages. The community's liturgy, since Vatican II, has been inspired by the Anglican liturgy.

1924/1949—Monastère Sainte-Françoise-Romaine (France)

Community of oblate sisters of Bec Abbey at the Monastery of Sainte-Françoise-Romaine. Founder: Mother Marie-Elisabeth of Wavrechin (Cormeilles-en-Parisis, 1924); prioress: Mother Marie-Placide Cazenave. "Following our brothers, our community established itself in Bec in 1949. We make our profession at the altar of the Abbey. We join the choir of monks for the major Sunday offices and feast days of the church in the church of Bec Abbey, two kilometers away."

1940—Community of Taizé (France)

Ecumenical community of men made up of brothers belonging to a variety of Protestant churches and to the Catholic Church.

Founder: Brother Roger; current prior: Brother Alois. Before Vatican II Taizé was a Protestant community. In 1969 Catholic brothers were able to become members. Taizé thus became an ecumenical community, a sign anticipating reconciliation between Catholics and Protestants. Br. Roger wrote: "Marked by the witness of the life of my grandmother, and still young, I found, by following in her footsteps, my own identity as a Christian by reconciling within myself the faith of my Protestant origins and the mystery of the Catholic faith, without breaking fellowship with anyone at all."

1951—Community of Pomeyrol (France)

Community of women of the churches of the Reformation.

Founder: Antoinette Butte; current prioress: Sister Danielle. Beginning in 1929 the community developed little by little in the region of Paris, a little seed of the church, born of its torment and its renewal, because of the distress of the world.

1953—Monastery of the Epiphany in Eygalières (France)

Community of Catholic nuns. Founder: Sister Simone; current prioress: Sister Dominique. Sister Simone lives today at the Hermitage of Dormition in Peyremale (Gard, a region of France). It's a Catholic community which, since Vatican II, has integrated the contributions of Eastern traditions (Syrian and Byzantine) into its liturgy as well as its monastic life.

1955—Community of Imshausen (Germany)

Protestant community of brothers and sisters. Founders: Sister Vera von Trott and Brother Hans Eisenberg; current leaders: Sister Angelika and Father Philipp. Beginning in 1931 the community developed little by little. The first monastic commitments of sisters and brothers took place in 1955. Attentive to the call of God as well as to the questions and sufferings of our times, the sisters and brothers seek to respond together with their prayers and their lives.

1968—Community of Bose (Italy)

Monastic community of men and women from different Christian churches. Founder and current prior: Father Enzo Bianchi moved to Bose in 1965 where he was joined by the first brothers and sisters in 1968. It's a community which seeks God in celibacy, brotherly fellowship, and obedience to the Gospel, involved in spiritual companionship with men and women, and at their service.

1998—Monastery of the Holy Cross in Rostrevor (Northern Ireland)

Community of Benedictine monks. Founder and current prior: Brother Marc-Ephrem Nolan. "Our particular mission is to contribute to the reconciliation between Catholics and Protestants in this country marked by reciprocal violence and stained with the blood of Christian brothers and sisters."

Bibliography

"A Retreat House in Switzerland." *Veillez!* (January 1936) 16.
Aubert, Alexandre. "Léopold Micheli au Jeunesse-Club (1903–1910)." In *Léopold Micheli, 1877–1910*, edited by Frédéric Gardy, 33–40. Geneva: A. Kündig, 1911.
Bardet, André. *Un Combat Pour L'Église: Un siècle de mouvement liturgique en Pays de Vaud*. Lausanne: Bibliothèque Historique Vaudoise, 1988.
Beaumont, Marguerite de. *Lectures quotidiennes de l'Avent pour préparer Noël*. Lausanne: Éditions La Concorde, 1932.
———. *Prépare-toi à célébrer Pâques: suis le chemin des béatitudes*. Lausanne: Éditions La Concorde, 1935.
Beaumont, Marguerite de, and Christianne Méroz. *Du grain à l'épi . . . recueil de souvenirs*. Areuse: Communauté de Grandchamp, 1995.
[Beaumont, Marguerite de, ed.] *Lettres de Sœur Geneviève*. Grandchamp: privately printed, 1964.
Benedict. *Holy Rule of Saint Benedict*. Translated by Boniface Verheyen. Atchison, KS: St. Benedict's Abbey, 1949. http://www.ecatholic2000.com/benedict/rule.shtml.
Berchtold, Alfred. *La Suisse romande au cap du XXe siècle*. Lausanne: Payot, 1963.
Bertell, Rosalie. *Planet Earth: The Latest Weapon of War*. London: Women's Press, 2000.
Berthoud, Dorette. *Les Indiennes Neuchâteloises*. Boudry: La Baconnière, 1951.
Bethge, Eberhard. *Dietrich Bonhoeffer: vie, pensée, témoignage*. Geneva: Labor et Fides, 1969.
Beyreuther, Eric. *Zinzendorf, l'apôtre de l'unité*. Geneva: Labor et Fides, 1967.
Bianchi, Enzo. *Si tu savais le don de Dieu*. Bruxelles: Éditions Lessius, 2001.
Birmelé, André. "Concorde de Leuenberg." In *Encyclopédie du protestantisme*, edited by Pierre Gisel. Paris: Labor et Fides, 1995.
Boissonnas, Gabrielle. *Expériences d'un évangéliste, Georges Boissonnas (1865–1942)*. Strasbourg: Éditions Oberlin, 1966.
Bonhoeffer, Dietrich. *Letters and Papers from Prison*. New York: Macmillan, 1967.
———. *Life Together*. San Francisco: Harper Collins, 1954.
———. *Résistance et soumission*. Geneva: Labor et Fides, 1973.
Bonhoeffer, Dietrich, et al. *A Testament to Freedom: The Essential Writings of Dietrich Bonhoeffer*. San Francisco: HarperSanFrancisco, 1990.
Borght, Eduardus A. J. G. van der. *Christian Identity*. Studies in Reformed Theology 16. Leiden: Brill, 2008.

Bossert, Marthe. *Cahier de Sr. Marthe.* Archives, Communauté de Grandchamp, Areuse, Switzerland.
Bourguet, Daniel. *Dieu au cœur de nos vies.* Lyon: Réveil, 2002.
Bourquin, Julien. *Des portes qui s'ouvrent ou La vie de Jules Paroz, 1824–1906: petit paysan, pédagogue, écrivain, directeur d'École normale.* Preface by G. Chevallaz. Neuchâtel: Delachaux et Niestlé, 1954.
Bovet, Félix, *Le comte de Zinzendorf.* Paris: Grassart, 1860.
———. *Lettres de Grandchamp et d'ailleurs.* Edited by Pierre Bovet. Neuchâtel: Éditions de la Baconnière, 1934.
Bovet, Pierre. *Un siècle de l'histoire de Grandchamp: entre la Fabrique d'Indiennes et la Communauté spirituelle.* Grandchamp: chez l'auteur, 1965.
———. *Vingt ans de vie: l'Institut J. J. Rousseau de 1912 à 1932.* Neuchâtel: Delachaux et Niestlé, 1932.
Brocher, Sara. *La Doctoresse Champendal.* Geneva: n.p. 1968.
Brother Johannes. "Christophorus." *Quarterly Review of the Community of the Resurrection* 423 (2008) 16–18.
Bundy, David. "Pietist and Methodist Roots of the Société des Missions Évangéliques de Paris." *The Asbury Journal* 70 (2015) 28–54.
———. "Should the Methodists Get all the Credit? The Methodist Crisis in Neuchâtel, 1820–1830." *Methodist History* 54/3 (2016) 180–91.
Burki, Bruno. "Liturgie et communauté monastique: l'exemple de la Communauté de Grandchamp dans le protestantisme francophone de Suisse." *Célébrer* 266 (1997) 9–13.
Butte, Antoinette. "Projet de retraite spirituelle durant l'été." *Veillez!* (April 1930) 12–13.
———. *Semences: méditations, lettres, témoignages.* Cahiers de Pomeyrol 9. Strasbourg: Oberlin, 1989.
C. "18–21 septembre." In *Sainte-Croix 1906*, 5–10. Saint-Blaise et Roubaix: Foyer solidariste de librairie et d'édition, 1906.
Carmel of St. Rémy/Stânceni, eds. *Qu'ils soient Un! Mélanges offerts en hommage au métropolite Emilianos Timiadis par la Fraternité Saint-Élie.* Iasi: Trinitas, 2005.
———. *Toi, suis-moi, Mélanges offerts en hommage à Élisabeth Behr-Sigel par la Fraternité Saint-Élie.* Iasi: Trinitas, 2003.
Carr, Thomas M. *Voix des Abbesses du grand siècle: la prédication au féminin à Port-Royal; contexte rhétorique et dossier.* Tübingen: G. Narr, 2006.
Centre Unité Chrétien, ed. *L'œcuménisme spirituel de L'Abbé Couturier aux défis actuels. Actes du colloque universitaire et interconfessionnel Nov. 2002.* Lyon: Profac, 2002.
Clark, Walter Houston. *The Oxford Group: Its History and Significance.* New York: Bookman, 1951.
Clifford, Catherine E. *The Groupe des Dombes: Dialogue of Conversion.* New York: American University Studies, 2005.
Colomb, Gustave. "Un siècle de prédication protestante, d'Adolphe à Wilfred Monod." In *Recueil de travaux.* Lausanne: F. Rouge, 1937.
Communauté de Taizé. *Louange des Jours.* Taizé: Les Presses de Taizé, 1971.
———. *Office de Taizé.* Taizé: Les Presses de Taizé, 1963.
———. *The Rule of Taizé in French and in English.* Taizé: Les Presses de Taizé, 1961.
———. *The Rule of Taizé in French and in English.* Taizé: Les Presses de Taizé, 1967.
———. *The Sources of Taizé.* Chicago: GIA, 2000.

Cornuz, Michel. *Soeur Minke de Grandchamp, Entretiens. Itinéraires spirituels.* Petite Bibliothèque de Spiritualité. Geneva: Labor et Fides, 2011.
Couturier, Paul, and Maurice Villain. *Œcuménisme spirituel: les écrits de l'abbé Paul Couturier.* Tournai: Casterman, 1963.
Cullis, Charles. *Dorothea Trudel; Or, The prayer of faith, showing the remarkable manner in which large numbers of sick persons were healed in answer to special prayer.* Boston: Willard Tract Repository, [1872].
Curtis, Goeffrey. *Paul Couturier and Unity in Christ.* London: SCM, 1964.
Dieterlen, Pierre. *Arnold Bovet, sa vie, son œuvre.* 2nd ed. Neuchâtel: Attinger, 1905.
Église et Liturgie. *L'Office divin de l'Église Universelle: Services du matin, de midi et du soir pour chaque jour de la semaine.* Paris: Éditions Je Sers, 1943.
Encrevé, André. "Le Réveil en France (1815-1850)." *Bulletin de la Société de l'Histoire du Protestantisme en France* 155 (2009) 529-40.
Evdokimov, Paul. *Les âges de la vie spirituelle.* Bruges: Desclée de Brouwer, 1964.
———, et al. *Ages of the Spiritual Life.* Crestwood, NY: St. Vladimir's Seminary Press, 1998.
Faith and Order. *Baptism, Eucharist and Ministry.* Geneva: WCC, 1982.
Fatio, Olivier. "Dominicé, Max." *Dictionnaire historique de la Suisse.* January 24, 2006. http://www.hls-dhs-dss.ch/textes/f/F11105.php.
Fernand-Laurent, Jean. *Que tous soient un . . . en sommes nous proches?* Saint-Maurice: Saint Augustin, 2003.
Fernex, Solange. *La vie pour la vie.* Bats, FR: Éditions Utovie, 1985.
Foucauld, Charles de. *Crier l'Évangile.* Mayenne: Nouvelle Cité, 1974.
Fouilloux, Étienne. *La pensée catholique française entre modernisme et Vatican II (1914-1962).* Paris: Desclée de Brouwer, 1998.
Freedman, Estelle. "Separation as Strategy: Female Institution Building and American Feminism." *Feminist Studies* 5 (1979) 513-29.
García Hernando, Julián. *Pluralismo religioso en España.* Madrid: Sociedad de Educación Atenas, 1981.
Gardy, Frédéric, ed. *Léopold Micheli, 1877-1910.* Geneva: A. Kündig, 1911.
Gaulué, Fabien, "Vers un monastère réel de l'unité chrétienne." In *L'œcuménisme spirituel de Paul Couturier: aux défis actuels. Actes du colloque universitaire interconfessionnel Nov. 2002,* edited by Centre Unité Chrétien, 131-56. Lyon: Profac, 2002.
Gamonnet, Étienne. *Lettres de Marie Durand (1715-1776).* Montpellier: Presses du Languedoc, 1986.
Gonzalez-Balado, J. L. *The Story of Taizé.* Oxford: Mowbray, 1980.
Goss-Mayr, Hildegard. *Oser le combat non-violent aux côtés de Jean Goss.* Paris: Cerf, 1998.
Gower, Nancy Sanders. "Reformed and Ecumenical: The Foundations of the Community of Taizé." PhD diss., Fuller Theological Seminary, 2010.
Grensted. L. W. *What Is the Oxford Group?* New York: Oxford University Press, 1933.
Groupe des Dombes. *For the Conversion of the Churches.* Paris: Centurion, 1991.
———. *Mary in the Plan of God and the Communion of Saints.* New York: Paulist, 2002.
Gruner, Paul. *Arnold Bovet, ein Vorkämpfer des Blauen Kreuzes.* Bern: Blaukreuzverlag, 1953.
Hammann, Gottfried. "Grandchamp, communauté de." *Dictionnaire historique de la Suisse.* July 17, 2007. http://www.hls-dhs-dss.ch/textes/f/F27805.php.

Hollander-Lafon, Magda. *Quatre petits bouts de pain: Des ténèbres à la joie.* Paris: Albin Michel, 2012.
Isaac, Bishop of Nineveh. *The Ascetical Homilies of Saint Isaac the Syrian.* Boston: The Holy Transfiguration Monastery, 1984.
John XXIII. *Encyclical Letter Pacem in Terris: On Establishing Peace in Truth, Justice, Charity, and Liberty.* New York: Paulist, 1963.
John Paul II. *Encyclical Letter Ut unum sint: On Commitment to Ecumenism.* Vatican City: Libreria Editrice Vaticana, 1995.
Keller, Rosemary Skinner. "Creating a Sphere for Women." In *Women in New Worlds,* edited by Hilah H. Thomas and Rosemary Skinner Keller, 246–60. Nashville: Abingdon, 1981.
Kerber, Linda K. "Separate Spheres, Female Worlds, Woman's Place: The Rhetoric of Women's History." *Journal of American History* 17 (1988) 9–39.
Kober-Gobat, M. *Samuel Zeller in Männedorf: eine Skizze seines Lebens und Wirkens.* Basel: Kober C. F. Spittlers Nachfolger, 1912.
Kobia, Samuel. "Celebrating Life: Report of the General Secretary. Porto Alegre, Brazil: WCC 9th Assembly, 14–23 February 2006." *Ecumenical Review* 58 (2006) 28–48.
Lagny, Gustave. *Le Réveil de 1830 à Paris et les origines des Diaconesses de Reuilly.* Paris: Édition Association des diaconesses, 1958.
Laplane, Sabine. *Frère Roger de Taizé: Avec presque rien . . .* Paris: Cerf, 2015.
Latourette, Kenneth Scott. *The Nineteenth Century in Europe.* New York: Harper, 1959.
Laufer, Véronique. *Aux origines des "Dames de Morges" et des Retraites de Granchamp: Helene Laufer et Genevieve Micheli.* Morges: n.p., 2012.
Laufer, Véronique, ed. "Témoignage de Véronique Laufer." In *Une vocation de femme: Geneviève Micheli. Journeé commémorative du 7 août 1994, marquant le cinquantième anniversaire de l'arrivée de Geneviève Micheli à Grandchamp,* edited by Jean-Louis Leuba et al., 45–74. Areuse: Communauté de Grandchamp, 1996.
Leonard, Émile. *Déclin et renouveau (XVIIIe–XXe siècle). Histoire générale du protestantisme.* Vol. 3. Paris: Presses Universitaires de France, 1964.
Leuba, J.-L. et al. *Une vocation de femme: Geneviève Micheli. Journeé commémorative du 7 août 1994, marquant le cinquantième anniversaire de l'arrivée de Geneviève Micheli à Grandchamp.* Areuse: Communauté de Grandchamp, 1996.
Masuy, Danielle. *Georges Liengme: l'homme, sa méthode, son enseignement pour une psychothérapie chrétienne, Vaumarcus-La Rochelle, 1908–1936.* Geneva: n.p., 1982.
Méroz, Christianne. "Liminaire." In *Du grain à l'épi . . . recueil de souvenirs,* by Marguerite de Beaumont. Areuse: Communauté de Grandchamp, 1995.
Merton, Thomas. *Faith and Violence: Christian Teaching and Christian Practice.* Notre Dame: University of Notre Dame Press, 1968.
Messie, Gérit. *Les Diaconesses de Reuilly.* Paris: Cerf, 1992.
Mesters, Carlos. *La mission du people qui souffre, la non-violence des pauvres dans les quatre chants d'Isaïe.* Paris: Cerf, 2000.
Meyer, Lucy Ryder. *Deaconesses: Biblical, Early Church, European, American, with the Story of How the Work Began in the Chicago Training School . . . and the Chicago Deaconess Home.* Cincinnati: Cranston & Stowe, 1892.
Micheli, Geneviève. *Message de Sœur Geneviève Micheli.* Areuse: Communauté de Grandchamp, 1986.
———. *Silence dans nos vies: Message aux femmes de pasteurs du Canton du Vaud—1938.* Areuse: Communauté de Grandchamp, n.d.

Monod, Wilfred. "Les Veilleurs." *Revue du Christianisme social* 46 (April 20, 1933) 7–28.

Monod, Wilfred, and Theodore Monod. *Livre de Prière: lumière, flamme, parfums*. Geneva: Éditions Labor, [1937].

Mouttapa, Jean. *Un Arabe face à Auschwitz. La mémoire partagée*. Paris: Albin Michel, 2004.

Müller, Jean-Marie. *Témoins de la non-violence: les moines de Tibhirine*. Paris: Éditions du Témoignage chrétien, 1999.

Murray, Paul, ed. *Receptive Ecumenism and the Call to Catholic Learning*. Oxford: Oxford University Press, 2008.

Pacot, Simone. *L'Évangélisation des profondeurs*. Paris: Cerf, 1997.

———. *Ose la vie nouvelle! Le chemin de nos Pâques*. Paris: Cerf, 2003.

———. *Reviens à la vie!* Paris: Cerf, 2002.

Paquier, Richard. "Avant-Propos." In *L'Office divin de chaque jour*, 5–12. Neuchâtel: Delachaux et Niestlé, 1949.

Paul VI. *Declaration on the Relation of the Church to Non-Christian Religions—Nostra Aetate*. http://www.vatican.va/archive/hist_councils/ii_vatican_council/documents/vat-ii_decl_19651028_nostra-aetate_en.html.

Paupert, Jean Marie. *Taizé et l'Église de demain*. Paris: Fayard, 1967.

Pyronnet, Joseph. *Prier 15 jours avec Gandhi*. Montrouge: Nouvelle Cité, 1998.

Rambert, Eugène. *Alexandre Vinet: histoire de sa vie et de ses ouvrages*. Lausanne: G. Bridel, 1875.

Reeuwijk, Dick van. *Opstand der Georgiërs, Sondermeldung Texel*. Rev. ed. Den Burg: Het Open Boek, 2001.

Robert, Daniel. *Les Églises Réformées en France 1800–1830*. Paris: Presses Universitaires de France, 1961.

Roser, Henri. *Le Chrétien devant la guerre*. Geneva: Labor & Fides, 1953.

Rougemont, Gilberte de, Sœur de Grandchamp, and Ginette Bovet. *La Geste des Bovet de Grandchamp*. Areuse: Communauté de Grandchamp, 1992.

Sainte-Croix 1906. À la mémoire de Gaston Frommel. Saint-Blaise et Roubaix: Foyer solidariste de librairie et d'édition, 1906.

Schildgen, Robert. *Toyohiko Kagawa: Apostle of Love and Social Justice*. Berkeley, CA: Centenary, 1988.

Schlup, Michel. "Félix Bovet, bibliothécaire, professeur et historien (1824–1903)." In *Biographies neuchâteloises*, edited by Michel Schlup, 3:51–56. Hauterive: G. Attinger, 2001.

Schutz, Roger. *Communauté de Cluny, notes explicatives*. Lyons: n.p., 1941.

———. *Vivre l'aujourd'hui de Dieu*. Taizé: Les Presses de Taizé, 1959.

[Schutz, Roger] A Swiss student. "Switzerland." *Federation News Sheet*, November 1940, 4.

Second Vatican Council. *Dogmatic Constitution on the Church, Lumen gentium*. Vatican City: 1964.

Senft, Ernest-Arved, and Eugène Reichel. *Souvenir du jubilé missionnaire de l'Église des Frères célébré à Montmirail le 21 août 1882*. Peseux: Bureau du Journal de l'Unité des Frères, 1882.

Senft, W. *Ceux de Montmirail. Esquisses historiques*. Neuchâtel: Delachaux et Niestlé, 1947.

Shoufani, Emile. "Memory for Peace: A Project to Promote Tolerance and Understanding." In *Our Memory of the Past and for the Future*, edited by Richelle Budd Caplan, 73-76. Cedex, FR: Council of Europe, 2005.

Simon, Charlie May. *A Seed Shall Serve—A Story of Toyohiko Kagawa, Spiritual Leader of Modern Japan*. New York: Dutton, 1958.

Sophrony, Archimandrite. *The Monk of Mount Athos: Staretz Silouan, 1866-1938*. London: Mowbray, 1973.

Suenens, L. J. *Une nouvelle Pentecôte*. Paris: Desclée de Brouwer, 1974.

Taylor, Richard K. *Love in Action: A Direct-Action Handbook for Catholics Using Gospel Nonviolence to Reform and Renew the Church*. Philadelphia: Taylor, 2007.

Tertulllian. *The Apology of Tertullian for the Christians*. Edited and translated by T. Herbert Bindley. London: Parker, 1890.

Timar, Monika. *Journal 1957-1962*. Paris: Nouvelle Cité, 1989.

Toulat, Jean. *Un combat pour l'homme: le général de Bollardière*. Paris: Centurion, 1987.

Villain, Maurice. *L'Abbé Couturier*. Paris: Casterman, 1957.

Viviers 1973: Rencontre Charismatique Interconfessionnelle. Valence-sur-Rhône: n.p., 1974.

Vries, Minke de. *Chemin de Croix*. Areuse: Communauté de Grandchamp, 1995.

———. *Christen zijn vandaag: Monastieke inspiratie*. Forward by Enzo Bianchi. Tielt: Lannoo, 2009.

———. "L'accompagnement spirituelle de l'Abbé Couturier et la Communauté de Grandchamp." In *L'œcuménisme spirituel de Paul Couturier aux défis actuels: Actes du colloque universitaire interconfessionnel Nov. 2002*, edited by Centre Unité Chrétien, 119-30. Lyon: Profac, 2002.

———. *Mijn leven in Grandchamp: Monastiek leven in een open gemeenschap*. Forward by Enzo Bianchi. Preface Nancy S. Gower. Utrecht: Uitgeverij Kok, 2015.

———. *Vers une gratuité féconde: l'expérience œcuménique de Grandchamp*. [Les Plans sur Bex; Paris]: Éditions Parole et Silence, 2006.

———. *Verso una gratuità Feconda: L'avventura ecumenica di Grandchamp*. Preface by Enzo Bianchi. Sentinelle di Frontera 17. Milan: Paoline, 2008.

Ware, Kallistos. *The Inner Kingdom*. London: Cassell, 2000.

Weber, Hans-Ruedi. *The Courage to Live: A Biography of Suzanne de Dietrich*. Geneva: WCC, 1995.

Wernle, Paul. "Les Frères Moraves en Suisse Romande au XVIII siècle." *Revue de théologie et de philosophie* 6 (1918) 118-42.

Westphal, Geneviève. "En guise de remerciements (In Thanks)." November 10, 2011. Grandchamp Archives.

———. *Nos fondatrices . . . et nous*. Lausanne: n.p., 2001.

World Council of Churches. *The Church: Towards a Common Vision*. Geneva: WCC, 2013.

Yoder, John Howard. *The Politics of Jesus*. Grand Rapids: Eerdmans, 1972.

Zee, Henri Antony van der. *The Hunger Winter: Occupied Holland, 1944-45*. London: Norman & Hobhouse, 1982.

Archives and Special Collections

Archives Cantonal Vaudoises, Lausanne, Switzerland.

Archives, Communauté de Grandchamp, Areuse, Switzerland.

Bibliothèque Cantonale et Universitaire, Riponne, Lausanne, Switzerland.

Bibliothèque de la Société de l'Histoire du Protestantisme français, Paris, France.

Bibliothèque des Cèdres, Lausanne, Switzerland.

Bibliothèque publique et universitaire de Neuchâtel, Switzerland.

Index

Abécassis, Armand, 156
Abraham, 113, 117, 150, 157, 171
Agapia, monastery, 140, 141, 146
Alfredinho, Father, 109, 185
Algeria, viii, 36, 46, 62–63, 85, 95, 100, 103n33, 108, 132, 153n28, 168–69, 171, 173–75, 178–79
Algiers, 33, 173–74, 178
Allmen, Jean-Jacques von, 86n6
Alois, Brother of Taizé, 69, 194
Amiel, H. F., 4
Anglican Church, vii, 32, 44, 46, 59, 60, 63, 67, 88, 100, 139, 140, 166, 193
Anne-Emmanuelle, Sister of Grandchamp, ix, 183, 184–85
Anne-Geneviève, Sister of Grandchamp, 174
Assaily, Nafez, 151
Assisi, 9, 12, 190
Auschwitz, 43, 138, 147–49, 201

Babut, Amy, 4
Baptists, 80, 85
Barth, Karl, 36, 159
Beatitudes, 9, 10, 13, 15, 26, 32, 60, 61, 99, 118, 133, 135, 142, 143, 145, 147, 151, 183
Béatrice, Sister of Grandchamp, 32
Beauduin, Dom Lambert, 63–64, 70n69

Beaumont, Marguerite de, 5, 9–32, 49, 52–55, 62, 64, 65, 67, 71, 72, 74, 79, 165
Bec Helouin, 8, 63, 157, 164, 169, 193
Benedictine, 28, 50n16, 114n54, 197
Benin, 183
Bernard de Clairvaux, 13
Bertell, Rosalie, 134
Bethlehem, 152, 153, 166, 167, 172
Bianchi, Enzo, Father, 41, 128, 169, 195, 202
Blumhardt, Johann Christoph, 36
Bobrinskoy, Boris, 101, 140
Boegner, Marc, 64
Boissonnas, Georges, 7, 77
Bon Secours (Good Help), 8, 9, 26
Bonhoeffer, Dietrich, ix, 44, 57, 64, 88, 104, 108, 113, 132n82, 161, 197
Bossey. *See* Ecumenical Institute of Bossey.
Bourguet, Daniel, 60, 181, 198
Bovet family, 1–5, 10–12, 14–15, 19, 21, 50–52, 199, 201
Bovet, Amy, 4, 11–12, 14–15
Bovet, Arnold, 3, 199
Bovet, Felix, 3–4, 11, 21, 51, 198, 201
Bovet, Jacques, 4
Bovet, Mathilde, 4, 11–12
Bovet, Philippe, 2–4
Bovet, Pierre, 2, 4, 14, 52, 198
Brazil, 89, 109, 183, 185, 186
Breck, Jean, 135
Bria, Ion, 140

INDEX

Brothers of St. Michael (*Evangelische Michaelsbruderschaft*), 60
Bruners, Father Wilhelm, 151
Buber, Martin, 159
Bucer, Martin, 56
Buddhists, 182
Bundy, David, xi, 2n6, 198
Burki, Bruno, 86
Burnat, Irène, 19–20, 29, 45, 52–53, 65, 72, 75, 79
Butte, Antoinette, 5, 8, 11, 20, 27n162, 53n26, 65, 167, 194

Caffarel, Henri, 164
Calvin, John, 6, 9, 163
Camara, Dom Helder, 108, 111
Cand, Robert, 85
Catherine of Siena, 13
Catholic Church, 10, 26, 46, 56, 64n49, 70n68, 85, 88, 108, 147n16, 193
Chagall, Marc, 149
Champendal, Dr. Marguerite (*La Doctoresse*), 8–10, 30, 198
Charmes, Union of Prayer, 156, 163, 164
Checkpoint Watch, 152, 172
Children of Abraham, 157, 171, 177
Chouraqui, André, 153, 159
Christianne, Sister of Grandchamp, 175
Christmas, 10, 97, 116, 136, 169, 182
Claire, Sister of Grandchamp, 168
Clement, Olivier, 140
Cleopas, Father, 141, 146
Cluj-Napoca, 142–43
Cluny, Community of, 26n149, 27, 28n163, 29, 61n43, 123n63, 201
Communität Christusbruderschaft in Selbitz, 59
Community of L'Arche de Lanza del Vasto, 132–33, 136
Concord of Leuenberg, 85
Conference of European Churches (KEK), 90
Congar, Yves, O.P., 64
Congress of Orthodox Women, 141
Corbon, Father, 140, 168

Council of [Catholic] European Bishops' Conferences (CCEE), 90, 191
Couturier, Abbé Paul, 20–21, 23, 26–28, 45, 47, 52n24, 53, 63n48, 64, 68, 69–76, 162, 198, 199, 202
Curtis, Geoffrey, 64, 75, 199

Dallière, Louis, 156n37, 163
Dames de Morges (*Morgiennes, Responsables*), 7, 10, 11–17, 21, 26, 29, 31–33, 51n19, 52n21, 200
Deaconesses of Reuilly (*Diaconesses de Reuilly*), 58, 63, 92, 200
Diakonia, 58, 167
Dietrich, Suzanne de, 29, 57, 59, 64, 89, 202
Divine Liturgy, 101, 109, 140, 141, 154n31, 156
Dombes (Abbey and Group), 20, 28, 45n7 and 8, 52n24, 60, 63, 72n76, 75n83, 163, 191, 198, 199
Dominicé, Max, 13, 52, 199
Dormitio Abbey, 153–54
Drobot, Marianne and George, 100
Du Pasquier, Marc, 15, 31
Durand, Marie, 56, 199

Easter, 10n8, 81, 82, 86, 92–97, 116, 124, 134, 145, 182, 183, 188
École Vinet, 5, 6
Ecumenical Center at Tantur, 152
Ecumenical Charter (Strasbourg), 91, 158, 191
Ecumenical Institute of Bossey, ix, 58, 68, 88–89, 144, 166–67
Edict of Nantes, 56
Église et Liturgie, 23, 26, 29, 31n178, 59, 66, 100n23, 199
Église Évangélique Libre, 6
Église Réformée Évangélique du Canton de Neuchâtel (EREN), 84–87, 89

INDEX

E.I.I.R. (Inter-confessional International Meetings of Religious), 141n5, 146, 166
Eisenberg, Brother Hans, 160–61, 170, 194
Éliane, Mother of the Carmel Saint-Elijah, 143–44
Élisabeth, Mother, founder of the Carmel Saint-Elijah, 144
Emiliano, Monsignor, 144
Evdokimov, Paul, 8n49, 74, 89, 139, 140, 199
Exchaquet, Germaine (Madame Émile Exchaquet), 11, 31
Eygalières, Monastery. See Monastery of the Epiphany at Eygalières.

Faith and Order, viii, ix, x, 59, 82n91, 88n10, 89, 91, 101n27, 191, 199
Feast of Tabernacles, 177
Federation of Protestant Churches of Switzerland (FEPS), 32, 87
Fédération Universel d'Associations Chrétiennes d'Étudiants, known as the Fédé (World Student Christian Federation (WSCF), 6, 10, 24–25, 29, 64n53, 87, 201
Fernex, Solange, 134
Flearstift, 175–76
Fliedner, Theodore, 3, 57
Foucauld, Charles de, 46, 81n90, 199
Fourvière. See Jesuit Center, La Fourvière.
Franciscan, 9, 12, 19, 46, 53, 60, 139, 166, 172
François, Brother or Taizé, 41, 67–68, 129, 160
Frank, Anne, 148
Fraternity of Sainte-Élisabeth, 177
Fraternity of the Suffering Servant, 109, 183, 185–86

Gagnebin, Samuel, 4
Gautier, Hélene Laufer, 5–7, 11, 51n19
Gélineau, Joseph, 100
Genton, Rosette, 41, 66, 180

Geneva, 4, 6, 7–10, 13, 16, 18, 28, 29, 52, 64–65, 76, 78, 84, 88, 96, 140, 146, 162, 182
Geneviève, Mother. See Micheli, Geneviève de Lacroix.
Gandhi, 57, 111n47, 152, 201
Gibbard, Father, 67, 188
Goss, Hildegard, 133, 135, 150
Goss, Jean, 41, 132–35, 199
Gratry, Joseph, 13
Groot, Maria de, 175

Hamer, Jerome, O.P., 89
Hans, Brother. See Eisenberg, Brother Hans.
Hanukkah, 177
Hazim, Monsignor, 141
Herrnhut, 3, 57
Hillesum, Etty, 148
Hiroshima, 43, 90, 126, 137
Hollander-Lafon, Magda, 147–49, 200
Huguenots, 22, 56

Indiennes, 2, 197, 198
Institut Saint-Serge, 63, 140
International Fellowship of Reconciliation (IFOR), 133, 150
International Movement for Reconciliation (MIR), 132, 150
International Union of Superiors General, 58
Invisible Monastery, 24, 26, 29, 71–74
Irmtraud, Sister of Grandchamp, 140
Islam, 157, 173
Istina, 70

Jacoba, Sister of Grandchamp, 109, 155, 158–59
Janny, Sister of Grandchamp, 183, 185–86
Jerusalem, 33, 85, 96, 131, 147, 149–59, 165, 171–72
Jesuit Center, La Fourvière, 70
Jeunesse-club (Youth Club) Geneva, 7, 197
Jews, 1, 64, 80, 124n65, 147, 149, 151–57, 171, 172, 182

Judaism, 51, 56, 68, 156–58, 172, 177
Justin, Father, 145

Kaire, 67, 167
Kaiserswerth, 2, 3n10, 51
Kessler, Colette, 156
King, Martin Luther Jr., 57
Kobia, Samuel, 184n11, 185, 200
Kunz, Fredy, 185n14
Kwast, Barbara, 177, 182

Lacroix, Genevieve de, 5, 7–9, 32n188
Landau, Dalia and Yehezkel, 151
Lansu, Paul, 150
Lasserre, Jean, 132, 133
Laurent, Sister of Grandchamp, 32
Lausanne, 5, 6, 59, 140
Lebanon, 33, 36, 39, 63, 96, 100–101, 129, 132, 140–41, 149, 159, 168
Lenoir, Évangéline, 31
Lenoir, Madame, 11
Leuba, Jean-Louis, 86n6, 89, 200
Life and Work, viii, 60n42, 88n10, 89
Little Brothers and Sisters of Jesus, 46, 54, 62, 63, 92, 108, 153, 168, 169
Lowe, Christopher, 139
Luther, Martin, 55, 56, 108, 118, 163
Lutheran, vii, 36, 56, 57, 58n36, 59, 60, 80, 84, 85, 106, 141, 152
Lyon, 20, 63n48, 68, 69n66

Machsom (Checkpoint) Watch, 152
Madagascar, 185
Magdeleine, Sister, 168
Mannedorf, 3, 200
Marie-Madeleine, Sister of Grandchamp, 139
Maatje, Sister of Grandchamp, 153, 171–72
Menchu, Rigoberta, 109
Mennonite, 35, 84, 105, 133–34
Menoud, Philippe 86n6
Merton, Thomas, 133
Methodists, 6n35, 80, 84, 85, 87, 170, 184n11, 198
Micheli, Geneviève de Lacroix, 5, 7–32, 36, 41–43, 48, 50, 52n24, 53–54. 62, 64–67, 70n67, 71, 72, 74, 76–79, 86, 89, 98, 102–3, 123–24, 132, 139, 159–61, 162–63, 165, 167–70, 179–80, 200
Micheli, Léopold, 7, 197, 199
Miskotte, Kornelis Heiko, 36
Moltke, Helmuth James Graf von, 161
Monastero di Bose, 41, 92, 128, 158, 169, 192n7, 195
Monastery (Carmel) of Saint Elijah, 143–44
Monastery of Sainte-Françoise-Romaine, 8, 18, 48n14, 53, 165, 193
Monastery of the Epiphany at Eygalières, 41, 156, 158, 168, 194
Monastic Family of Bethlehem, 167
Monod, Théodore, 5, 60, 201
Monod, Wilfred, 5, 8, 10, 13, 14, 16, 18, 23n138, 31n179, 60, 64, 72, 99, 198, 201
Montmirail, 2, 32, 201
Montricher, 6, 7, 15n90,
Moravian, 2, 3, 6, 32, 57, 105n39
Moses, 57, 113, 155, 188
Mouttapa, Jean, 147
Müller, Franz, O.P., 41, 140
Müller, Jean-Marie, 133, 201
Mumm, Bertha, 2
Muslims, 1, 80, 109, 151, 152, 154, 172–75, 182
Myriam, Sister of Grandchamp, 139

Nazis, 25, 44, 62, 88, 124n65, 160
Netherlands, 35, 57, 85, 142, 171, 175–76, 182, 183
Neuchâtel, 1, 2, 3, 6, 15n90, 84–86, 89, 96, 101, 107, 132, 140, 142, 145, 169, 176
Nicholas de Flue, 22
Nicole, Pierre, 13

Ordo Pacis, 59
Orthodox Church, 96, 104, 141, 143, 146
Oxford Group, 15–16, 35, 198, 199
Oxford Movement, 59

INDEX

Pacot, Simone, 68N63, 136–37
Paquier, Richard, 29, 201
Palestinian, 150, 152–54, 157–58, 172
Paris, 5, 7–10, 17, 33, 36, 53, 57, 58n35, 62, 65, 70, 74n79, 89n12, 96, 101n27, 140, 142n8, 147–48, 194
Paroz, Jules, 3, 198
Pascal, Blaise, 13
Passover, 96, 106, 177
Pax Christi, 150
Peace Now, 152
Pentecost (Pentecôte), 22n130, 83, 95, 115, 116, 118, 130, 145, 154, 163, 165, 202
Pentecostal, 16
Pétavel, Abram-François, 2
Peugeot, Émile, 2
Philoxenia, 139
Pierrette, Sister of Grandchamp, ix, xi, 36, 68, 80, 95
Pierre-Yves, Brother of Taizé, 67
Pietism, 57
Plămădeală, Anthony, 140–41
Pomeyrol, 5, 18, 20, 21, 27, 32, 53, 58, 59, 63–69, 102n29, 157, 167, 168, 194, 198
Poor Clares, 140, 164
Pope John XXIII, 47, 57, 190n2, 200
Pope John Paul II, ix, 87, 103n31, 130, 158, 163, 190
Port Royal, 21, 22, 27n159, 198
Protestantse Kerk in Nederland (PKN), 85
Pury, Roland de, 70
Pyronnet, Joseph, 110, 112, 112n49, 130, 132, 136

Rabaut, Paul, 22
Rabbis for Human Rights, 152, 172
Ramallah, 152, 153
Reformed Church, 5, 10, 19, 23, 29, 31, 35, 51, 60, 64n54, 79, 84, 85, 105, 106, 140, 142, 143, 145, 147, 163
Renée, Sister of Grandchamp, 67, 168, 173–74
Renoux, Christian, 150

Retreat/*Retraite*, 11, 12, 15–16, 22, 29–31, 32–33, 40, 50–53, 58, 62–63, 65, 67, 72, 74–76, 78, 80, 95, 100, 102, 106, 109, 115, 117, 127, 129, 135–39, 141, 160, 163, 165–66, 169, 174, 182, 185
Retraites de Grandchamp, 11, 12–13, 15–16, 19, 29, 52n21, 53, 165
Réveil, 2, 5,7, 10, 51, 58n35 and 36, 199, 200
Ronnefeldt, Clemens, 150
Rosé, Alma, 148
Rosen, David, 153
Roser, Henri, 132, 201
Rossier, Madame Alfred, 11
Rougemont, Gilberte de, 2, 3, 31
Rougemont, Madame de, 31
Rousseau Institute, 4, 198
Rousseau, Dom Olivier, 89, 107
Rublev, 100, 118
Rumi, 153

Sabbah, Michel, 150, 152, 164n51
St. Elizabeth/St. John in the Desert, 153, 159, 172
Saint Seraphim de Sarov, 187
Sainte-Croix, 6, 7, 143, 144
Saint-Ouen (Paris), 33, 62–63
Salameh, Noah, 153
Salvation Army, 35
Sarah, 113, 176
Saussure, Jean de, 16, 18–20, 23–24, 26, 52, 89
Schneider, Marguerite, 31
Schutz, Roger (Brother Roger, founder of Taizé), xi, 6, 23–30, 32, 46, 60, 61n43, 64–69, 88, 110, 123n63, 157n38, 166, 179–80, 194, 200, 201
Servants of Unity. 60–61, 66n61, 108, 139, 177, 179–81
SDC (Service des Contemplatives de Suisse Romande), 91–92
Shoufani, Father Émile, 147, 202
Sihastria Monastery, 141, 146
Silouan, *starets*, 103, 129, 141, 202
Sisters of Casteller Ring, 59

Sisters of Darmstadt, 59
Sisters and Brothers of Gnadenthal, 59
Sisters and Brothers of Imshausen, 59, 90, 159–62, 170, 194
Sisters of Saint-André, 67, 68, 166–67
Sisters of Strasbourg (Servants of the Poor), 57, 58
Soeurs Blanches, 63
Sonnenhof, viii, 33, 62, 67, 80, 119, 139, 159, 183
Sophrony, Father, 129, 141, 202
Soutter, Noémi, 17n107, 21, 31
Souvairan, Pierre, 28–29
Stein, Edith, 148
Sufi, 151, 153, 174
Suso, Heinrich, 13
Swiss Reformed Church, 1, 63
Sylvie, Sister of Grandchamp, 100, 139

Taizé, Community of, xi, 6, 23–30, 32, 41, 45, 46, 52n22, 59, 60–61, 63–69, 71n74, 75, 83n92, 86, 88, 97, 100, 101n28, 102n29, 110n45, 119n58, 123, 125, 129, 156, 157, 160, 166, 170, 179, 181, 182, 183n10, 193–94, 198, 199, 200, 201
Tel Aviv, 63, 132, 147, 154, 159
Ten Commandments, 177
Tersteegen, Gerhard, 57
Third Order of Unity (*Tiers ordre de l'unité*), 60, 62, 66, 177, 182–83
Thurian, Max, 23–24, 26–30, 46, 66
Tibhirine, Monastery of, 95, 108, 151, 174, 201
Timotei, Father, 140, 146
Toledo, Françoise de, 135
Trott, Adam von, 159
Trott, Vera von (Frau Vera, founder of the Community of Imshausen), 41, 116, 159–62, 170, 194
Tudor, Alexandru, 142
Tutu, Desmond, 90

Vatican II (Second Vatican Council), ix, 46, 47, 71, 74n79, 89n12, 107, 129, 157, 163–64, 168, 193, 194, 199, 201
Veilleurs, 5, 9, 12, 13, 14, 15, 16, 18, 19, 22, 23, 26, 27, 29, 52, 60, 64, 65, 99, 201
Venite Adoremus, 59
Vera, Frau. *See* Trott, Vera von.
Vernet, Sophie, 6, 15n90
Vinet, Alexandre, 6, 13, 201
Visarion, Father, 146
Visser 't Hooft, Willem, 29, 64, 88
Viviers, 164, 167, 202
Voillaume, René, 46, 47
Vries, Minke de, 16n102, 33, 35–36, 199, 202

Wavrechin, Elisabeth de, 8, 9, 18, 53, 165, 193
Weber, Hans-Ruedi, 41, 89, 202
Week of Prayer for Christian Unity, 45n7, 89, 147, 169–70
Westphal, Geneviève, 7n39, 11n62, 33, 202
Westphal, Martha, 177, 179
Women in Black, 152
World Council of Churches, 58, 67–68, 84, 87, 88, 89, 139, 166, 183, 184–85
World Health Organization, 182
World War, 17, 32, 35, 43, 47, 59, 64, 67, 87–88, 131, 132n84, 134, 138, 160

YMCA, 87, 89
Yoder, John Howard, 133, 202
Yom Kippur, 177

Zander, Leon, 89, 139
Zinzendorf, 3, 57, 105n39, 197, 198
Zougby, Zougby, 153
Zwingli, 163